AIN'T MY AMERICA

AIN'T MY AMERICA

The Long, Noble History
of Antiwar Conservatism and
Middle American Anti-Imperialism

Bill Kauffman

Metropolitan Books
Henry Holt and Company
New York

m

Metropolitan Books
Henry Holt and Company, LLC
Publishers since 1866
175 Fifth Avenue
New York, New York 10010
www.henryholt.com

Metropolitan Books® and m® are registered
trademarks of Henry Holt and Company, LLC.

Library of Congress Cataloging-in-Publication data

Kauffman, Bill, date.
  Ain't my America: the long, noble history of antiwar conservatism and
middle American anti-imperialism / Bill Kauffman.
       p.   cm.
  Includes index.
  ISBN-13: 978-0-8050-8244-9
  ISBN-10: 0-8050-8244-1
  1. Conservatism—United States.   2. Imperialism.   3. United States—Foreign
relations—20th century.   4. Peace movements—United States.   I. Title.
  JC573.2.U6K38   2008
  303.6'6—dc22   2007025894

First Edition 2008

Designed by Meryl Sussman Levavi

Printed in the United States of America

1   3   5   7   9   10   8   6   4   2

To Marie (On Wisconsin!)
and
Ken (Ayo Gernank!)

The price of empire is America's soul and that price is too high.

—Senator J. William Fulbright

A sense of the past is far more basic to the maintenance of freedom than hope for the future.

—Robert Nisbet, *The Quest for Community*

It's a dream
It's only a dream
And it's fading now . . .

—Neil Young

CONTENTS

AIN'T MY
AMERICA

INTRODUCTION: I'LL JUST STAY HERE, THANKS

LEFT STANDS FOR peace, right for war; liberals are pacific, conservatives are bellicose. Or so one might conclude after surveying the dismal landscape of the American Right in the Age of Bush II.

Yet there is a long and honorable (if largely hidden) tradition of antiwar thought and action among the American Right. It stretches from ruffle-shirted Federalists who opposed the War of 1812 and civic-minded mugwump critics of the Spanish-American War on up through the midwestern isolationists who formed the backbone of the pre–World War II America First Committee and the conservative Republicans who voted against U.S. involvement in NATO, the Korean conflict, and Vietnam. And although they are barely audible amid the belligerent clamor of today's shock-and-awe Right, libertarians and old-fashioned traditionalist conservatives are among the sharpest critics of the Iraq War and the imperial project of the Bush Republicans.

Derided as *isolationists*—which, as that patriot of the Old Republic Gore Vidal has noted, means simply people who "want no part of foreign wars" and who "want to be allowed to live their own lives without interference from government"[1]—the antiwar Right has put forth a critique of foreign intervention that is at once gimlet-eyed, idealistic, historically grounded, and dyed deeply in the American grain. Just because Bush, Rush, and Fox are ignorant of history doesn't mean authentic conservatives have to swallow the profoundly un-American American Empire.

Rooted in the Farewell Address of George Washington, informing such conservative-tinged antiwar movements as the Anti-Imperialist League, which said no to U.S. colonialism in the Philippines, finding poignant and prescient expression in the extraordinary valediction in which President Dwight Eisenhower warned his countrymen against the "military-industrial complex," the conservative case against American Empire and militarism remains forceful and relevant. It is no museum piece, no artifact as inutile as it is quaint. It is plangent, wise, and deserving of revival. But before it can be revived, it must be disinterred.

A note, first, on taxonomy. To label is to libel, or at least to divest the subject of individuating contradictions and qualifications. I have found that the most interesting American political figures cannot be squeezed into the constricted and lifeless pens of *liberal* or *conservative*. Nor do I accept the simpleminded division of our lovely and variegated country into *red* and *blue,* for to paint Colorado, Kansas, and Alabama requires every color in the spectrum. *Right* and *Left* have outlived their usefulness as taxonomic distinctions. They're closer to prisons from which no thought can escape.

Yet the terms are as ubiquitous as *good* and *evil,* and in fact many on the Right do think, Latinately, of their side as dexterous and the Left as sinister. I say it's time for a little ambidexterity. So my "Right" is capacious enough to include Jeffersonian libertarians and Jefferson-hating Federalists, Senators Robert Taft and George McGovern (yes, yes; give me a chance), dirt-farm southern populists and Beacon Streeters who take hauteur with their tea and jam, cranky Nebraska tax cutters and eccentric Michigan tellers of ghostly tales, little old ladies in tennis shoes marching against the United Nations and free-market economists protesting the draft. My subjects are, in the main, suspicious of state power, crusades, bureaucracy, and a modernity that is armed and dangerous. They are anti-expansion, pro-particularism, and so genuinely "conservative"—that is, cherishing of the verities, of home and hearth and family—as to make them mortal (immortal?) enemies of today's neoconservatives.

Above all, they have feared empire, whose properties were enumerated well by the doubly pen-named Garet Garrett: novelist, exponent of free enterprise and individualism, and a once-reliable if unspectacular stable horse for the *Saturday Evening Post.* Writing in 1953, he set down a quintet of imperial requisites.

1. The executive power of the government shall be dominant.
2. Domestic policy becomes subordinate to foreign policy.
3. Ascendancy of the military mind, to such a point at last that the civilian mind is intimidated.
4. A system of satellite nations.
5. A complex of vaunting and fear.[2]

Between "*Constitutional, representative, limited* government, on the one hand, and Empire on the other hand, there is mortal enmity,"[3] wrote Garrett, who did not burst with confidence that the former would vanquish the latter. He wrote in the final days of the Truman administration. The executive bestrode the U.S. polity. Militarism and the cult of bigness held sway. The blood rivers of Europe had yet to run dry. More than fifty thousand American boys had died—for what?—on the Korean peninsula. Truman had refused to obtain from Congress a formal declaration of war; future presidents would follow suit. The dark night of Cold War was upon us. This was what our forebears had warned against.

Why did these men (and later women) of the "Right" oppose expansion, war, and empire? And, in contemporary America, where have all the followers gone?

From the Republic's beginning, Americans of conservative temperament have been skeptical of manifest destiny and crusades for democracy. They have agreed with Daniel Webster that "there must be some limit to the extent of our territory, if we are to make our institutions permanent. The Government is very likely to be endangered . . . by a further enlargement of its already vast territorial surface."[4] Is it really worth trading in the Republic for southwestern scrubland? Webster's point was remade, just as futilely, by the Anti-Imperialist League. It was repeated by those conservatives who supplied virtually the only opposition to the admission of Hawaii and Alaska to the Union. As the Texas Democrat Kenneth M. Regan told the House when he vainly argued against stitching a forty-ninth star on the flag, "I fear for the future of the country if we start taking in areas far from our own shores that we will have to protect with our money, our guns, and our men, instead of staying here and looking after the heritage we were left by George Washington, who told us to beware of any foreign entanglements."[5]

Expansion was madness. John Greenleaf Whittier compared its advocates to hashish smokers.

> *The man of peace, about whose dreams*
> *The sweet millennial angels cluster,*
> *Tastes the mad weed, and plots and schemes,*
> *A raving Cuban filibuster!*[6]

George W. Bush, it is rumored, preferred coke to hash, but his utopian vision of an American behemoth splayed across the globe would be, to conservatives of eras past, a hideous nightmare.

Robert Nisbet, the social critic who was among the wisest and most laureled of American conservatives, wrote in his coruscant *Conservatism: Dream and Reality* (1986): "Of all the *mis*ascriptions of the word 'conservative' during the last four years, the most amusing, in an historical light, is surely the application of 'conservative' to the [budget-busting enthusiasts for great increases in military expenditures]. For in America throughout the twentieth century, and including four substantial wars abroad, conservatives had been steadfastly the voices of non-inflationary military budgets, and of an emphasis on trade in the world instead of American nationalism. In the two World Wars, in Korea, and in Viet Nam, the leaders of American entry into war were such renowned liberal-progressives as Woodrow Wilson, Franklin Roosevelt, Harry Truman and John F. Kennedy. In all four episodes conservatives, both in the national government and in the rank and file, were largely hostile to intervention."[7]

In the two decades since Nisbet's observation the historical amnesia has descended into a kind of belligerent nescience. Today's self-identified conservatives loathe, detest, and slander any temerarious soul who speaks for peace. FDR and Truman join Ronald Reagan in the trinity of favorite presidents of the contemporary Right; those atavistic Old Rightists who harbor doubts about U.S. entry into the world wars or our Asian imbroglios (scripted, launched, and propagandized for by liberal Democrats) are dismissed as cranks or worse. Vice President Dick Cheney, lamenting the August 2006 primary defeat of the Scoop Jackson Democratic senator Joseph Lieberman, charged that the Democrats wanted to "retreat behind our oceans"[8]—which an earlier generation of peace-minded Republicans had considered a virtuous policy consistent with George Washington's adjuration to avoid entanglements and alliances with foreign nations.

Felix Morley, the *Washington Post* editorialist who would have been a top foreign-policy official in the Robert Taft administration, wrote in 1959: "Every war in which the United States has engaged since 1815 was waged in the name of democracy. Each has contributed to that centralization of power which tends to destroy that local self-government which is what most Americans have in mind when they acclaim democracy."[9] Alas, Dick Cheney, the draft-dodging hawk, the anti-gay-marriage grandfather of a tribade-baby, is not an irony man.

I will consider the anti-expansionists of the early Republic in the first chapter. My focus in this book, however, is on "conservative" anti-imperialists of the twentieth century—the American Century, as that rootless son of missionaries Henry Luce dubbed it. The men and women whom I shall profile regarded Lucian expansion, conquest, and war—whether in the Philippines in 1900 or Vietnam in 1968—as profoundly un-American, even anti-American. The American Century, alas, did not belong to the likes of Moorfield Storey, Murray Rothbard, or Russell Kirk. But the American soul does.

These brave men and women also insisted, in the face of obloquy and smears, that dissent is a patriotic imperative. For questioning the drive to war in 1941, Charles Lindbergh would be called a Nazi by the FDR hatchet man Harold Ickes, and for challenging the constitutionality of Harry Truman's Korean conflict, Senator Robert Taft would be slandered as a commie symp by *The New Republic*. Patrick J. Buchanan would be libeled as an anti-Semite for noting the role that Israel's supporters played in driving the United States into the two (the first two?) invasions of Iraq, and the full range of anti–Iraq War right-wingers would be condemned as "unpatriotic conservatives" by *National Review* in April 2003. Same as it ever was. As Senator Taft lamented in January 1951 during the brief but illuminating "Great Debate" over Korea and NATO strategy between hawkish liberal Democrats and peace-minded conservative Republicans, "Criticisms are met by the calling of names rather than by intelligent debate."[10]

In pre-imperial America, conservatives objected to war and empire out of jealous regard for personal liberties, a balanced budget, the free enterprise system, and federalism. These concerns came together under the umbrella of the badly misunderstood America First Committee, the largest popular antiwar organization in U.S. history. The AFC was formed in 1940 to keep the United States out of a second European war that many Americans feared would be a repeat of the first. Numbering eight hundred thousand members who ranged from populist to patrician, from Main Street Republican to prairie socialist, America First embodied and acted upon George Washington's Farewell Address counsel to pursue a foreign policy of neutrality.

As the America Firsters discovered, protesting war is a lousy career move. Dissenters are at best calumniated, at worst thrown in jail: for standing against foreign wars and the drive thereto Eugene V. Debs was imprisoned (World War I), Martin Luther King Jr. was painted red and spied upon (Vietnam War), and those who have spoken and acted against the Bush-Cheney Iraq War have been subject to a drearily predictable array of insults and indignities.

It has long been so. Edgar Lee Masters, the *Spoon River Anthology* poet and states'-rights Democrat who threw away his career by writing a splenetic biography of Abraham Lincoln decrying Honest Abe as a guileful empire builder, recalled of the Spanish-American War: "There was great opposition to the war over the country, but at that time an American was permitted to speak out against a war if he chose to do so."[11] Masters had lived through the frenzied persecutions of antiwar dissidents under the liberal Democrat Woodrow Wilson. He had little patience with gilded platitudes about wars for human rights and the betterment of the species. He knew that war meant death and taxes, those proverbial inevitabilities that become shining virtues in the fog of martial propaganda. Masters, in the argot of today's war party and its publicists, was a traitor, a cringing treasonous abettor of America's (and freedom's!) enemies.

Yet Masters and his ilk were American to the core, and the antiwar Middle Americanism they represented has never really gone away. It surfaced even during Vietnam, that showpiece war of the best and brightest establishment liberal Democrats. Although most conservative Republicans were gung-ho on Vietnam, discarding their erstwhile preference for limited constitutional government, the right-wing antiwar banner was carried by such libertarians as

Murray Rothbard (who sought, creatively, to fuse Old Right with New Left in an antiwar popular front) and the penny-pinching Iowa Republican congressman H. R. Gross, who said nay to the war on the simple if not wholly adequate grounds that it cost too much.

The Iraq wars of the Presidents Bush have rekindled the old antiwar spirit of the Right, though it is easy to miss in the glare of the bombs bursting in the Mesopotamian air. Indeed, Bush Republicans and pro-war Democrats have fretted mightily over recent surveys from the Council on Foreign Relations showing that the American people are reverting to—horrors!—*isolationism,* which the CFR defines invidiously as a hostility toward foreigners but which I see as a wholesome, pacific, and very American reluctance to intervene in the political and military quarrels of other nations.

The old American isolationism endures, despite the slurs, despite its utter absence within the corridors of power. President George W. Bush, as messianically interventionist a chief executive as we have ever endured, took out after the bogeyman in his 2006 State of the Union address: "Our enemies and our friends can be certain: The United States will not retreat from the world, and we will never surrender to evil. America rejects the false comfort of isolationism."[12] And America, or rather its masters, chooses the bloody road of expansion and war.

The men who write the words that thud from Bush's mouth felt compelled to rebuke nameless isolationists because, as a Pew Research Center survey of October 2005 found, 42 percent of Americans agreed that the U.S. "should mind its own business internationally and let other countries get along the best they can on their own." As a Pew press release noted, over the last forty years "only in 1976 and 1995 did public opinion tilt this far toward isolationism."

Democrats were "twice as likely as Republicans to say the U.S. should mind its own business internationally," a sign of just how successful Bush and the neoconservatives have been in re-shaping the GOP mind, as it were. (A decade earlier, Pew found no substantial difference in isolationist attitudes among Republican and Democratic partisans.)

Despite the Wilsonian tattoo issuing from the White House and repeated assertions that the U.S. military is constructing a democratic Middle East, Pew found that "promoting democracy in other nations" comes in dead last in the foreign-policy priorities of Americans. Only 24 percent of respondents affirmed that goal, as compared to 84 percent who favored "protecting jobs of American workers" and 51 percent who placed "reducing illegal immigration" atop their list.[13] These latter two are classic themes of the isolationist Right, as embedded, for instance, in the presidential campaigns of Patrick J. Buchanan.

There is nothing freakish, cowardly, or even anomalous about these Middle Americans who are turning against foreign war. They are acting in the best traditions of their forebears. But those forebears have been disgracefully forgotten. The history of right-wing (or decentralist, or small-government, or even Republican) hostility to militarism and empire is piteously underknown. The traditions are unremembered. Which is where this book comes in.

The Bush-whacked Right is incorrigibly ignorant of previous "Rights." For all they know, Robert Taft may as well be Che Guevara. Yet there is a good deal of subsurface grumbling by the Right, among Republican operatives (who understand the potential of an anti-interventionist electoral wave); D.C.-based movement-conservatives, who recall that in the dim mists of time they once spoke of limited government as a desideratum; and at the grassroots level, where once more folks are asking the never-answered question of the isolationists: why in hell are we over there?

Bill Clinton lamented after his 1997 State of the Union address, "It's hard when you're not threatened by a foreign enemy to whip people up to a fever pitch of common, intense, sustained, disciplined endeavor."[14] Old-style conservatives would deny that this is *ever* a legitimate function of the central state. "Sustained, disciplined endeavor" driven by a populace at "fever pitch" and organized by a central state is fascistic. It ill befits the country of Ken Kesey and Bob Dylan and Johnny Appleseed. It sure as hell ain't my America.

I should own up to my own biases. I belong to no political camp: my politics are localist, decentralist, Jeffersonian. I am an American rebel, a Main Street bohemian, a rural Christian pacifist. I have strong libertarian and traditionalist conservative streaks. I am in many ways an anarchist, though a front-porch anarchist, a chestnut-tree anarchist, a girls-softball-coach anarchist. My politics are a kind of mixture of Dorothy Day and Henry David Thoreau, though with an upstate New York twist. I voted for Nader in 2004 and Buchanan in 2000: the peace candidates. I often vote Libertarian and Green. I am a freeborn American with the blood of Crazy Horse, Zora Neale Hurston, and Jack Kerouac flowing in my veins. My heart is with the provincial and with small places, and it is from this intense localism that my own isolationist, antiwar sympathies derive. I misfit the straitjackets designed by Fox News and the *New York Times*. So does any American worth the name.

You can have your hometown or you can have the empire. You can't have both. And the tragedy of modern conservatism is that the ideologues, the screamers over the airwaves, the apparatchiks in their Beltway viper's den, have convinced the Barcalounger-reclining *National Review* reader that one must always and forever subordinate one's place, one's neighborhood, whether natal ground or beloved adopted block, to the empire.

It isn't true! It never has been true. There is nothing conservative about the American Empire. It seeks to destroy—which is why good American conservatives, those loyal to family and home and neighborhood and our best traditions, should wish, and work toward, its peaceful destruction. We have nothing to lose but the chains and taxes of empire. And we have a country to regain.

1

"THE GREATEST CURSE THAT EVER BEFELL US":
AN EMPIRE IS BORN

"I ABOMINATE AND detest the idea of a government, where there is a standing army,"[1] George Mason, father of the Bill of Rights, told the 1788 Virginia convention on the adoption of the federal Constitution. His view was not anomalous; militarism was.

If things have not turned out quite the way the founders anticipated, perhaps James Madison & Company miscalculated the proper balance between the national and the local. Elsewhere in that speech Mason proposed giving states an explicit veto over the federal government's power to send state militia beyond a state's borders. In reply, Madison—after agreeing that "a standing army is one of the greatest mischiefs that can possibly happen"— dismissed Mason's concerns as alarmist. "Can we believe that a government of a federal nature, consisting of many coequal sovereignties, and particularly having one branch chosen from the people, would drag the militia unnecessarily to an immense distance?" said Madison. "This, sir, would be unworthy the most arbitrary despot."[2]

True, true, though the act is eminently worthy of the administration of George W. Bush, which has called well over half of the four hundred thousand members of the state National Guards— descendants of the militia—to active duty for the Iraq War. And when in the mid-1980s the governors of Minnesota and Massachusetts challenged the authority of Ronald Reagan's Department of Defense to send state National Guard units to Honduras, presumably to assist in the overthrow of the government of Nicaragua, the Supreme Court (*Perpich v. Defense,* 1990) upheld the right of the central government to send Guardsmen wherever the hell it wishes, even over the objections of state governors. So much for federalism. So much for Madisonian guarantees.

It wasn't supposed to be this way. Ignore the neoconservative gleet about America the world policeman. Neutrality, abstention from foreign quarrels, minding our own business—these, and not perpetual war in service of American Empire, are our birthright.

George Washington's Farewell Address, which bore the editorial mark of Alexander Hamilton and James Madison and thus was as close to an expression of early American political omnifariousness as one might find, still stands as a sacred text among conservative critics of empire.[3] One doubts if any secular sutra has ever been violated with such brutal regularity as has the Farewell Address, especially in its foreign-policy injunctions. Washington warns posterity against "foreign alliances, attachments, and intrigues" and "those overgrown military establishments which, under any form of government, are inauspicious to liberty, and which are to be regarded as particularly hostile to republican liberty." His hobgoblins are today's establishment.

"Observe good faith and justice toward all nations. Cultivate peace and harmony with all," instructs Washington, and one can see the eyes roll and mouths curl into snickers in the offices of the *New Republic.* George Washington, peacenik appeaser of Islamofascism! The father of our country emphasizes that "nothing is more essential than that permanent, inveterate antipathies against particular nations and passionate attachments for others should be excluded, and that in place of them just and amicable feelings toward all should be cultivated." In language the modern restatement of which would exile the sayer to that Coventry populated by "xenophobes," Washington counsels, "Against the insidious wiles of foreign influence (I conjure you to believe me, fellow-citizens) the jealousy of a free people ought to be *constantly* awake, since history and experience prove that foreign influence is one of the most baneful foes of republican government . . . Excessive partiality for one foreign nation and excessive dislike of another cause those whom they actuate to see danger only on one side, and serve to veil and even second the arts of influence on the other. Real patriots who may resist the intrigues of the favorite are liable to become suspected and odious, while its tools and dupes usurp the applause and confidence of the people to surrender their interests." This message was *not* brought to you by Fox News.

Washington's valedictory amounts to a repudiation of U.S. foreign policy from 1917 to the present. He cautions explicitly against engagement in transatlantic affairs, for "Europe has a set of primary interests which to us have none or a very remote relation. Hence she must be engaged in frequent controversies, the causes of which are essentially foreign to our concerns." Neutrality is the ideal, and an achievable one. "It is our true policy to steer clear of permanent alliances with any portion of the foreign world," writes Washington. This is not isolation or autarky, though these policies have been urged, with considerable eloquence, by the pacific throughout our history. Rather, Washington insists, "The great rule of conduct for us in regard to foreign nations is, in extending our commercial relations to have with them as little *political* connection as possible."[4]

There is a reason, you see, why the National Endowment for Democracy, which since 1983 has spent upwards of $1 billion rigging foreign elections and fossicking about in tramontane sinkholes, does not brand the likeness of George Washington on its policy papers. Nor is the author of that classic anti–imperialist statement, the Declaration of Independence, in the pantheon of the warmakers.

Thomas Jefferson encapsulated his philosophy of defense in 1799: "I am for relying, for internal defence, on our militia solely till actual invasion, and for such a naval force only as may protect our coasts and harbours from such depredations as we have experienced: and not for a standing army in time of peace which may overawe the public sentiment; nor for a navy which by it's [*sic*] own expences and the eternal wars in which it will implicate us, will grind us with public burthens, & sink us under them. I am for free commerce with all nations, political connection with none, & little or no diplomatic establishment, and I am not for linking ourselves, by new treaties with the quarrels of Europe."[5]

Jefferson's anathema upon standing armies—not to mention the kind that march and kill—was of a piece with what the colonial historian Merrill Jensen (a South Dakota farmboy and classic embodiment of the University of Wisconsin history department's Upper Midwest populism) called the "all-prevailing distrust of standing armies in time of peace."[6]

James Madison, in his *Notes of Debates in the Federal Convention of 1787*, noted that "armies in time of peace are allowed on all hands to be an evil,"[7] as casually as if he were mentioning, in passing, that the delegates, to a man, eschewed the clap.

No such unanimity existed, however, in the matter of expansion, and it was here that the "conservative" case against empire, based on the trinity of scale, place, and economy, found its republican groove. Growth may be, as Edward Abbey liked to say, the ideology of the cancer cell, but those who have challenged the growth of the American imperium have tasted oblivion's dust. Early critics of American expansion have been flushed down the memory hole with cloacal efficiency. These Little Americans need not be slandered or caricatured; they are forgotten, sunken deep into Lethe.

Is there a word for the lamenting of the passage of things that have not only not yet passed but that have not even yet begun? I have the affliction. I sorrow over the end of autumn in early September, or, come Thanksgiving eve, the terminus of another Christmas. Our forebears—my forebears; yours, too, if you set your sights nigh enough—had the same premonitions of Republic's end. We were on the verge of empire, said the Anti-Federalists of 1787. As did the critics of the War of 1812, the Mexican War, the Civil War, the Spanish-American War, and so it goes and so it goes and so it goes, until at one point we really did cross over into Empire's snare, and the lamenters of the passage of those things that have not only not yet passed but that have not even yet begun were confirmed as prophets.

Some saw the shadows falling in 1803.

When in 2003 a bicentennial hullabaloo surrounded the Louisiana Purchase, one might well have thought that Thomas Jefferson's land deal, like the Interstate Highway System and National Administrative Assistants Day, enjoyed unanimous support. Opponents of Jefferson's French real-estate steal, which doubled the American realm for a mere $15 million, have faded to an invisibility rivaling that of contemporary Franco-American culture. (SpaghettiOs excepted, of course.)

Yet this was no bland triumph of consensus politics.

The Senate ratified the Louisiana Purchase by a vote of 24–7, and the House voted to pay for it by 90–25. So who were these skinflints and skeptics?

Many had read their Montesquieu, who wrote, "It is natural for a republic to have only a small territory, otherwise it cannot long subsist."[8] The country was already too large, they suspected, and further expansion would swell it past the point of viability. John Dawson, the law partner of James Monroe (our only Anti-Federalist president), had argued during the ratification of the Constitution (which he opposed) that "no government formed on the principles of freedom can pervade all North America."[9]

The splenetic Massachusetts Federalist Fisher Ames scoffed

that Louisiana was "a great waste, a wilderness unpeopled with any beings except wolves and wandering Indians."[10] It was too extensive to govern. The United States, he marveled, was "rushing like a comet into infinite space."[11] And for what? Ames, a first-class hater of Jefferson and "Imperial Virginia," slyly asked, "Having bought an empire, who is to be emperor?"[12] and the answer was embedded in the question.

Foes of the Purchase were concentrated in the Northeast, where the Mississippi River was considered a parvenu not fit to wash the Hudson's banks. Besides, they could count. Two by two, as the states of the West inevitably entered the Union, would Jefferson's Republicans build an impregnable Senate majority. New England, cradle of the Revolution, would be reduced to a factious province.

The Yankees struck the occasional prescient note, warning that Louisiana would plant "the seed of division" in the American soil. The enlarged country would be too big, its sections too various, to exist under any common government beyond the loosest confederation. As the Connecticut Federalist representative Roger Griswold asserted, "It is not consistent with the spirit of a republican government that its territory should be exceedingly large, for as you extend your limits you increase the difficulties arising from a want of that similarity of customs, habits, and manners so essential for its support."[13]

The spirit of separation, condemned by New Englanders with bombast and cannonblast threescore years later, was fanned by her representatives in the wake of the Purchase. The atrabilious Federalist Timothy Pickering, who despised "the Moonshine philosopher of Monticello,"[14] dreamed of a northern confederacy, "exempt from the corrupt and corrupting influence and oppression of the aristocratic Democrats of the South."

"There will be—and our children at farthest will see it—a separation," predicted Pickering.[15] He spoke not in sadness.

The Louisiana Purchase was one of those agenda-bending flashpoints at which the parties reverse roles with head-spinning alacrity. The Federalists, usually friends to a powerful central government, stood up for parsimony and strict construction of the Constitution, while Jefferson and the Republicans, whose belief in limited government was such that they would be virtually barred from public debate in this first decade of the twenty-first century, pushed through a mammoth land purchase that Jefferson privately conceded to be "beyond the Constitution."

Principles were as elastic as national boundaries. As the historian Jon Kukla writes in *A Wilderness So Immense,* "Only five years earlier, Jefferson's party had championed states' rights and strict construction in the Virginia and Kentucky Resolutions of 1798. Now their words could have been scripted by the Hamiltonian Federalists."[16]

The Louisiana Purchase showed Jefferson at his slipperiest. Bothered by the extraconstitutional nature of what he had done, he fiddled with an authorizing amendment until Treasury Secretary Albert Gallatin and others persuaded him that the power to acquire territory was "implied" by the power to make treaties. After a bit of throat clearing, President Jefferson concluded that "the less that is said about any constitutional difficulty, the better."[17] The amendment stayed in his desk.

I do not mean to make the paradoxical Mr. Jefferson, whose reputation is in deep slough in our Hamiltonian age, the villain of the piece. No president, not even Washington in his Farewell Address, left us so many statements and restatements of the antiimperial, antimilitarist nature of his imagined America. He counseled repeatedly against involvement in European affairs, and as an old man, the melancholic Monticelloan devised a brilliant "ward republic" scheme by which political responsibilities would be decentralized to an almost revolutionary extent. Its adoption would have redeemed the promise of the Revolution. But Jefferson did

favor hemispheric expansion, well beyond the bounds of the original thirteen and across the Mississippi River, even down into Cuba,
as the "empire for liberty" would fill with tillers in the soil, "the
chosen people of God," the American farmer. "The mobs of great
cities" are to the body politic as "sores [are] to the strength of the
human body," he wrote in *Notes on the State of Virginia*.[18] An abun-
dance of arable land—however obtained—was essential to the national health.

Two years after Mr. Jefferson and Congress bought a new
America, the scheme's eloquent defender in the House of Representatives, John Randolph of Virginia, reverted to strict constructionist principles, saying that "the Louisiana Purchase was the
greatest curse that ever befell us." Though Randolph would later
declare, "Louisiana is not my country,"[19] the bazaar of expansion
had a no-returns policy. The thing was done. Limits—a sine qua
non of conservatism—had been transcended. There would be
consequences.

Henry Adams wrote that "the Louisiana treaty gave a fatal
wound to 'strict construction.' "[20] Conventional historians insist
that this was a case of justifiable homicide if ever there was one:
an expanding nation needed an expansive Constitution. Infinite
space awaited.

Infinite space, alas, invites the infinite state. The Anti-
Federalists, those critics of the Constitution with whom Jefferson
had much in common, had warned that the document's ambigu-
ities (for what is not subsumed under "general welfare"?) were
big enough to drive a standing army through.

Which was all to the good in the minds of such southern expansionists as John C. Calhoun of South Carolina, who exulted
in the wake of his passionately desired War of 1812, "Let us conquer space."[21]

Or if not space, how about Canada?

Let us first take a poetical interlude.

Would you like to hear my "Ode to the Genesee River," upon whose sylvan banks I brood? All right, I shan't subject you to my versifying. (Do not call me poetaster!) But in the prelude to the War of 1812, when next the conservative critique of expansion and war would surface, one of America's great men of letters cut his political eyeteeth in defense of those classical liberal (which is to say, in a later context, conservative) tenets of peace and free trade.

Once upon a time in America, poets engaged in public discourse and sought consulates instead of endowed chairs. Whitman's lodestar was free trade, Whittier's abolition, and James Russell Lowell's the prosier cause of civil service reform. But it was a child who led them.

In 1808, in the Berkshires of western Massachusetts, there lived a thirteen-year-old boy who had never been beyond Hampshire County. His name was William Cullen Bryant; his father, a physician, served in the state legislature as an arch-Federalist and enemy of all things Jeffersonian. Cullen read by firelight the contents of his father's library: Pope's *Iliad,* devotional verse, and of course the Federalist papers—the newspapers, that is, in vitriolic reams.

Bryant was the most precocious adolescent in the history of American letters. He was a frail, nervous, delicate lad, prone to headaches, who, had he been born into our time, would have been sent immediately to right field. While his playmates frolicked "'neath yon crimson tree,"[22] Cullen stewed over the hated Jefferson's Embargo Act of 1807 and its successor embargoes, which forbade commerce with warring England and France. Though the president was responding to British depredations on the high seas, Federalist New England (and the sui generis John Randolph, he of the Louisiana Purchase volte-face) feared the suffocating effects of this autarkic measure. Jefferson considered the embargo an alternative to war; the Federalists thought it a prelude—and with an ulterior motive. The southern planter states, the Yankees feared, were exploiting British misbehavior at sea as an excuse to bind and choke the northern commercial states.

Most fathers of American poets have disdained their sons' callings as disreputable, unmanly, and foolishly improvident; Dr. Bryant did not. So impressed was he with Cullen's rhymes that in the spring of 1808 he secured the Boston publication of *The Embargo, or Sketches of the Times: A Satire by a Youth of Thirteen*. Its 244 lines took up ten pages and sold—quite well—for twelve and one-half cents a copy.

The boy poet sings of "commerce" and "agriculture" as "the blessing of mankind":

Who hand in hand, and heav'n-directed, go
Diffusing gladness through the world below.

But then along comes Jefferson, "the scorn of every patriot name," whose embargo is the "curse of our nation, source of countless woes/From whose dark womb unreckon'd misery flows."

The cessation of trade desolates the nation. The "bold Sailor from the ocean torn" (yes, rhymesters, he was "forlorn") cannot feed his "starving children." The farmer, "since supporting trade is fled . . . cheerless hangs his head." He watches "his hoarded produce rot," while "debts follow debts, on taxes, taxes pour." As for laborers:

In vain Mechanics ply their curious art,
And bootless mourn the interdicted mart.

The tone here is libertarian: the purity of laissez-faire has been mucked and soiled, and now hell is upon the land. The meddling president "wisely regulating trade—destroys." Bryant's verses might have been repeated by the free-market critics of the periodic embargoes (against Japan, Cuba, Iraq) that became a tool of twentieth-century U.S. diplomacy.

The callow poet works himself into a frenzy over Jefferson. "Go, wretch, resign the presidential chair," he spits. Then:

Go, scan, Philosophist, thy . . . charms
And sink supinely in her sable arms.[23]

The ellipses refer to Sally Hemings, of course, Jefferson's rumored slave inamorata, and one can almost picture the teenage Bryant luxuriating in his stash of *National Geographics*.

That a lad of so tender an age wrote such competently venomous verse inspired wonder. One critic foresaw "a respectable station on the Parnassian mount" for Bryant once he reached shaving age.[24]

The embargo was followed by war, as embargoes are wont to be. *The Embargo* led to puberty—and then fame, when in 1817 Cullen's snooping father discovered a sheaf of poems buried in a desk and sent them to the *North American Review*. "Thanatopsis," a meditation on death composed when Bryant was seventeen, became the most celebrated American poem of its era.

Concluding that "poetry and starvation" are twins,[25] William Cullen Bryant forsook his place as the bard of the Berkshires (and town clerk of Great Barrington) for New York City, where for almost fifty years he was editor and part owner of the *Evening Post*. From "Thanatopsis" to "Headless Body Found in Topless Bar" is a frightful plunge, but then think what Rupert Murdoch might have done with the Sally Hemings roorback.

The *Evening Post*'s doctrine—liberty and freedom of exchange—was pure Jefferson, and Bryant forever rued his intemperate poem. Parke Godwin, his son-in-law and biographer, related, "I once asked him if he had a copy of 'The Embargo.' 'No,' he answered testily; 'why should I keep such stuff as that?' "[26]

Bryant may have been irascible, but he was not inconstant. In his seventies, approaching his old friend Thanatos, he was president of the Free Trade League. Like his comrade Whitman, who insisted that "tariff taffy gives me the belly-ache,"[27] Bryant always regarded free trade as "the natural workings of this beneficent system of Providence."[28]

Upon Bryant's death in 1878, he was eulogized as our foremost champion of the philosophy of Thomas Jefferson. The few who recalled *The Embargo* pardoned Bryant his youthful indiscretion, his boyhood pumpkin smashing. After all, it was only poetry.

The Most Unpopular War

If John Randolph woke late to the unconstitutional nature of the Louisiana Purchase, he was lying in wait for the next expansionist spasm: the War of 1812.

"Black Jack"[29] Randolph is a strange and luminous comet streaking across the American sky, leaving as his legacy only the afterglow of brilliance. Descended of Pocahontas and John Rolfe, he is regal and he is feral. "Only a Randolph is good enough for a Randolph" went the Virginia adage, and the resultant intermarriage and madness and mossy languor rivaled Poe's House of Usher. Indeed, the Randolph plantation had an apposite name: Bizarre.

Randolph had been kicked out of William and Mary for dueling over the correct pronunciation of a word. (Jack won, wounding the "fleshy portion" of his foe's backside,[30] which suggests either that the ass-clipped student turned or that Randolph stopped counting too soon.)

Randolph was a habitual opium user, a bachelor who seems to have nurtured a crush on Andrew Jackson. Alan Crawford, a historian of old Virginia and the author of a vastly entertaining book (*Unwise Passions*) on the incest-and-infanticide scandal of cousin Nancy Randolph and brother Richard Randolph, unearthed a letter in which Randolph suggests "Greek love" to a no doubt dumbfounded and thoroughly unaroused Old Hickory.[31]

Crawford describes Jack Randolph in Congress: "He would saunter into the House chamber and nonchalantly drape his long legs, encased in sleek white riding boots, over the bench in front of him. He would study his gloves or gaze at the ceiling or peruse a book of verse or even affect sleep. Sometimes he had his dogs with him, and he would pay more attention to them than to his colleagues."[32] (Of one, he memorably snapped, "Like rotten mackerel by moonlight, he shines and stinks.")

Randolph was not the sort of man you'd choose for an enemy. He once said of his political opponents: "It is a mere waste of time to reason with such persons. They do not deserve anything like serious refutation. The proper arguments for such statesmen are a strait-waistcoat, a dark room, water, gruel, and depletion."[33] He would not chitchat amiably around the muffin table at a Brookings symposium.

His most sympathetic explicator has been Russell Kirk, the man of letters who taught traditionalist conservatives their patrimony at midcentury—albeit with an Anglophonic clip—and published a fine volume, *John Randolph of Roanoke: A Study in American Politics* (1951), in which he considers Randolph's lonely anti-expansion stance as perfectly natural, for men of "sturdy conservative convictions . . . were naturally lovers of tranquility and foes of aggression."[34]

Presaging the eloquently desperate fight of old American conservatives against the annexation of the Philippines in the early twentieth century, John Randolph was set firmly against expansion, whether to the west or the north or the south. He desired no new states. (Kentucky, he said, with fine aristocratic distaste, was the

"Australia of Virginia.")[35] The United States were a decentralized federation; the Constitution, he believed, would prove sorely inadequate to the task of governing a continental power. He would declare in 1822, "No government, extending from the Atlantic to the Pacific, can be fit to govern me or those whom I represent."[36] He was right. A nation stretching three thousand miles over mountain and prairie and desert is ungovernable from a single city set on a coastal swamp. Or at least it cannot be governed with a sensitivity to local conditions, an intelligent awareness of the cultural diversity inherent in any healthy society. It can be governed by the brute force of an Internal Revenue Service and a Department of Homeland Security, but it cannot sustain the Republic's spirit.

Randolph's exertions of wit, bile, despair, and savagery—his country was slipping away from him, and its polity was but a quarter of a century young—mark his as among the most valorous if forgotten campaigns against war. He stood for peace and free trade and "was the foe of all proposals for hostilities or foreign entanglements."[37]

A Tertium Quid, he led a small band of Old Republicans who viewed with meet suspicion standing armies, the tariff, the shadow of imperialism, and the embargo of their erstwhile ally Jefferson. They were, in the matter of national government, libertarians, though in the case of Randolph the slave owner, he well understood the iniquity of the peculiar institution but resigned himself, too easily, to acquiescence. Above all, the Old Republicans execrated the devil militarism. A standing army was "not only a useless and enormous expense" but a dagger pointed at the fair bosom of liberty.[38]

In 1810 Randolph had proposed that the navy sell *all* its gunboats and discharge the crews—and the measure almost carried in those disarming days. Not for Black Jack & the Quids the effete Eurodreams of thalassocracy!

The causes of the War of 1812 ranged from British impressment of American seamen (perhaps a thousand a year, though admittedly many of those seamen were of recent or nonexistent American vintage) to British interference with U.S. ports and maritime commerce to a ravenous desire of some Americans for Canada. The war might even have been avoided had the dashing if dotty Samuel F. B. Morse invented his telegraph a generation earlier. Given more alacritous communication, news of the June 23 repeal of the British Orders-in-Council (which barred neutrals such as the United States from trading in continental ports) might have reached Washington in time for the Potomac war fever to pass. Or perhaps no, since John C. Calhoun and Speaker of the House Henry Clay were hell-bent for the national glory that noncombatants believe to be the spoils of war.

A word about Black Jack's bête noire: Kentuckian Henry Clay, Speaker of the House and later senator, did his part to mold us into a less idiosyncratic country, forbidding Randolph from bringing his dogs onto the House floor. On the other hand, even an apostle of growth like Henry Clay would come to see limits to the American imperium. In 1852 he declared, "Far better is it for ourselves . . . and for the cause of liberty, that, adhering to our wise, pacific system, and avoiding the distant wars of Europe, we should keep our lamp burning brightly on this western shore as a light to all nations, than to hazard its utter extinction amid the ruins of fallen or falling republics in Europe."[39] This once was the consensus view of Americans, whether agrarians or Federalists, hot-blooded slavocrats or moralistic Yankees. Avoid Europe. Within a century anyone expressing the Clay opinion was maligned as unfit for participation in the national discussion, or echo chamber.

As for John C. Calhoun, the South Carolina Yalie, the Calhouns had come across the sea from Donegal in 1733, but to Black Jack they were fresh off the boat—jabbering foreigners, arrivistes hardly fit for positions of responsibility in Randolph's America. No war hawk of middling station would cast aspersions on his love of country! Referring to Calhoun, Randolph sneered, "I must be content to be called a tory by a patriot of the last importation."[40] Ouch!

Anent the War of 1812, Randolph would have no guff about impressment and the defense of national honor. These were irritations, to be sure, even sore vexations, but hardly worth going to war. Expansion, he thought, was the real motive. "Agrarian cupidity, not maritime right, urges the war," he said.[41] The old land hunger was aiming its esurient maw northward, to British Canada.

The British presence on our northern border had long rankled. Just as Florida to the south looked like an orange that would inevitably fall into our union, so too did the Great White North. As early as 1810, Henry Clay, then in the Senate, informed his colleagues, "The conquest of Canada is in your power."[42]

The murmurs of manifest destiny grew audible. A rare New England expansionist, Representative John A. Harper of New Hampshire, exulted that "the Author of Nature has marked our limits in the south, by the Gulf of Mexico; and on the north, by the regions of eternal frost."[43] Those who lived closest to the eternal frost—for instance, the peaceable citizens of western New York—had little stomach for an invasion of Canada, toward which they bore no ill will. But theoreticians banged the war drums, as theoreticians are wont to do. One expansionist gushed in the *Nashville Clarion* of April 28, 1812, "Where is it written in the book of fate that the American republic shall not stretch her limits from the capes of the Chesapeake to Nootka sound, from the isthmus of Panama to Hudson bay?"[44]

Fate does like to dillydally, so the hawks were happy to help it along. Few of those bellowing for British blood lived on the front lines. And if maritime disputes were the primary cause of the war, asked the historian Julius W. Pratt in 1925, why "was war to redress those grievances opposed by the maritime section of the nation?"[45] Anglophilia was one explanation: some Federalists would no more fight England, whatever the provocation, than they would lash a slave. But Pratt uncovered evidence of a quid pro quo of sorts: southern expansionists supported northern designs on Canada in the expectation that war with England would segue into war with England's ally Spain, one consequence of which would be U.S. conquest of Florida and the Southwest.

Former president Jefferson believed that "the cession of Canada," which would drive Great Britain from the continent, "must be a *sine qua non* at a treaty of peace." The mother country's "insults and injuries" had become intolerable; so had its sponsorship of hostile Indians who "tomahawk our women and children."[46] (Secretary of State Monroe, soon to be the last of the Jeffersonian presidents, did not share his fellow Virginian's insistence upon taking Canada.)

The House approved President Madison's message of war on June 4, 1812, by an unimpressive margin of 79–49, and the Senate followed thirteen days later by a fairly narrow vote of 19–13. Rather like the Mexican War of a later generation, this was almost purely a sectional war supported by the South and opposed by New England. "Except Pennsylvania," wrote Henry Adams, "the entire representation of no Northern State declared itself for the war; except Kentucky, every State south of the Potomac and the Ohio voted for the declaration."[47] All thirty-one Federalists in the Congress, including the nine from the South, said no to Mars, as did twenty-two Republicans (all but four from the North).

Samuel Eliot Morison called it "the most unpopular war that this country has ever waged."[48] New Englanders responded with talk of secession, Old Republicans à la Randolph stressed the fatal link between militarism and liberty, and the expected volunteers never showed. Congress authorized a fifty-thousand-volunteer

force, but only ten thousand men signed up. The Madison administration then proposed a draft, which—in eras not consecrated to
servility—has been the surest way to galvanize Middle American
antiwar sentiment.

A young New Hampshireman named Daniel Webster was
elected to Congress as an antiwar Federalist in 1812 and then re-
elected in 1814 on "the American Peace Ticket." On December
9, 1814, Black Dan delivered a timeless speech against the conscription sought by Madison and Calhoun. He thundered:

> Is this, sir, consistent with the character of a free government? Is
> this civil liberty? Is this the real character of our Constitution? No
> sir, indeed it is not. The Constitution is libelled, foully libelled. The
> people of this country have not established for themselves such a
> fabric of despotism. They have not purchased at a vast expense of
> their own treasure and their own blood a Magna Charta to be
> slaves. Where is it written in the Constitution, in what article or
> section is it contained, that you may take children from their par-
> ents, and parents from their children, and compel them to fight the
> battles of any war in which the folly or the wickedness of govern-
> ment may engage it? Under what concealment has this power lain
> hidden which now for the first time comes forth, with a tremen-
> dous and baleful aspect, to trample down and destroy the dearest
> rights of personal liberty? Who will show me any Constitutional
> injunction which makes it the duty of the American people to sur-
> render everything valuable in life, and even life itself, not when the
> safety of their country and its liberties may demand the sacrifice,
> but whenever the purposes of an ambitious and mischievous gov-
> ernment may require it?[49]

Black Dan is still waiting for a reply.

The governors of Massachusetts and Connecticut rebuffed
Madison's request for militia, apparently in ignorance of the ju-
risprudential principles that would guide the Supreme Court in
Perpich v. Defense. Disaffection in New England produced the Hart-

ford Convention, a gathering of Yankee delegates in which secession was whispered, if not endorsed, and a series of quite excellent
constitutional amendments were proposed, foremost a requirement
that the approval of two-thirds of each house of Congress was
necessary to a declaration of war. The Treaty of Ghent, a sort of
call-it-a-draw end to the war, was signed on Christmas Eve 1814,
and General Andrew Jackson's boys won their rousingly anti-
climactic Battle of New Orleans on January 8, 1815, so when the
Hartford men wrapped up their work in January 1815 they were
jeered as traitors, backstabbers, effete cut-and-runners not fit to
pour Old Hickory's tea.

But the most forceful foe of the War of 1812 had been Black
Jack Randolph, who, characteristically, twice challenged Webster
to duels, once in a debate over a sugar tariff.

On December 10, 1811, as the dogs of war strained at their
chains, Randolph took the House floor to descant darkly upon
the coming "war, not of defence but of conquest, of aggrandize-
ment, of ambition; a war foreign to the interest of this country,
to the interests of humanity itself."

Randolph was no grubby partisan, shilling for war and conquest when his party was in power but donning the sash of peace
when the opposition had the votes. (See, in a later time, the
Democrats who supported the Clinton administration's attack on
Serbia but opposed the Bush administration's attack on Iraq, and
those Republicans who acted vice versa.) No, Randolph and his
comrades were "firm and undeviating Republicans who . . . now
dare, to cling to the ark of the Constitution, to defend it even at
the expense of their fame, rather than surrender themselves to the
wild projects of mad ambition!"

The true Republican genius distrusted—nay, despised—
standing armies. Such armies played offense, never defense. The
war hawks had their mean little eyes on Canada, or so Randolph
charged, and by fighting "a war for the acquisition of territory

and subjects" they would be giving the lie to the "doctrine that Republics are destitute of ambition—that they are addicted to peace."

Declaring himself the sworn foe of "standing armies, loans, taxes, navies, and war," Randolph asked, "Who would suffer" by war? "The people. It is their blood, their taxes, that must flow to support it."

"The Government of the United States," Randolph lectured, "was not calculated to wage offensive foreign war—it was instituted for the common defence and general welfare; and whosoever should embark it in a war of offence, would put it to a test which it was by no means calculated to endure."[50] The price of Canada, which he believed to be the hidden desideratum of the war hawks, was the Constitution. Just as the price of empire would later be America's soul.

Randolph lost his seat in the election of 1813, a martyr to the cause of peace. The people had spoken—the bastards! Black Jack wrote a friend, "No man can reproach me with the desertion of my friends, or the abandonment of my post in a time of danger and trial. 'I have fought the good fight. I have kept the faith.' I owe the public nothing."[51]

The public reciprocated. Randolph, Georgia, changed its name to Jasper in protest over Black Jack's peacemongering.

Randolph was a Virginian before he was an American, but then so did most Americans identity with state rather than with nation, for that was the heart of the federal system. (Even more so was it the heart of the Anti-Federalists' system, the Articles of Confederation, which the Constitution supplanted.) Nathaniel Hawthorne, the conservative Democrat and best friend of President Franklin Pierce, went so far as to say that "we never were one people, and never really had a country since the Constitution was formed."[52] By 1865 the question would be settled—we were, indeed, a country, albeit one fused at sword's point—but in 1812

Virginia and Massachusetts were separate countries bound by a Constitution that those two states had barely ratified.

John Greenleaf Whittier eulogized Randolph:

> *Too honest or too proud to feign*
> *A love he never cherished*
> *Beyond Virginia's border line*
> *His patriotism perished*
> *While others hailed in distant skies*
> *Our eagle's dusky pinion,*
> *He only saw the mountain bird*
> *Stoop o'er his old Dominion!*[53]

(The nationalist praises the eagle for its aggressiveness; the localist, the patriot of his state or, better, her village or pond or avenue, fears the bird of prey, the supper on carrion, and seeks to keep clenched its talons. The humble, ornery, esculent turkey is our feathered friend.)

"Remorse, remorse!" were Randolph's last words. "He was buried with his face to the setting sun," as Russell Kirk relates the legend, "so that he might keep his sharp eyes on Henry Clay and the West."[54] Little did Randolph dream that his grave vision might one day descry Old Glory flying over Hawaii, Guam, and the Philippines.

Expansion carried within the seeds of destruction. Libertarians and conservatives understood this, if progressives did not. John Lowell, Federalist kindred of the Massachusetts Lowells, went so far as to propose, in 1813, that "the original thirteen states" kick out the latecomers, renounce the Louisiana Purchase, and restore comity within a country of manageable size. Returning the United States to its eastern base, wrote Lowell, "appears to be the last hope of our country."[55]

It was not the last hope, of course, though we hear, again and again throughout our history, the dire warnings of Little Americans that expansion, conquest, and what was soon to be called manifest destiny will be the ruin of us yet. We acquired no territory by the Treaty of Ghent, which ended the war; the northern lands remained under British dominion. Great lakes made good neighbors.

Abe Lincoln's Finest Moment

Ralph Waldo Emerson prophesied of the Mexican War, "The United States will conquer Mexico, but it will be as the man who swallows the arsenic, which brings him down in turn. Mexico will poison us."[56] For once, Massachusetts and South Carolina, or at least their most prominent men, were in agreement. John C. Calhoun compared Mexico to a forbidden fruit, the eating of which would kill the Republic.

In retrospect, continentalism, even the absorption of Texas, makes a certain sense. Lord knows I have a deep sentimental attachment—nay, an abiding love—for the Lower 48. But to ignore the way in which the fruit was picked dishonors the faith of our fathers.

Like the War of 1812, the Mexican War galvanized the antiexpansionists of New England. Curiously, it was also opposed by Calhoun and an Illinois Whig congressman named Lincoln, neither of whom were noteworthy in antiwar causes before or after the 1840s. And while the poets of the North, from James Russell Lowell to Henry David Thoreau, sang songs of peace, a Brooklyn Democrat named Walter Whitman mongered war.

President James K. Polk, the Tennessee Jacksonian who was tormented by diarrhea during his single and eventful term in the White House, is typically awarded the grade of "near great" in those periodic presidential rankings by American historians. He is hard by the immortals because—not although—he, like almost all the "greats" and "near greats"—Lincoln, Theodore and Franklin Roosevelt, Wilson, Truman—waged war.

The casus belli of "Polk's war," as it came to be called, was a border incident provoked by his land-covetous administration. The boundaries of the new state of Texas were in dispute; so were the sizes of damage claims lodged by American citizens against the bankrupt government of Mexico. After a series of diplomatic contretemps, Polk ordered U.S. soldiers under General Zachary Taylor through the heart of the disputed territory to the Rio Grande. When a detachment from the Mexican side crossed the river in the attempt to break a U.S. blockade, shots were fired, and three Americans fell dead, far from home. A door had opened. We fell through, headfirst. The Polk Democrats drew up a kind of portmanteau bill: it authorized supplying the men at what was now the front, and it also declared that due to Mexican aggression a state of war existed between the two North American nations. Charles Francis Adams called this "one of the grossest national lies that was ever deliberately told,"[57] but presidents have been known to lie the country into war, and rare indeed is the member of Congress with the guts to stand up and call a lie a lie.

Congressional Democrats muffled debate on the war resolution, limiting consideration of this declaration of war to a mingy two hours. Courage, as is its wont, kept a safe distance from the halls of Congress. The House voted for war on May 11, 1846, by a vote of 174–14, and the Senate concurred the next day by 40–2. Massachusetts and Ohio supplied the majority of nays. (Protesting the reflectionless rush to an obvious land grab, several antiwar figures abstained or were absent, among them John C. Calhoun, who would argue, in part, from fiscal conservatism against a fellow southern Democrat's profligate war.)

Explaining the apparent disjunction between the overwhelming vote for the Mexican War and the widespread opposition that was soon to develop, the historian Frederick Merk noted "a momentary hysteria on the part of the public which Polk converted into a stampede."[58] When honor is at stake or perceived to be at stake, men fight. An admirable trait—for men, that is, whose means of inflicting damage are mean. Nations, with their comparatively limitless capacity for wrack, are—or ought to be— another story. As the Georgia Whig Alexander H. Stephens, future vice president of the Confederacy and harsh critic of the war, explained in a discourse on "national greatness," a theme revisited by neoconservatives of our own day, "Fields of blood and carnage may make men brave and heroic, but seldom tend to make nations either good, virtuous or great."[59]

I admire extravagantly Texas writers (Elmer Kelton) and singer-songwriters (Townes Van Zandt, Alejandro Escovedo) and even the occasional politician (Congressman Ron Paul, the rancher-historian and states'-rights Democrat J. Evetts Haley), but let's face it: Texas has almost been more trouble than it's worth. Its annexation in 1845 led to the eventual war with Mexico; its presidents (LBJ and the two Bushes) have waged costly wars of aggression against nations that posed no threat to these United States. As Gene McCarthy joked to me in a 1996 interview, "A Mexican cartoonist said, What's your position on the return of the Panama Canal? I said I would do it but to offset it you would have to take Texas. He said, We'll take the land but not the people. So it may be good policy: . . . give 'em half of Texas. We took it from you, and we'll give it back to you."[60]

McCarthy, as a retired pol not worried about reelection, could afford to tell the truth. Despite the harrumphing about national honor, all sides to the debate in 1846–47 understood that this was a war for expansion. In the revealing toast of Polk's vice president, George M. Dallas, "A more perfect Union; embracing the entire North American continent."[61] Perhaps extending slavery westward was a subreason for the war; perhaps not. For there were fierce critics of Polk's war who defended the peculiar institution, and among the hawks were such lovers of humankind as Walter Whitman. The Pennsylvania Democrat David Wilmot sought, with his Wilmot Proviso, to bar slavery from any territory acquired from Mexico, but as fire bells clanged in the night his proposal failed again and again. For whom did the bells toll? For union, for union.

The war was driven by the ideology of manifest destiny—the notion, in its most naively appealing form, that so effervescent was the American spirit that it could not be contained in the constrictive old wineskins but needed a continent, perhaps even a continent and a half, over which to spill. "All Mexico!" cried the destinarians. Eight million Mexicans were to be swallowed whole. The New York City litterateurs grouped around the *New York Morning News* editor John L. O'Sullivan under the "Young America" umbrella waxed rhapsodic over westward expansion at sword's point, though as usual the martial Manhattans never did get around to enlisting in the crusade.

O'Sullivan's fellow editor James Gordon Bennett of the *New York Herald* spoke for the ink-stained imperialists on the eve of war: "The minds of men have been awakened to a clear conviction of the destiny of this great nation of freemen. No longer bounded by those limits which nature had in the eye of those of little faith [in] the last generation, assigned to the dominion of republicanism on this continent, the pioneers of Anglo-Saxon civilization and Anglo-Saxon free institutions, now seek distant territories, stretching even to the shores of the Pacific; and the arms of the republic, it is clear to all men of sober discernment, must soon embrace the whole hemisphere, from the icy wilderness of the North to the most prolific regions of the smiling and prolific South."[62]

No longer bounded by limits. Is there a more succinct expression of anticonservative philosophy? Manifest destiny was the

pipe dream of epicene East Coast intellectuals for whom America
was not so much a country as it was an idea, a sort of viscous
rolling blob capable of absorbing foreign peoples, sovereign republics, and anything else that got in its way. Their ilk, alas, would
reappear throughout our history.

Our destiny was not so manifest to everyone. Abraham Lincoln was elected to the House of Representatives as an antiwar
Whig in 1846, a midterm midwar election that, as with the election of 2006, produced a new Congress controlled by the opposition party. The Whigs gained thirty-eight seats; the citizenry
had awaked to the Polkian prevarications. In fact, Lincoln was
among those approving a House resolution praising the soldiers—
"supporting the troops" has always been a wise political move—but
condemning "a war unnecessarily and unconstitutionally begun
by the President of the United States."[63]

Going beyond the usual disapprobative limits, Ohio senator
Thomas Corwin, a conservative anti-expansionist Whig, delivered what still ranks as one of the most incendiary peace speeches
in congressional history when on February 11, 1847, he told a
hushed Senate, "If I were a Mexican, I would tell you, 'Have you
not room in your own country to bury your dead men? If you
come into mine we will greet you with bloody hands, and welcome you to hospitable graves.' "[64]

Talk about not supporting the troops!

Corwin ripped into Polk as if possessed by the avenging
ghosts of 1776. The president—"His Majesty"—had lied a nation into war, effectively bypassed the constitutional requirement
that such a declaration come from Congress, and was building a
"most odious, most hateful despotism" under which a president,
accountable to no one, least of all a meek and compliant Congress, might order troops "to Mexico, to Panama, to China."
Americans, no longer vigilant guardians of their liberties, had
"torn that written Constitution to pieces, scattered its fragments

to the winds, and surrendered themselves to the usurped authority of ONE MAN."[65]

The senatorial courtesies Corwin dispensed with. Senator Lewis Cass (D-MI), the mediocrity who recited expansionist slogans in pursuit of the 1848 Democratic presidential nomination, was "red with the blood of recent slaughter, the gory spear of Achilles in his hand and the hoarse clarion of war in his mouth."[66]

Offer Mexico peace, Senator Corwin urged; wash the blood from our hands and renounce any territorial ambitions.

Corwin's address was a sensation. He joked that his effigy blazed in town squares from Maine to Texas, yet the freshman senator was also boomed for president by his many new admirers. He was gutsy; he was eloquent; he was a spellbinder. (President Rutherford B. Hayes said many years later, "Corwin was one of the most wonderful talkers I have ever met.")[67] A rooted son of Lebanon, Ohio, the husband of an impressive woman kin to the Randolphs of Virginia, Corwin did not suffer for his speech. In fact, Millard Fillmore would appoint him secretary of the treasury in 1850. But the Ohioan knew well that a marble pose was not his fate: he had been too honest, his wit too biting. He once told an aspiring orator: "Never make people laugh. If you would succeed in life, you must be solemn, solemn as an ass. All the great monuments are built over solemn asses."[68]

Echoing Corwin, the Congregationalist minister Samuel J. May of Syracuse pleaded with his flock to not submit to the "fell delusion that patriotism demands of them to sacrifice themselves on the plains of Texas."[69] God intends for you to be something more than a slain soldier or a butcher of men. Heed not the calls of the warites. Easy, I suppose, for an old man to preach; harder for blood-stirred youths to absorb.

The vehemence with which Reverend May, Thomas Corwin, and other dissentients expressed themselves was a subject of wonder for the historian Charles J. DeWitt. Writing in 1933, DeWitt remarked, "A most unusual thing is the lack of press and speech censorship during the Mexican War. Statements were both written and spoken which during the World War would have gained their perpetrators imprisonment or fine for seditious utterance."[70] Men spoke freely once in this America, consecrated as it was to liberty and to conscience. We forget that. Today a Thomas Corwin could kiss his career good-bye after delivering so blistering an assault on a war and a president. In antebellum America, he wound up in Millard Fillmore's cabinet.

Under the Treaty of Guadalupe Hidalgo of 1848, Mexico ceded one-third of its territory to the United States. As if to rebut the charge that these were ill-gotten gains, the administration insisted upon paying Mexico $15 million for the cession. The pretty fiction is that these lands were bought, not stolen.

Among those voting against the treaty was Daniel Webster: a peace man in 1814 and still in 1847. His son Ned, the black sheep of the family who had compared himself to the prodigal son, was an organizer of a company of Massachusetts volunteers. Ned died of typhoid eight miles outside of Mexico City. His father would be unconsoled by unctuous assurances that the boy had died for his country. His country? Hell, Black Dan thundered in denouncing the Treaty of Guadalupe Hidalgo, we had squandered men and millions to gain a "monstrosity," an "enormity," a "disfiguration" of the Republic. The lands acquired by the treaty "are not worth a dollar; and we pay for them vast sums of money!"[71] Not to mention sons.

The Vermont Whig congressman George Perkins Marsh—etymologist, naturalist, diplomat—was a polymathic Little American. He disdained the Southwest as an "apple of discord" upon which the Republic would choke. Political association ought to conform to geographic boundaries, argued Marsh. Like John Lowell during the War of 1812, Marsh saw no reason to expand the Union beyond the original thirteen states. Far-flung empires connected only by the thin cable of a coercive central state were unnatural, incoherent, and unhappy. Small is beautiful; large is ugly, and brutal withal. "The citizens of the little republic of San Marino, and of the duchy of Tuscany,"[72] are happy and prosperous in their insularity, said Marsh. So could be the United States, if we let pass the mania for growth.

There was no indignity in smallness. The best New Englanders knew this. Thoreau had traveled widely in his own backyard, and Marsh, as a five-year-old boy in Woodstock, Vermont, had learned that each acre of woods contains a glorious profusion of the distinct and the unduplicable. He recalled, "My father pointed out the most striking trees as we passed them, and told me how to distinguish their varieties. I do not think I ever afterward failed to know one forest tree from another."[73] He was a man who could see the forest only because of the trees.

John Greenleaf Whittier looked to the west and saw

> *Great spaces yet untravelled,*
> *great lakes whose mystic shores*
> *The Saxon rifle never heard,*
> *nor dip of Saxon oars;*
> *Great herds that wander all unwatched,*
> *wild steeds that none have tamed,*
> *Strange fish in unknown streams,*
> *and birds the Saxon never named;*
>
> . . . .
> *all these ye say are ours?*[74]

They were indeed. The dismembered Mexico had become, overnight, part of America. Though a pure-hearted abolitionist, Whittier gives a foretaste of the racialism that is undeniably present in later anti-expansionist movements, particularly the opposition to the annexation of the booty from the Spanish-American War. It's not that fear of the adulteration of old Anglo-Saxon stock was the prime afflatus of the anti-expansionists and the anti-imperialists, but it was present and must be admitted, if not excused. It would be unjust to make of Mexicans American subjects, but whether they could be made citizens was by no means obvious to the peace party of 1848.

Manifest destiny, we must recall, was ordained not by God but by jingoes. And it wasn't all that manifest to many Americans. "Civilization, religion, education, and manners are all injured by the inordinate increase of 'frontier life' among us," wrote E. L. Godkin, the laissez-faire editor of the *Nation*, shortly after the Civil War. "Every interest of our society calls for more condensation of our people and less expansion of our territory."[75]

Contiguous expansion makes a certain sense, even to a Little American like myself. Virginia leads to Tennessee, which connects with Arkansas, which abuts Texas. There is about the concatenation an undeniable coherence—a manifest practicality, if not destiny. But to covet islands across a sea, or even oceans distant—this was madness. Or at least it was un-American.

The Conquest of the United States by Spain

The high-water mark of naked U.S. imperialism—and anti-imperialism as well, for the reaction was torrid, even from codfish Congregationalists—came at the end of the nineteenth century, as the mauve decade flashed carmine red. A rich blend of Gold Democrats and buckskin western populists, New England conservatives and Republican regulars, frontier humorists and rarefied Harvardians joined—no, that verb implies too much cohesion; rather, they agitated in fraternal disconcert—in opposition to the expansionist aftermath of the Spanish-American War.

The anti-imperialists of 1899–1902 remain the least studied but most articulate, passionate, and desperate antiwar proponents in our history. They spoke for a Little America, a land of creeks, not oceans; shops, not factories; modesty and sly humor, not bluster and brass. Or at least most of them did. The immigrant steel tycoon Andrew Carnegie, who helped to bankroll the cause, declared, "I am no 'Little' American, afraid of growth, either in population or territory, provided always that the new territory be American and that it will produce Americans, and not foreign races bound in time to be false to the Republic in order to be true to themselves."[76]

The lines had been drawn five years earlier in the Hawaiian sands, during the waning days of the gilded age of President Benjamin Harrison. The 1893 overthrow of Queen Liliuokalani by plotters backed by the U.S. minister and absentee owners of the not-so-sweet Sugar Trust presented the expansionists with a charming polyglot colony (and U.S. coaling station that was the gateway to the Orient) whose rulers were begging to be annexed. Harrison complied, sending a treaty to the Senate in mid-February, just days before his term expired and he was to return to Indianapolis and eventual marriage to his late wife's niece (much to his children's disgust). But Grover Cleveland, the once and future president, would not be swept along in the mad rush to plant the flag on Molokai. Cleveland withdrew the treaty.

Expansionists—intellectual admirals eager to spangle their uniforms while achieving seafaring supremacy, missionary progressives ready to teach the paganry the rudiments of tithing and toothbrushing—threw a collective hissy fit.

Cleveland, "the Buffalo lilliputian," and his fellow Democratic reactionaries, charged one Republican paper (the *New York Commercial Advertiser*), were shattering "the dream of an American republic at the crossroads of the Pacific" (whose dream was *that?*) and handing back the islands to "native rule, ignorant, naked, heathen[s]" with their "superstitious orgies."[77]

Let us now praise corpulent men. Grover Cleveland was the last of the laissez-faire Democrats (or Bourbon conservatives, as his populist critics would say) and the closest thing to a nineteenth-century classical liberal (which is to say, in twentieth-century terms, conservative) president we ever had.

As governor of New York he had even vetoed a bill that would have permitted his hometown of Fayetteville "to borrow money for the purchase of a new steam fire engine."[78] So he was hardly the sort to undertake spendthrift nation building across the seas.

In his first inaugural address he repeated the Jeffersonian pledge of "peace, commerce, and honest friendship with all nations; entangling alliance with none."[79] This wasn't the usual ghostwritten, cliché-ridden bullshit.

"Cleveland was essentially an isolationist and uninterested in military and naval affairs," writes the presidential historian Henry F. Graff.[80] By junking Harrison's Hawaii annexation treaty, Cleveland revealed "his unyielding opposition to imperialist tendencies, Latin-American or Pacific adventures, and overseas entanglements in general,"[81] observed Allan Nevins.

To Grover Cleveland and patriots of the old America, the idea of incorporating into U.S. territory "islands of the sea more than two thousand miles removed from our nearest coast"[82] was madness. It flouted tradition; it was of dubious constitutionality; it denied the importance of propinquity in political relationships. Why should a continental nation accumulate insular possessions? Imperial annexationists had to wait for Cleveland's Republican successor, William McKinley—a Civil War brevet major, not so incidentally, which means that unlike the draft-dodging shirker Cleveland, he had seen, firsthand, how to fly Old Glory over people who hated that striped banner.

Intoxicated by the exotic bounty of the Spanish-American War, the McKinley administration also succeeded in the annexation of Hawaii in July 1898. The flag, severed from its staff, now waved in any vagrant breeze.

Former president Cleveland issued a statement to the Associated Press declaring that "ever since the question of Hawaiian annexation was presented," he had been "utterly and constantly opposed to it."[83] He minced no words. "Our interference in the revolution of 1893 was disgraceful," and the absorption of these Pacific islands would be "a perversion of our national mission."[84] When Hawaii was annexed, Cleveland announced himself "ashamed of the whole affair."[85]

It's not that he or his confreres were head-in-the-sand ostriches of the interventionist caricature; rather, Cleveland, the free trader, would have agreed with the individualist sociologist William Graham Sumner, who said that if "we could have free trade with Hawaii while somebody else had the jurisdiction, we should gain all the advantages and escape all the burdens."[86]

And what burdens they were! Just twoscore years after their absorption into the American Empire, Hawaii and the Philippines were to prove the "back door to war." The historian John Lukacs has ventured that "one may even speculate that had Hawaii remained a Pacific kingdom the tragedy at Pearl Harbor or perhaps even a Japanese-American war might not have occurred—but that carries speculation too far."[87] Ah, what the hell. Let's carry it all the way to the end zone. If the anti-imperialists had carried the day, and no American flag had ever flown over Hawaii, the Philippines, Guam, or any other mass of land in the Pacific, it's tough to discern any reason why the United States and Japan would have gone to war in 1941. More than one hundred thousand American lives would not have been lost. All we would have had to do was give up Jack Lord.

Southern Democrats, who in the twentieth century would act as an almost solid bloc for every war, supplied the majority (75) of the 91 votes against the annexation. Race, unquestionably, was a factor in the anti-annexationist calculus. Hawaii was a mélange of natives, Chinese, Japanese, Portuguese, and a smattering of white Americans. Its people seemed unassimilable. By contrast, every member of the Manhattan congressional delegation voted with the imperialists. The city of New York had recently swallowed Brooklyn in pursuit of municipal hugeness. Skyscrapers were blotting out the sun. Bigness was in fashion. Why not extend America as far as it could stretch?

"There will be no war with Spain while I am President,"[88] declared Grover Cleveland, and there wasn't. But Cleveland, unlike the next upstate New Yorker to take the presidential oath, Franklin D. Roosevelt, obeyed George Washington's two-term precedent. And Uncle Jumbo's men stood by him: eight members of Cleveland's cabinet also denounced the nation's imperialist turn under McKinley.

The "splendid little war," in Secretary of State John Hay's phrase, from which the United States emerged militarily triumphant but morally defeated (William Graham Sumner called it "the conquest of the United States by Spain") lives today only in the thrasonical tales of Theodore the Rough Rider. Of this bespectacled Harvard boy, Republican kingmaker Mark Hanna, a reluctant imperialist himself, is said to have blurted out to the reporter Arthur Dunn at the 1900 GOP convention in Philadelphia at which TR was nominated for vice president: "Don't you understand that there is just one life between this crazy man and the presidency if you force me to take Roosevelt?"[89]

Like Poe's red death, the Spanish-American War happened in the blink of an eye. The USS *Maine* blew up (we know not why) in Havana Harbor on February 15, 1898, killing 260 Americans; on May 1, Commodore George Dewey and his tars sank the Spanish fleet in Manila Bay. Two months later, Teddy Roosevelt led his Rough Riders up San Juan Hill. With only 300-plus battle deaths in a handful of skirmishes, the United States defeated Spain in less than half a year.

The stated purpose of the war was to liberate Cuba from Spanish tyranny—a reason plausible on the surface, though southern Democrats had sought to acquire Cuba in the 1850s as lebensraum for slavery. A decadent and popish Old World nation had no rightful place in the western hemisphere. Even Mark Twain agreed, saying, "[I have] never enjoyed a war . . . as I am enjoying this one."[90] The Spanish-American War happened so fast that opposition never really organized. But then came the cleanup, which begat the mess. The misheard voice of the Lord— or was it the seductive voice of the Prince of Lies?—served as the deus ex machina. As President McKinley told an enrapt audience of visiting Methodist missionaries, he walked the White House floor night after night, praying for guidance. What ought he to do with this Filipino bounty that God, in the guise of Admiral Dewey, had delivered unto him? He couldn't remand our little brown brothers back to Spanish custody, and they sure weren't capable of self-government, no matter what Jefferson wrote in the Declaration. So there really was "nothing left for us to do but to take them all and to educate the Filipinos, and uplift and Christianize them, and by God's grace do the very best we could by them, as our fellow-men for whom Christ also died."[91]

The occupying U.S. forces refused to permit General Emilio Aguinaldo, the admirable leader of the Filipino rebels, to assume the office of president. Spain ceded the Philippines to the United States, which in turn did not cede them to the Filipinos. The rebels turned their guns upon the American occupiers. Boys from Indiana and Kentucky were halfway around the globe suppressing indigenous patriots in what would sprawl into a three-year guerrilla war in which two hundred thousand Filipinos would die. Mark Twain now proposed that the skull and crossbones replace the Stars and Stripes.

Robert L. Beisner, who in *Twelve Against Empire: The Anti-Imperialists*, recalled the recusants in the new church of Theodore Rex, declared, "In less than a year a strong but largely self-contained America had changed into a far-flung empire already harassed by a colonial rebellion."[92] Or as Felix Morley, who was born in the pre-imperial year of 1894, would write ruefully, "The deeper result [of the Spanish-American War] was to make Washington for the first time classifiable as a world capital, governing millions of people overseas as subjects rather than as citizens. The private enslavement of Negroes was ended. The public control of alien populations had begun."[93]

The Treaty of Paris, signed on December 10, 1898, gave Cuba a nominal independence and transferred the Philippines, Puerto Rico, and Guam to the United States for $20 million—a violation of contiguity, of common sense, and of the Constitution, which had not contemplated the acquisition of territories except those intended for eventual statehood, which these new possessions most certainly were not. Republicans, the party of nationalist consolidation in the 1860s, were now the party of extranational conquest. The Treaty of Paris was approved by the Senate, 57–27. The opponents included two Republicans: George Frisbie Hoar of Massachusetts and Eugene Pryor Hale of Maine.

These anti-imperialists "are still a reminder of the value of conservative dissent," writes Beisner.[94] Theodore Roosevelt called them "unhung traitors,"[95] but they acted as honorable, befuddled, exasperated men who went to sleep in a republic and woke up under the blistering sun of empire. "They thought that an imperialist policy ran counter to the political doctrines of the Declaration of Independence, Washington's Farewell Address, and Lincoln's Gettysburg Address," wrote Fred H. Harrington,[96] one of the few historians to examine this band of old Americans who refused to march to the martial drum of the new century.

The Anti-Imperialist League, coordinator of Little American dissent, was primarily a New England production; its matrix was the Massachusetts Reform Club, with all the high-mindedness that implies.

By the turn of the century, Anti-Imperialist Leagues had sprouted from Portland to Cleveland to Baltimore—a dozen cities in all. The league headquarters moved west, to Chicago, in October 1899, but unlike the antiwar movements that formed before each of the world wars, opposition to the imperialist aftermath of the Spanish-American War was strongest in the Northeast. The grandchildren of Lowells and Adamses (Brooks aside) were not going to give up the ghost that easily. And not all of these descendants quailed before radicalism. General William Birney, the son of James Birney (the Liberty Party's standard-bearer in 1840) and the president of the Washington Anti-Imperialist League, called for McKinley's impeachment, but the Congress has seen fit to institute such proceedings not for the launching of unconstitutional wars but only for graver violations of the public trust: Andrew Johnson's firing of Edwin Stanton, Richard Nixon's clumsy obstruction of an investigation into a political break-in, and Bill Clinton's fibbing about an adulterous blow job.

The Anti-Imperialist League was founded on November 19, 1898, in the office of Edward Atkinson, a vice president of the American Peace Society. Atkinson, a born and bred patriot of Brookline, Massachusetts, made his mint as treasurer and agent for several cotton mills. The father of nine, he was one of those indefatigable New England reformers whose belief in improvement and a reasonable return on the dollar followed him into his roles as "friend of the 'new' South, writer, tariff reformer, sound-money agitator, anti-imperialist, statistician, economist, dietician, inventor,"[97] and a pioneer in the field of fire insurance. His adherence to the free-trade faith brought him into conflict with his mostly protectionist and Republican manufactural brethren, but it was in 1898 that Atkinson took his stand as a peace capitalist.

Atkinson could never be caricatured as an autarkist, as were later antiwar businessmen. Foreign markets and robust international trade were his goals, but he did not wish the U.S. Navy to shell outsiders for those markets or U.S. taxpayers to shell out for them. He called battleships "commerce destroyers"[98] and would have seconded the libertarian maxim that if goods can't cross borders, troops will.

Of Atkinson, Beisner has written: "His views were usually buttressed by a mass of statistics that did not always prove what he thought they did but were impressive by virtue of their sheer bulk." He was a dull writer but a lively man. Atkinson invented the Aladdin Oven, earning himself the mock epitaph "He taught the American people how to stew."[99]

The acquisition of the Philippines radicalized Atkinson. An inveterate pamphleteer, he requested of the U.S. government the names of "five hundred or six hundred"[100] Philippine-based soldiers and officers so that he might send them his tracts against imperialism. The authorities were not amused. Starting at the top, he mailed pamphlets to Admiral Dewey and six other eminences abroad. The postmaster general ordered the Manila envelopes seized in San Francisco.

This brazenness proved too much for the genteel New England contingent of the league, so Atkinson shifted his efforts and not inconsiderable bankroll to the Chicago branch.

Like Atkinson, most of the anti-imperialists were partisans of a laissez-faire economy, though unlike Atkinson and the sugar daddy Andrew Carnegie, they made their pile the old-fashioned way: they inherited it. "Conservatives dominated the anti-imperialist movement," writes Beisner. "They were members of the old upper-middle and upper classes, conservative in social outlook and frequently aristocratic in demeanor. They took for granted that they could speak for the American conscience."[101] Their bloodlines often ran through abolition and mugwumpery; they considered themselves reformers, but those reforms were aimed at curbing the excesses of mobocracy. More than a few shuddered when in best nouveau riche fashion the steel magnate Carnegie proposed that he simply write a check for $20 million and thereby secure independence for the Filipinos. (One can imagine Ross Perot, whose 1992 presidential campaign played isolationism in a minor key, scribbling out a check for Kuwait.)

The fungibility of the Yankee dollar also amused Republican Speaker of the House Thomas B. Reed, whom the redoubtable Missouri Democrat Champ Clark described as "a self-made man who worshipped his Maker." The Speaker was a sardonic wit whose bitterness against the imperialists erupted in such wisecracks as his remark about a $300,000 appropriation for a Philadelphia museum: "This seems like a great waste of money. We could buy 150,000 Sulus with that."[102] Reed, alas, saved his antiimperial witticisms for private conversations and notes that no one would read till long after the battle was ended. It's so easy to be courageous in the den.

Yet rebel Republicans cut some of the sharpest and most poignant profiles in courage.

Among the most stalwart of these Republicans—indeed, a founder of the Grand Old Party—was the Vermont senator Justin S. Morrill, father of the land-grant college act. Morrill was a consistent anti-imperialist throughout his career: in best "Little Vermonter" tradition he argued against the annexation of San Domingo, Cuba, and Hawaii.[103] With all the vigor an eightyeight-year-old politico might muster, he criticized the Spanish-American War as a betrayal of the free-soil principles that had led him in the 1850s to organize the Vermont Republicans.

The anti-imperialist Republicans were, admittedly, of superannuated cast. The president of the Anti-Imperialist League was

George S. Boutwell, the ancient placeholder who had served as treasury secretary in the unfortunate administration of Ulysses S. Grant. Boutwell, bless his run-of-the-mill heart, found his voice and achieved a kind of anguished nobility at his life's end. Breaking with McKinley and the party he had served so faithfully if not always so well, Boutwell framed the question in this way: "Is it wise and just for us, as a nation, to make war for the seizure and government of distant lands, occupied by millions of inhabitants, who are alien to us in every aspect of life, except that we are together members of the same human family?"[104]

"Empire means vast armies employed in ignominious service" and "burdensome taxation at home," wrote Boutwell. In committing the Republic to an imperial course, President McKinley had "turned away from the history of America, he disdained our traditions, and he reversed the policy of a century."[105]

Boutwell abandoned his party in 1900, prophesying that "the reelection of McKinley would mean the abandonment of the republic and the acceptance of a colonial empire as the result of his policy."[106] It was a leap of faithlessness that few others were willing to make.

Senator George Frisbie Hoar (R-MA), sticking fast to the GOP, tried vainly to "persuade the Republican Party, or a sufficient number of Republicans, to adopt a sound and righteous policy."[107] (William A. Croffut, secretary of the Washington Anti-Imperialist League, quipped of Hoar's simultaneous support for McKinley and anti-imperialism that "nobody seems to be infringing brother Hoar's patent for denouncing the crime and praising the criminal.")[108]

There is an almost pitiful quality to Hoar's magnificent January 9, 1899, animadversion upon imperialism. Speaking in favor of the resolution of Senator George Graham Vest (D-MO)—Vest, by the way, is generally credited with fathering the aphorism that a dog is man's best friend—declaring that the Constitution does not confer upon the federal government the right to acquire colonies, Hoar first justifies a lifetime spent in service of the GOP: "I am one of those men who believe that little that is great or good or permanent for a free people can be accomplished without the instrumentality of party. And I have believed religiously, and from my soul, for half a century, in the great doctrines and principles of the Republican Party."

But now, having caught a frightful glimpse of his bride in the garb of the Whore of Babylon, he casts uxoriousness aside. It is time "to speak for my country, for its whole past and its whole future." A fateful, perhaps fatal, step is about to be taken. Even "the strongest frame may get mortal sickness from one exposure: the most vigorous health or life may be destroyed by a single drop of poison, and what poison is to the human frame the abandonment of our great doctrine of liberty will be to the Republic."

"Our danger today is from the lust of empire," roars Hoar. Denying that he is a "strict constructionist," an "alarmist," or, God forbid, a "States' rights man," the senator asserts that as a Federalist patriot, a Daniel Webster Republican, he must speak out before his party "will make of our beloved country a cheapjack country, raking after the cart for the leavings of European tyranny." Colonies require a standing army, which the founders regarded as an instrument of oppression. They require a "powerful navy" and systematized national plunder, which "is sure to make our national taxgatherer the most familiar visitant to every American home." By making mockery of the pretty phrases in the Declaration of Independence, by forsaking "the ancient path of republican liberty" for "the modern swamp and cesspool of imperialism," the empire builders were burying under their devilish edifice the birthright of every American.

Hoar did not understate the question: "Is there to be no place on the face of the earth hereafter where a man can stand up by virtue of his manhood and say, 'I am a man?'" The stakes, he told the Senate, were no less than the Republic itself. Empire or republic? The choice would resound unto "the great eternity of national life."[109]

It reverberates yet.

Hoar was consistent, courageous, and not a little frustrated. He fought U.S. imperialism in Puerto Rico as well as in the Philippines, for he did not agree that "the safety of the United States" was "in the least dependent on a little island down in the West Indies."[110]

He feared for his erring country: "You have no right to impose on an unwilling people your Constitution and your notions of freedom. When you say that freedom as we conceive it and not as the people of the Philippines conceive it, shall prevail, and that if it does not we are to force it on them at the cannon's mouth, I say that the nation which undertakes it will encounter the awful and terrible rebuke, 'Beware of the leaven of the Pharisees which is hypocrisy.' "[111]

Of George Frisbie Hoar, the poet Frances Bartlett predicted:

So stands Hoar now before his fellow-men,
True to that faith for which the fathers died!
And one day History, with iron pen,
Shall write on Time's stained leaves his name beside,
"Champion of Freedom's honor crucified,"
And centuries unborn shall say "Amen!"[112]

What charming faith the early anti-imperialists had in posterity! The nation had stumbled and sinned in the dark, but they believed that those of us a century hence, bathed in the light, would commission statues to "Hoar of Massachusetts."

Alas, the statues are all dedicated to Hoar's homonyms.

Hoar and Morrill and Boutwell were old men. Decrepit relics. The vascular young imperialists who rallied to the jingoistic calisthenics of Theodore Roosevelt ("Megaphone of Mars," as the novelist Henry Blake Fuller called him) had little patience for the vaporings of senescent haunts. Empire was for the fit and vigorous who would not be chained to a place; peace was for the old, the anile, the invalided.

To the Rooseveltian promise of a spanking new navy sailing the seven seas, conquering pagan natives and planting Old Glory on exotic atolls, the elderly anti-imperialists could answer with only the tattered rag of the thirteen-star flag. In vain did they protest against what would later be known as "preparedness."

"When we get our navy and send it round the world in search of imputations on our honor," wrote E. L. Godkin in 1896, "we shall have launched the United States on that old sea of sin and sorrow and ruffianism on which mankind has tossed since the dawn of history . . . We shall have abandoned as a failure the greatest experiment any government ever made."[113]

Edwin Lawrence (E. L.) Godkin was a founding editor of *The Nation* in 1865 and later editor in chief of the *New York Evening Post,* ancestor of the Murdochian tabloid rather in the way that Ernest Hemingway is the progenitor of Margaux. Godkin is yet another example of the complications of dividing sentient human beings into the cattle pens of "Left" and "Right." An Anglo-Irish immigrant, he was anti-imperialist, anti-expansion, and an advocate of free trade, economy in government, lenient treatment of the former Confederacy, and civil service reform. He denounced the graduated income tax as "socialistic" and a form of theft. He admired the classical liberal (which is to say conservative) Grover Cleveland above all the presidents of his era; in 1900, refusing to vote for the Democratic populist William Jennings Bryan, he supported the Gold Democrat John Palmer, candidate of the night-watchman-state Democracy.

Godkin's *Nation,* it should be remembered, upheld the ideals of free trade and limited government, not the democratic socialism it took up by the midpoint of the twentieth century. "I am," he confessed, "heart and soul, an American of the *vieille roche*"—an immigrant going old school! "American ideals were the intellectual food of my youth, and to see America converted into a senseless, Old World conqueror, embitters my age."[114] Godkin, like other old liberals, found himself adrift in the imperial sea. He was a Little American at the dawn of a century that fetishized bigness.

The historian William M. Armstrong, in his study of Godkin's thought, indicts his subject for "narrow conservatism,"[115] but what, may I crotchetedly ask, is so great about wideness?

So wondered another Celt, Bourke Cockran, the silver-tongued orator from Sligo, an Irish immigrant whose forensic skills, at bar and podium, led Winston Churchill to call his the "most original mind" he had ever met.[116]

Bourke Cockran was one of those tertium quids who enliven, even as they fail to cleanse, American politics. Speaker of the House Uncle Joe Cannon called him "the most unpredictable figure in American politics." He was a Tammany boss and then a reformer and then a Tammany man again. He was a Democrat for McKinley in 1896 because as a gold-standard capitalist he thought Bryan's bimetallism barmy. In 1900 he returned to the Democratic fold and supported Bryan as a fellow anti-imperialist. Cockran bolted the Democracy for Teddy Roosevelt's Wall Street–dominated Progressive Party in 1912. He was headstrong; he was contumacious; he was willing to take a hike. As his biographer James McGurrin concludes, "He hated to take orders, and he never followed the party line."[117]

Shane Leslie, Cockran's brother-in-law, wrote of him: "On two dogmas he never defaulted—Transubstantiation and Free Trade."[118] The tariff he judged "a legalized policy of public plunder," and U.S. membership in the League of Nations, he told the Senate Foreign Relations Committee, would be "an abomination."[119]

Cockran, as a Tammany man, loathed the Polly Purebred Cleveland. He spoke against his fellow New Yorker at the 1884 Democratic convention, telling delegates that Cleveland was no Samuel J. Tilden: "When the mantle of a giant falls upon a dwarf, he is bound to be smothered."[120] (With Cleveland, affectionately known as "Uncle Jumbo," no stranger to three hundred pounds, one doubts that he was ever again called a dwarf.)

But Cockran was with Cleveland on the matter of empire, saying, "I oppose the un-American policy of imperialism because the grounds on which its advocates support it are puerile, inconsistent and dishonest; because it is cowardly to invade the rights of the weak while respecting those of the strong; because it would divorce the American flag from the American Constitution by sending one where the other cannot go; because it is a policy of inconceivable folly from a material point of view, and a policy of unspeakable infamy from a moral point of view."[121]

The parallels with Pat Moynihan are limited, but they are there. Both were Irish Catholics whose papistry and paddyism were sources of electoral support and targets of WASP contempt. Cockran was a confirmed Wet, leader of the anti-Prohibition forces in the Congress until his death in 1923. Moynihan hadn't a dry bone in his body. But where Moynihan hesitated, thereby gaining renown if losing his soul, Cockran rushed in. He was, as Churchill wrote, a "pacifist, individualist, democrat, capitalist, and 'Gold Bug.' "[122] Does he contradict himself? Well, he contains multitudes. But that's what America was like. Men said, What the hell.

The Democratic platform of 1900, upon which Bryan ran and which Cockran supported, flatly stated, "We assert that no nation can long endure half republic and half empire, and we warn the American people that imperialism abroad will lead quickly and inevitably to despotism at home."[123] Bryan, like many other populists, had supported the war as an act of liberation and even raised a regiment therefore, but when the high-flown oratory of *Cuba libre* faded into peremptory colonial demands he pitched his tent on anti-imperial grounds.

Bryan made 1900 a referendum on imperialism—the only such vote we ever had, really, since subsequent war-shadowed elections featured nary an antiwar choice: Wilson vs. Hughes in 1916, FDR vs. Willkie in 1940, LBJ vs. Goldwater in 1964, Nixon vs. Humphrey in 1968, and Bush vs. Kerry in 2004. Bombs vs. Tanks. Carnage vs. Corpses. Death vs. Destruction. You pay for this, but they give you that. (I concede the special nature of the 1972 election, which is discussed in chapter 3.)

Bryan understood the stakes: "In the month of November, 1900, the future of the nation will be decided: Republic or empire? That is the question, the only question of any importance before the country. If any false financial or industrial policies are entered upon by a new administration, adequate corrections may be applied in four or eight years, but a policy by which Puerto Rico and the Philippines are incorporated in the Union, or attached to it as vassal dependencies, can never be reversed until this republic is numbered among the states that have fallen through an unjust and criminal greed for empire and power."[124]

The hypocrisy of the thing was just so damned rank. Seizing foreign lands and subjugating their people to "make them free." Saith Ernest Crosby, president of the New York Anti-Imperialist League, successor to Teddy Roosevelt's New York State Assembly seat, author of the broad satirical novel *Captain Jinks: Hero* (1902), which remains the bluntest anti-imperial fiction in the (pacific) canon, and a leading American anarchist of the conservative Tolstoyan variety:

> *I hate the oppressor's iron rod,*
> *I hate his murderous ships;*

But most of all I hate, O God,
The lie upon his lips![125]

Grover Cleveland looked on in impotent disgust as the "'round-up' and slaughter of Philipinos [*sic*] seemed to go merrily on." The yellow press appalled him with its bellowing insistence that "anybody who says this is not a Christian nation or that our President is not the very pink of perfection of a Christian, is a liar and an un-American knave."[126]

"The anti-imperialists viewed the world from a conservative framework," notes Robert Beisner.[127] They did not idealize the polyglot peoples of the new colonies; they simply wished to set them free. Most would have made very poor modern multiculturalists indeed: they frankly admitted the superiority of their own culture and doubted that anything beyond incoherence could result from a melding of diverse peoples.

Senator Hoar, a contrary descendant of patriots who fought at Concord at the rude bridge that arched the flood, had rather more enlightened racial attitudes than many of his compatriots. In 1902 he summed up the war and its aftermath: "We crushed the only republic in Asia. We made war on the only Christian people in the East. We converted a war of glory to a war of shame. We vulgarized the American flag. We introduced perfidy into the practice of war. We inflicted torture on unarmed men to extort confession. We put children to death. We established reconcentrado camps. We devastated provinces. We baffled the aspirations of a people for liberty."[128]

If Clevelands and Hoars did not wish to take up the White Man's Burden, neither were they eager to hasten a multicultural America. James T. DuBois, a U.S. consul general posted in Switzerland, composed a poem titled "Expansion" in which the bemused narrator encounters a series of exotic characters, clad outlandishly or barely at all, and upon asking, "Where you hail f'm, pardner?" is informed "Porto Rico, U.S.A.," "Honeyluler, U.S.A.," "Santiago, U.S.A.," and "Manila, U.S.A." The bestupored author concludes:

> *"Hully Gee," says I, "I never heard of*
> *These here cannibals before.*
> *Air these heathens yere all voters?*
> *Will we stan' fur enny more?*
> *Nex' you know you'll ask a feller*
> *Whur he's frum, he'll up an' say*
> *With a lordly kind o' flourish,*
> *'All creation, U.S.A.' "*[129]

Not bad foresight, DuBois. Honeyluler is a full-fledged city of the U.S.A. and Porto Rico would be had the Gingrich Republicans had their way in the mid-1990s.

This introduces, by way of doggerel, the nettling matter of American racial attitudes. Race is our "hidden wound," in Wendell Berry's phrase, though it never stays hidden for long, does it? In *The Nation*, E. L. Godkin warned that annexing Hawaii meant admixing "alien, inferior, and mongrel races to our nationality."[130] Eventual statehood for the islands would mean adding "ignorant, superstitious, and foreign-tongued" poi eaters to the electoral rolls.[131]

Imperialism worked an unsubtle alteration on American civilization. In the Senate this alloying was foreseen by the redoubtable Missouri Democrat Champ Clark, who asked, tongue in cheek but heart on sleeve, "How can we endure our shame when a Chinese senator from Hawaii, with his pigtail hanging down his back, and with his pagan joss in his hand, shall rise from his curule chair and in pidgin English proceed to chop logic with *George Frisbie Hoar* or *Henry Cabot Lodge*? O tempora, O mores!"[132]

The Spanish-American War brought within the American ambit persons of—however distinguished and venerable their culture—strikingly alien stock. "We regarded the United States as quite large enough for our civilizing activities," the novelist Hamlin Garland later recalled,[133] but the Roosevelts and Mahans and Beveridges did not.

Less delicately, the populist and racist South Carolina Democratic senator "Pitchfork Ben" Tillman threw in with the anti-imperialists because, he said, the white man will "walk on the necks of every colored race he comes into contact with." We had quite enough African Americans underfoot in freedom's land without "incorporating any more colored men into the body politic." So Tillman pleaded with other southern white supremacists to renounce colonies and object to "the subjugation of the Filipinos and the establishment of a military government over them by force."[134] If he didn't love his Filipino brothers and sisters, nor did he wish to rule them. Call it an early form of benign neglect.

If neither side distinguished itself by the elevated moral standards of the twenty-first century, when all men are brothers and peace rules our planet, at least the anti-imperialists wanted to leave the Filipinos alone rather than conquer and slaughter them. And the most racially enlightened Americans stood with the anti-imperialists, none more nobly than that consummate Bostonian Moorfield Storey.

Storey, a railroad lawyer who in his youth had served as famulus to Senator Charles Sumner, had married a woman whose family tree included Dolley Madison and Thomas Jefferson. He was an aristocrat aghast at the deformation of the national character preached by the likes of Theodore Roosevelt. Harvard man Storey protested mightily against his alma mater's participation in intercollegiate athletics. Not because he was a palsied ectomorph; on the contrary, Storey swam, fenced, and once walked forty miles in a single day. Rather, he feared that the cult of athletics and TR's perfervid gym-teacher routine would lead to American boys "grow[ing] up to believe that the strong warrior is the perfect type of man, and that the nation whose armies and navies make it the terror of its weaker neighbors, is the only great nation."[135]

Politically, Storey stood for free enterprise, states' rights, a low tariff, protection of the rights of African Americans (he was the first president of the NAACP), and an anti-imperialist foreign policy. Yet he just wasn't made for those times, or these either, perhaps. For he had "all of lost America in his eyes," as August Derleth said of Crazy Horse.[136]

Storey became president of the Anti-Imperialist League in 1905. The Philippines were ours, as were Hawaii and Puerto Rico. Most members of the league, said Storey, were "more anxious to get rid of the Islands for the sake of the United States than for the sake of the Filipinos."[137] (Storey, who cultivated an interest in the weal of small nations and people endangered by modernity, was an exception.) But Storey's denunciations of the imperial project knew no surcease, and he would stand, almost alone in public life, against U.S. interventions in Haiti, Nicaragua, Mexico, Panama, and the Dominican Republic. He faltered in 1917, endorsing U.S. entry into the Great War, but then that was a war of which New England approved, and Storey never pretended to be more than the product of the finest traditions of his region.

The opposition to the U.S. detour into empire had a literary tint. "Conservative" men of letters such as Henry Blake Fuller, William Vaughn Moody, and Thomas Bailey Aldrich (always there is the middle name; this was not a proletarian uprising) took pen in hand to protest this besmirching of American ideals.

Aldrich, the author of "Unguarded Gates," the classic poetic expression of immigration restriction ("O Liberty, white God-dess! is it well/To leave the gates unguarded?"),[138] went so far as to cast his ballot for the tarnished man of silver. "I would sooner vote for Bryan" than McKinley, he said in 1899. "To be ruined financially is not so bad as to be ruined morally."[139]

The appalling sight of U.S. soldiers suppressing a Filipino independence movement that was professedly based on the same self-evident rights proclaimed in the Declaration of Independence inspired *Liberty Poems* (1900), an anthology compiled by the New England Anti-Imperialist League, for as usual, the poets, especially the best poets, were disproportionately reactionary and antiwar.

I like especially the contribution of Corporal John Mulcahy.

Fighting in a blazing sun, in thickets,
   With a grim foe who well knows how to fight;
Standing in the rain when all our pickets
   Are destitute, and clothes are "out of sight";
Firing from the trenches hot and sizzling,
   And standing where the water's to the knees;
Fighting when the rain is pouring, drizzling,
   And parched troops are dying for a breeze;
   This is Empire.

Our flag floats o'er trenches damp, ill-smelling,
   And reeking with the odors of the dead,
While far and near yellow men loud yelling
   With sword and torch make all the vista red;
Fighting with fever, and, O God! with Death,
   In hospitals beneath a tropic sun,
No woman's hand to soothe the latest breath,
   When, far from home, the soldier's work is done;
   This is Empire.

Facing death in rice-fields which are shambles,
*   For yellow men who're fighting to be free;*
Here, amid the cactus and the brambles,
*   Old Glory seems ashamed across the sea;*
Dying here before malarial breezes,
*   That swamp across the camp-ground and the bay,*
Bringing here the fever quick that seizes
*   And lays the strong man low within a day;*
*   This is Empire.*

Sleeping in the marshes where the fevers
*   Prostrate the men in windrows at a breath,*
Hearing words of those who would deceive us
*   With promises that we are near the death;*
Fighting when there's never hope of winning,
*   With elements upon the other side;*
And while Death and Pestilence sit grinning
*   O'er flooded fields where gallant men have died;*
*   This is Empire.*

Fighting niggers who themselves are fighting
*   For the same cause our fathers fought to save;*
Fighting in a way that is forever blighting
*   The fairest heritage our fathers gave;*
Fighting in a cause that is forever grabbing,
*   The cause that is the old-time robber's still;*
Fighting in a cause that's only stabbing
*   The one we battled for at Bunker Hill;*
*   This is Empire.*[140]

Mulcahy was a classically American character. A New York
City orphan who picked up, Alger-like, and moved to Chicago on
his own at the age of ten, he caught a ride west as a teenager and

spent his adulthood as "a steeple painter, cowboy, preacher, and poet," according to the Nevada historian Howard Hickson.[141] In 1898, legend—if not the army roster—has it that Mulcahy joined the First U.S. Cavalry (the Rough Riders) and fought under the bullyragging Teddy Roosevelt. "Broncho Jack" lived until 1938, an itinerant poet-preacher best known for such works as "Death of Cherokee Charlie Snead at Elko Nev." The Republic was on its way to joining Cherokee Charlie Snead—but not without Broncho Jack's bitter protest.

The finest literary work to emerge from the anti-imperialists was William Vaughn Moody's "An Ode in the Time of Hesitation." Moody, who upheld "the old conservative positions of laissez-faire government and nonintervention,"[142] was an Indiana boy, a poet and dramatist who taught at Harvard and the University of Chicago. He shunned political action, preferring to give the world "not a syllogism, but a song."[143] He was mildly pro-Spanish-American War, but the refusal of the United States to turn the Philippines over to the Filipinos disgusted him. In the "Ode,"[144] he measured the decay of American ideals by appealing to the example of Robert Gould Shaw, the Boston gentleman, "this delicate and proud New England soul,"[145] who fell on July 18, 1863, while leading the first enlisted Negro regiment, the 54th Massachusetts.

In "On a Soldier Fallen in the Philippines," Moody urges us never to let the deceased know of the rotten cause for which he gave his life. The last two stanzas read:

> *Toll! Let the great bells toll*
>   *Till the clashing air is dim.*
> *Did we wrong this parted soul?*
>   *We will make it up to him.*
> *Toll! Let him never guess*
>   *What work we sent him to.*

Laurel, laurel, yes;
  He did what we bade him do.
Praise, and never a whispered hint
  but the fight he fought was good;
Never a word that the blood on his sword
  was his country's own heart's-blood.

A flag for the soldier's bier
  Who dies that his land may live;
O, banners, banners here,
  That he doubt not nor misgive!
That he heed not from the tomb
  The evil days draw near
When the nation, robed in gloom,
  With its faithless past shall strive.
Let him never dream that
  his bullet's scream went wide of its island mark,
Home to the heart of his darling land
  where she stumbled and sinned in the dark.[146]

The Hoosier Moody rang the death knell for the old America when the Megaphone of Mars won the presidential election of 1904 over the phlegmatic Wall Street Democrat Alton B. Parker. Moody wrote despairingly that "the vision in the light of which our country was created and has grown great, will soon fade, and one more world-dream will have been found impossible to live out . . . Our different destiny may be greater, but the America that we have known and passionately believed in, will be no more."[147]

It is striking just how often conservatives and poets and American romantics (often one and the same) have descried in the battle fog of war the end of their country. The smoke had barely cleared from Manila Bay when Godkin was predicting "how this 'imperialist' movement will end. The history of America under it will, in all human probability, be that of a calamity greater by far than the fall of the Roman Empire."[148]

But who bothered to listen? The Philippines, Puerto Rico, Guam, Hawaii: the Stars and Stripes rippled incongruously in the tropical island breezes. Empire was upon us.

2

"IT'S NOT OUR FIGHT":

SAYING NO TO WORLD WARS

THE FIRST AND in may ways climacteric "liberals' war" was the First World War. Woodrow Wilson had narrowly defeated the internationalist Republican Charles Evans Hughes by running on the slogan "He Kept Us Out of War," but like FDR and LBJ in subsequent generations, he took his reelection as license to plunge the nation into a foreign conflict he had pledged to avoid.

Unlike the foreign wars of the century ultimo, the United States did not ship its boys Over There in 1917 for purposes of conquest or coaling stations. No, this was more high-minded than such buccaneering. If the occupation of the Philippines had been justified as a civilizing act, a gift to our brown-skinned brothers by the armed agents of Methodism, Americans entered the First World War largely because, in Herbert Agar's phrase, Woodrow Wilson "and his countrymen were destined to teach the whole world how to govern itself."[1] Prussian militarism was run amok. Heretofore the United States, in obedience to the injunctions of its founders, had ignored the periodic wars of the Old World. But we were now a World Power, and no self-regarding World Power could stay out of the fray.

This was "Our War for Human Rights," as one of the numerous propaganda books of 1917 put it. The Germans, a warlike race "obsessed with the spirit of militarism,"[2] must be crushed by a militarized America so that "the principles of liberty for which

[America] has ever stood may be perpetuated throughout the world."[3] In 1898 we had pried Cuba free from under the Spanish boot heel. If territories exotic had been our reward, well, so much the better. But we fought to make others free—just as Christ had, according to Julia Ward Howe's anthem of 1862. Now was the time to die, or at least send the twenty-year-old sons of strangers across the sea to die, once more to make men free.

The war marked a decisive rejection of the traditional—that is, Washingtonian—U.S. policy of neutrality. The home front was militarized—Prussianized—to a degree almost unimaginable: conscription was imposed, taxation became burdensome, industries were effectively nationalized, and freedom of speech was drastically curtailed by the Espionage and Sedition acts. And oh how quiescent the conservatives had become.

The models of Atkinson and Carnegie, men of business who saw war as a drain on both the American soul and the U.S. Treasury, were outmoded. The days were past when a Carnegie might effuse, "Favored land, may you prove worthy of all your blessings and show to the world that after ages of wars and conquests there comes at last to the troubled earth the glorious reign of peace. But no new steel cruisers, no standing army. These are the devil's tools in monarchies; the Republic's weapons are the ploughshare and the pruning hook."[4] The pragmatic businessman of 1917 looked beyond mere domestic concerns. Even Carnegie himself called upon Americans to bury the plowshare and unsheath the sword.

William Randolph Hearst was among the few men of power and prominence to stand against Mr. Wilson's War to End All Wars. So did Henry Ford, who in December 1915, at the urging of the pacifists Jane Addams and (Hungarian) Rosika Schwimmer, had chartered a widely ridiculed "Peace Ship," whose beatific passengers hoped to convince the warring parties to "get the boys out of the trenches by Christmas."[5] They left Hoboken, landed in Stockholm a month later, and earned nothing but mockery. If this was naïveté on the high seas, so be it, but Ford's intentions were benign. Undeterred by the ridicule, Ford continued to speak against U.S. involvement in the Great War: "For months the people of the United States have had fear pounded into their brains by magazines, newspapers and motion pictures. No enemy has been pointed out. All the wild cry for the spending of billions, the piling up of armament and the saddling of the country with a military caste has been based on nothing but *fiction*."[6]

Fittingly, the House declared war (and how quaintly constitutional *that* sounds in our day) on Good Friday, April 6, 1917, by a vote of 373–50, with nine members abstaining.

Of the fifty representatives who told Europe no, the Yankees are *not* coming, thirty-two were Republicans, sixteen were members of Mr. Wilson's Democratic Party, and one each was Socialist and Independent. Except for the Socialist Meyer London of Manhattan's Lower East Side, the Northeast, especially New York City, was solidly for war. The most antiwar state in the South was Mississippi, with three representatives and one senator voting no. The Wisconsin and South Dakota House delegations voted against war, as did Nevada's lone representative.

The opposition to the war came mostly from farmers, old-school classical liberals, pacifists, Main Street Republican isolationists, and socialists. The balance tilted leftward, as the balance of a similar peace coalition would list rightward when it came time to fight the drive toward U.S. intervention in the next world war.

Majority Leader Claude Kitchin (D-NC) was among the fifty who took their stand for American neutrality. With considerable poignance, not to say prescience, he predicted, "I know that for my vote I shall be not only criticized but denounced from one end of the country to the other. The whole yelping pack of defamers and revilers in the Nation will at once be set upon my heels. My friends, I cannot leave my children land and riches—I cannot leave them fame—but I can leave them the name of an ancestor who, mattering not the consequences to himself, never dared to hesitate to do his duty as God have him to see it."[7]

Kitchin won reelection, and should these United States ever again resemble a republic, his bulkily handsome form will be carved in marble and placed among the statuary of those who cut authentic profiles in courage.

Kitchin, the proud descendant of Confederates and Farmers' Alliance populists, was hardly the sort of Democratic congressional leader to play handmaiden to Parson Wilson. He was "too much of a free-trader, too much of an agrarian, [and] too anti-militaristic"[8] in the assessment of his biographer. He was an American suffused with the spirit of '76, which was antithetical to the spirit of '17.

The New York press flayed Kitchin without mercy or verity. It hit him with everything but the sink from you-know-where. He was a hayseed, a rube, a committer of "moral treason"[9] in the curiously twenty-first-century locution of the *New York World*. The *New York Times* demanded his resignation in an editorial. He was, sniffed the *Times,* "unpatriotic."[10] In *Collier's,* Mark Sullivan, the pompous retailer of conventional wisdom (and isn't that position always well paid and amply filled?), sneered that the North Carolinian was "a simple and ignorant man."[11] For his part, Kitchin took the heat and deflected the poison darts of the martial intellectuals, saying that "it takes neither moral nor physical courage to declare a war for others to fight."[12]

The Illinois Republican Fred A. Britten spoke metaphysically of a disjunction between elite and popular opinion that would recur in later wars: "The truth of the matter is that ninety per cent of your people and mine do not want this declaration of war and are distinctly opposed to our going into that bloody mire on the other side. There is something in the air, gentlemen, and I do not know what it is, whether it be the hand of destiny of some superhuman movement, something stronger than you and I can realize or resist, that seems to be picking us up bodily and literally forcing us to vote for this declaration of war when way down deep in our hearts we are just as opposed to it as are our people back home."[13]

Isaac Sherwood (D-OH), a veteran of the Civil War's Fourteenth Regiment, Ohio Volunteer Infantry, called upon the ghosts of his fallen comrades: "As I love my country, I feel it is my sacred duty to keep the stalwart young men of today out of a barbarous war 3,500 miles away in which we have no vital interest."[14]

Some conservatives appealed to the Lord—"Let us not declare war in the hour they crucified the Prince of Peace," begged Representative William E. Mason (R-IL)[15]—but Golgotha had nothing on Capitol Hill.

The Senate had voted on April 4, 1917, by 82–6, to declare war on Germany. The six senators who shouted nay were the progressive Republicans George Norris of Nebraska and Robert La Follette of Wisconsin; Asle J. Gronne, Republican of reliably isolationist North Dakota; and the Democrats Harry Lane (OR); William J. Stone (MO), chairman of the Foreign Relations Committee, who stood alone in his fiefdom against the war declaration; and James K. Vardaman (MS). (Thomas P. Gore, populist Democrat of Oklahoma and grandfather of the novelist and isolationist Gore Vidal, was absent but sent word that he, too, would have voted no.)

"We ought to remember the advice of the Father of our Country and keep out of entangling alliances," expatiated Norris in a language that was obsoleting even as the words debouched from his mouth. "Let Europe solve her problems as we have solved ours. Let Europe bear her burdens as we have borne ours."[16]

American flag lapel pins had been distributed to members before the president spoke to Congress on April 2, 1917, requesting a declaration of war. It took a certain obdurate courage to refuse to wear the colors; Senator La Follette was among the refusers, as was the Mississippi senator Vardaman. (Wilson had called for "stern repression" of disloyalty in his speech of April 2—a Prussian formulation that ought to have set American throats to gagging.)[17]

A word about Senator James K. Vardaman, who comes down to us as a vile racist in the worst Mississippi gutter stream of Theodore Bilbo and John Rankin. He was that—lynch law was good law to the "White Chief"—but in his finest hour Vardaman sacrificed his career for peace. Vardaman was born in 1861, a year pregnant with significance, and though without money or station he would make his way as a lawyer and newspaper editor until in 1903 he was elected governor of Mississippi. He took a populist's interest in enriching the schools (for white children at least) and bringing absentee corporations to heel, and when he was elected to the U.S. Senate he was that rare southern Democrat who found kinship with such progressive Republicans as Robert La Follette and George Norris. William Alexander Percy, Walker's guardian, called him in *Lanterns on the Levee* "a kindly, vain demagogue unable to think, and given to emotions he considered noble,"[18] but when Mr. Wilson declared his war, and the South went marching solidly behind him, James K. Vardaman stood alone against the crimson tide. (Though virulently antiblack, Vardaman was a consistent foe of anti-Semitism, calling Jews "that wonderful people who have made the greatest fight against great odds that any race on earth has ever made."[19] In 1922 he would denounce Henry Ford for littering his *Dearborn Independent* with "slanderous ignorant persecution of the Jews." He urged Ford to let the Jews alone and instead try to solve "the negro problem in the South"[20]—not, we may be sure, with high-paying factory jobs but with more efficiently produced garrotes.)

With his shoulder-length hair and elegant carriage (Theodore Bilbo, his bitter rival, jested that "Jim . . . even surpasses the Queen of Sheba with the talcum on his face and toilet water on his hair"),[21] Vardaman cut a memorably anachronistic profile. Prefiguring Huey Long and J. William Fulbright, he was that rare southern anti-imperialist. Senator Vardaman urged self-government for the Philippines, and though his view was partially colored by his "fear of racial amalgamation," as the historian Joseph E. Fortenberry has written,[22] he also spoke the language of the "moralistic isolationist."[23] "The men and women who conceived our form of government and constructed our Constitution never dreamed we would engage in the business of holding subject provinces," said Vardaman. "It is therefore our duty to get out of the Philippine Islands and come back to stay."[24]

He could make anti-imperialist noises on such peripheral matters without incurring the wrath of the Democracy, but his straightforwardly isolationist and libertarian objections to U.S. intervention in the Great War brought down upon his pomaded head a shit storm of obloquy.

He was vilified as "Kaiser Vardaman" and the "Kaiser-loving betrayer of the American people," but he replied simply, "Now these are my views; if it be treason, make the most of it."[25] He opposed not only the war but its shackling accoutrements, including the Espionage and Sedition acts and conscription. He voted against appropriations for the army and navy and damned "the un-American principle of compulsory military training."[26]

Shortly before the April 1917 declaration of war, a delegation of Vardaman's friends implored him to vote with the president. He was unmoved. One of the delegation reported, "He replied that his position on the war was the result of extensive investigation, great study, and mature deliberation and that his loss of his seat in the United States Senate was nothing as compared with the loss of lives and liberty and opportunities which would follow such a war."[27]

Vardaman told the Senate, "I do not feel like sacrificing a million men . . . in order to liberate Germany from the cruel domination of kings, without first consulting the people who are to be sacrificed for the deliverance."[28] True to the populist faith, Vardaman speculated that if "the plain, honest people, the masses who are to bear the burden of taxation and fight the Nation's battles, were consulted—the United States would not make a declaration of war against Germany today."[29]

He lost his seat in 1918 to the hawkish (and of course also segregationist) Democrat Pat Harrison. There was only one issue: the war. Varadaman understood that standing athwart the empire would destroy his career. How easy it would have been to trim, to temporize, to dissemble, to quietly slip out of the peace camp and vote for Death. But to his eternal credit, he did not. He left the Senate urging all nations to ban conscription and permit their citizens to vote in referenda before going to war.

His biographer, William F. Holmes, concluded of Vardaman's "baffling and paradoxical" career that "he proved his integrity and dedication to principle, as he pursued the lonely course of opposing America's entry into war."[30]

Does this excuse his race-baiting? Of course not. That was despicable. But segregationists, too, were capable of heroism. As the Drive-By Truckers sing, it's the "duality of the Southern thing," and it appeared in spades in the former Georgia congressman Tom Watson, the Jeffersonian populist who by the teens had curdled into a Jew-baiter and Negro-hater of unusual ferocity. In 1917 Watson regained, for the nonce, his agrarian libertarian voice.

> Upon the pretext of waging war against Prussianism in Europe, the purpose of Prussianizing this country has been avowed in Congress . . .
>
> On the pretext of sending armies to Europe, to crush militarism there, we enthrone it here.
>
> On the pretext of carrying to all the nations of the world the liberties won by the heroic lifeblood of our forefathers, we first deprive our own people of liberties they inherited as a birthright.[31]

While nationalist Republicans refused to swallow whole the Wilsonian war aims—Senator Warren G. Harding (R-OH) told colleagues that he was not "voting for war in the name of democracy . . . It is my deliberate judgment that it is none of our business what type of government any nation on this earth may choose to have"[32]—they faltered before reaching a stage of full-bore opposition. Antimilitarism, though in the American marrow, had acquired an unpatriotic taint. Its expression was ceded to the prairie populists and the socialists. The Left distinguished itself in 1917, while the Right, as it would in future conflicts, threw in with a liberal war president. That it took Socialists to circulate a pamphlet with the libertarian title *No Conscription, No Involuntary Servitude, No Slavery* is an indictment of the individualistic Right. Shame on Main Street for its silence.

The extent—and the pettiness—of the "stern repression" demanded by that liberal Democratic paragon Woodrow Wilson still amazes. Men and women who spoke against the draft and the war were prosecuted and jailed for their exercise of what had been, pre-Wilson, First Amendment liberties. The cases, many collected by Gilbert C. Fite and H. C. Peterson in *Opponents of War, 1917–1918* (1957), have not lost their power to appall. Walter C. Matthey of Iowa was sentenced to a year in jail for *applauding* an anticonscription speech. Walter Heynacher of South Dakota was sentenced to five years in Leavenworth for telling a young man that "it was all foolishness to send our boys over there to get killed by the thousands, all for the sake of Wall Street." The South Dakota farmer Fred Fairchild was sentenced to a year and a day in Leavenworth for saying, "If I were of conscription age and had no dependents and were drafted, I would refuse to serve. They could shoot me, but they could not make me fight." Abraham Sugarman of Sibley County, Minnesota, was sentenced to three years in Leavenworth for arguing that the draft was unconstitutional and remarking, "This is supposed to be a free country. Like Hell it is."[33]

These stories go on and on, stretching from here to Leavenworth, and when the civil libertarian is tempted to call George W. Bush the worst president in our history, she would do well to remember Woodrow Wilson, who makes Bush look like a pro bono lawyer for the ACLU.

The old America simply would not do; it must be remade. As Robert Nisbet wrote in *Twilight of Authority* (1975), "To have waged war with volunteers only, with business as usual at home, with the social and cultural pursuits of the American people untouched, was, as we know very well indeed today, utterly out of the question. If an army was to be manufactured for export to Europe in a war that a very large number of the American people considered none of America's business, then a new nation had to be manufactured: economically, politically, culturally, and, not least, psychologically."[34]

The range and audacity of the Wilsonian reconfiguring of America staggers the imagination. But then again, as Wilson said, "It is not an army we must shape and train for war, it is a nation."[35]

Some trivial acts of Germanophobia are faintly risible: Sauerkraut became liberty cabbage, hamburger was Anglicized as Salisbury steak. Others are sickening: States and cities banned German language in the schools, Mozart and Bach were driven out of symphony repertoires, and the president's house intellectuals whipped up "hatred of the enemy and of the home-grown isolationist or pacifist."[36] Vice President Thomas Marshall proposed that anyone not "heartily in support of the Government in this crisis" be stripped of his citizenship.[37] The doctrine of neutrality handed down by George Washington was scorned as the creed of pinks and traitors and goldbricks.

The president's minister of propaganda, George Creel, deputized about seventy thousand "Four Minute Men" to harangue audiences with four-minute war rants at movie theaters, sporting events, civic clubs, and anywhere else civilians gathered. The Espionage and Sedition acts drawn up by the Wilson administration and passed by a compliant Congress resulted in the jailing of twelve hundred Americans, martyrs to freedom of speech, among them the great Socialist leader Eugene V. Debs, a front-porch patriot of

Terre Haute, Indiana, whose postwar pardon Wilson refused to grant. (Debs was released by a kinder, better man, Warren G. Harding of Marion, Ohio.)

The economy was collectivized in a manner that might be called fascistic in the pre-Nazi sense of the word: that is, it was centralized under a tripartite administration of government, big business, and, to a much lesser extent, labor unions. Prices of wheat, coal, copper, iron, steel, food, and any other product with even a tenuous relationship to "national defense" were set by the federal government, which essentially nationalized the railroad, shipping, telegraph, and telephone industries. It was in this mephitic fog that Randolph Bourne coined his aphorism "War is the health of the state."

The yeomanry was impressed—as in impressment. In *Country People* (1924), the Iowa novelist Ruth Suckow depicted the bewilderment of her German farmers as the United States approached the European bloodbath. "They were a conservative bunch," writes Suckow of her Iowa husbandmen. "They said that this country would never be involved. They were opposed to that."[38]

But we went, afire with hatred of the butchering Hun. The sons of Suckow's farmers were conscripted into Mr. Wilson's army, though in the hearts of the fathers there burned "a deep opposition to the draft. To have someone tell his boys to do this and that! To take away his help on the farm just when he needed it most! To have somebody just step in and tell them where they had to go! Was that what happened in this country? Why had his people left the old country, then, if things were going to be just the same?"[39] Why, indeed? (As Speaker of the House Champ Clark had said, "In the estimation of Missourians there is precious little difference between a conscript and a convict.")[40]

The ghost of Daniel Webster stood beside these conservative Iowans, but if the godlike Daniel could chase the devil out of the Granite State, as Stephen Vincent Benét had it, he could not derail the progressive project of world war and compulsory military service. The cult of the nation-state held sway. Iowa children, their home education banned, their locally run rural district schools under siege by consolidators, were pledging allegiance to an indivisible nation in words penned by the socialist Francis Bellamy, a votary of the "Nationalist" creed of his cousin Edward, an authoritarian whose novel *Looking Backward* (1887) had envisioned the whole of America conscripted into an "Industrial Army" in which toil was mandatory, for wise rulers had "simply applied the principle of universal military service . . . to the labor question."[41] That Bellamy's horrific world was considered a utopia rather than a dystopia suggests the extent to which great Americans like Huck and Jim were no longer floating down the mainstream.

To the blustery paragon of progressivism, Theodore Roosevelt, "Any man who says, 'I didn't raise my boy to be a soldier' isn't fit for citizenship. That statement is on the same moral level with saying, 'I didn't raise my girl to be a mother.' "[42]

Mothers were brood sows. Sons were herded into the abattoir. Only cowards squealed.

Smearing Middle America

Fascism, or the specter thereof, stoked the interventionist fires on the Left in the 1930s, just as communism did on the Right of the 1950s. The rude implication was that patriots who opposed sending American boys across the sea to fight Franco in 1937 or Hitler or Tojo in 1941 were cryptofascists. (In fact, many Middle Americans for peace worried that militarism would breed fascism on the home front.) The same dreary scene played out in the 1950s, though this time the fascist-baiters were themselves red-baited. As for the lawn-mowing Ohio Rotarians of the peace party . . . well, don't bother looking for their story on the History Channel.

Not all isolationists were muck-bound provincials. Robert Taft was the son of a president, after all, and Representative George Holden Tinkham (R-MA), whom Representative Hamilton Fish (R-NY) said "believed honestly and sincerely in almost complete isolation," was a blueblood Bostonian, *Mayflower* descendant, social equal of Cabots and Lodges, "official Leopard Champion of East Africa," and frequent safari hunter whose skill at shooting leopards, elephants, rhinoceri, zebras, cheetahs, ibex, oryx, hartebeests, and all manner of fauna led the right-wing activist and historian William K. Shearer, a founder of the George Wallace vehicle the American Independent Party, to marvel, "Left to his own devices, he might well have destroyed all animal life on earth."[43]

Will Lang, profiling "Tinkham the Mighty Hunter" in *Life* in December 1940, said of the bald, bearded Smith Brother lookalike that he was "above all an individualist and non-conformist."[44] Despite his magnificently aristocratic gesture of going off to Africa to hunt big game during election season, Tinkham served twenty-eight years in Congress, a rock-ribbed Republican representing a Democratic district, casting negatives whenever the belligerent or spendthrift specter of internationalism raised its head. He despised Prohibition, the segregationist South, and "international bankers." He regretted very much his vote in favor of the First World War, which he called "the greatest disaster that ever occurred to our Republic. It should never be allowed to happen again."[45]

"The key to me is that I am an *old* American," he declared,[46] à la E. L. Godkin, and if that made George Holden Tinkham a man out of time, perhaps even a man without a country, so be it.

Middle American anti-imperialism came in many varieties, from "I won't have my son die for foreigners" to the impishly witty projects of upper-middle-class collegians. Take, for instance, the Veterans of Future Wars, which within months of its creation at Princeton in 1936 by the students Lewis Jefferson

Gorin Jr. and Thomas Riggs Jr. boasted 584 chapters across the country.

This alternative VFW—slogan: "We will make the world safe for hypocrisy!"—demanded payment of one-thousand-dollar war bonuses to students in advance of the next European war. Founded "partly in a spirit of high jinks and partly in a spirit of protest against the glorification of war," hailed by conservatives as a "heaven-sent" spoof of Rooseveltian profligacy and militarism,[47] the Veterans of Future Wars parodied martial superpatriots, deskbound saber rattlers, and the greed of such veterans' groups as the American Legion and the Veterans of Foreign Wars. James E. Van Zandt, national commander of the adult VFW, spat that the kids were "too yellow to go to war."[48] The kids, for that matter, saluted each other in a pastiche of Nazism and New Dealism, with "hand outstretched, palm up and expectant."[49] (War is expensive, and the bills keep coming due for decades after the armistice. A policy of preemptive fiscal conservatism would stop war before it started.)

A ladies auxiliary, born at Vassar and known as the "Association of Gold Star Mothers of Future Veterans," requested tours of France to inspect "the future burying ground of our dead."[50] The engineers at Rensselaer Polytechnic Institute launched the Future Profiteers; the young ladies at Sweetbriar College formed a companion organization, the Future Golddiggers, whose task would be "to sit on the laps of future profiteers while they drink champagne during the next war."[51] Students at the City College of New York set up Foreign Correspondents in Future Wars; their claim upon the treasury would be "to establish training courses for members of the association in the writing of atrocity stories and garbled war dispatches for patriotic purposes."[52] Rutgers students had the same idea with their "Association of Future War Propagandists."

The student VFW, like the America First Committee to come, endorsed a national referendum on any congressional declaration of war. Known as the Ludlow Amendment, this last-gasp populist attempt to subject the warmongering of the East Coast to the approval of South Dakota and Oklahoma failed by 209–188 in a House procedural vote in December 1937. A 1938 Gallup Poll found that 68 percent of Americans supported the amendment, but they were the 68 percent that doesn't count within the councils of state.

The Ludlow Amendment seems to us today a virtual jacquerie, a fantastic notion of the farthest fringe. Yet it attracted widespread support in the mid-1930s among hinterlands conservatives. They wanted peace, and they were not above using direct democracy to get it.[53]

Sponsor Louis Ludlow (D-IN) was a Jeffersonian Democrat, a critic of the New Deal as an unconstitutional centralization of power. His allies were Main Street Republicans of the Midwest, prairie populists and radicals of the Upper Midwest, and the remnant of Jeffersonian Democrats holding on like purple asters against the November chill. These same people would form the core of the America First Committee.

America First was very much a Middle American production, with its heart in Chicago. It was not in any way pro-fascist or pro-Nazi, though of course anyone who opposes a war in modern America gets tagged as an enemy symp. (Ask Gene Debs, ask the Berrigans, ask Martin Luther King Jr.)

Midwestern businessmen formed the committee's backbone: General Robert E. Wood, chairman of Sears, Roebuck; R. Douglas Stuart Jr., grandson of the cofounder of Quaker Oats; the textile manufacturer William H. Regnery; Jay C. Hormel of the meatpacking company; Sterling Morton of the salt company. The committee's house organ was the *Chicago Tribune* of Colonel Robert McCormick, the English-boarding-school-educated publisher who snapped the lion's tail con brio.

The AFC was founded in September 1940 at Yale Law

School, of all places, by a set of men who went on to great establishment success. They included Potter Stewart (Supreme Court justice), Sargent Shriver (George McGovern's running mate in 1972), Gerald Ford (!), Kingman Brewster Jr. (Yale president), and the aforementioned Bob Stuart (Quaker Oats CEO and Reagan's ambassador to Norway). Ford, amusingly, was the first to drop off the executive committee: he was afraid that being involved with an antiwar group might cost him his job as assistant football coach. Courage sharpens its profile!

The America First Committee was the largest (eight hundred thousand members) antiwar organization in U.S. history. Its members ranged from Iowa Republicans to Wyoming socialists. John F. Kennedy was a donor, as was his reptilian father. Many of the finest writers in America sympathized with (or joined) America First—Sinclair Lewis, Edmund Wilson, Robinson Jeffers, E. E. Cummings, William Saroyan, John P. Marquand, a young Kurt Vonnegut, and Gore Vidal—while the leading pro-war authors were such toadies as Archibald MacLeish (or macarchibald maclapdog macleish, as Cummings called him). The aviator Charles Lindbergh was the AFC's most popular speaker.

Their principles were from the American bedrock.

1. The United States must build an impregnable defense for America.
2. No foreign powers, nor group of powers, can successfully attack a *prepared* America.
3. American democracy can be preserved only by keeping out of the European war.
4. "Aid short of war" weakens national defense at home and threatens to involve America in war abroad.[54]

Armed neutrality, in short, though the AFC cooperated with pacifists and indeed featured such exponents of nonviolence as the novelist Kathleen Norris on its national committee. Committee members professed the following creed, which was as American as, well, George Washington:

I believe in an impregnable national defense.

I believe that we should build it thoroughly, soundly, and immediately, but not hysterically.

I believe we should keep our country out of the Old World's everlasting family quarrels. Our fathers came to America because they were sick of them. Let's not stick our necks back into them.

I believe in the preservation of this Republic. Embroiled again in European affairs, we shall lose it. We shall be destroying the heritage our fathers fought for and sacrificed to leave us. In an effort to destroy totalitarianism, we shall be forced into totalitarianism ourselves. George Washington warned us of this day. His advice is better today than when he gave it.

I believe that no man nor group of men—no foreign power nor group of powers—will ever attack a prepared America.

I believe that our job is clear before us. Let's not give our defenses away, nor destroy the best defense we possess—plain, ordinary American common sense. Hysteria and fear are poor substitutes. They have no place in our history.

I believe that no man here, nor any group of perhaps sincere, but obviously propaganda-bewildered citizens, should be permitted to divert us from our first duty to our country and our children—the defense and preservation of America and all that it represents.

I believe that our job is right here at home. It's big enough for all our energies. Sympathetic as we all may be with unfortunate nations overseas, we must remember that we stand alone. Europe and Asia cannot be expected to fight our battles. They never have and they never will. No nation will survive which depends on another to fight its battles.

I believe that our best contribution to a sorry, troubled world is an America to which men and nations can repair for help, guidance, and inspiration for the restoration of civilization—an America strong and unafraid.[55]

Okay, it lacks the poetry of the Nicene Creed, not to mention the brachylogical oomph of the Boy Scout Oath. But you get the point.

That point was blunted and buried on December 7, 1941, and although many America Firsters suspected that FDR welcomed the Japanese attack on Pearl Harbor as a "back door to war," the committee disbanded after briefly considering the possibility of remaining alive as a civil liberties watchdog in the midnight of wartime. U.S. participation in World War II would have the inestimable benefit of helping to defeat the European terror of Nazi Germany. (It also bolstered Joseph Stalin.) But the AFC, as its name declared, placed the concerns of America first, and the domestic fallout of the Second World War harmed small-town and rural America especially, in ways that we seldom bother to acknowledge but that I will detail in chapter 5.

America First spoke for Middle America. When the Gallup pollsters asked Americans, "Would you vote to go into the war or stay out of the war?" the proportion answering "stay out" was 84 percent in June 1940 and 79 percent as late as October 1941.[56]

America First even sang in the accents of Middle America.

Picture, if you will, the preteen Ruth Palmer of Aberdeen, South Dakota, who appeared throughout her landlocked state in 1940 singing "Just Stay This Side of the Pond," composed by her farmer-father, Irwin H. Palmer.

Little Ruth, draped in cape and topped by a feathered marching band cap, sang her song at state fairs, Kiwanis and American Legion conventions, and Fourth of July celebrations across the Upper Midwest, from Pierre to Minneapolis. She belted it out over the radio in what was the last time South Dakota would be heard from on the question of war and peace until 1972, when George McGovern asked his countrymen to come home from across the seas. Little Ruth sang with all her heart:

If war is on across the pond,
And submarines are lurking in the ocean
Let them be, don't try to cross the sea
They will surely get you,
Take this message from me.

The Eagle screams, there's danger drawing nigh.
War clouds are in the sky
Now there is room in the good old U.S.A.
A grand place for you and me.
If war should come within our border lines,
We'll give our lives to save our flag from harm
We pray for hands, not arms across the sea
Just stay this side of the pond.

And if our boys go over again,
Just let them take our war promoters with them.
They will see what war can really be
They will praise their freedom this side of the sea.

The Eagle screams . . .[57]

Ruth was unheeded. What did South Dakota know? The nation went to war, leaving this side of the pond for good.

Little Ruth sang for Middle America. She sang for peace, for minding our own business, for Aberdeen, for all the men and boys whose lives might be spent baling hay or plowing fields or even fucking their brains out instead of moaning pathetically, limblessly, dicklessly, in veterans' hospitals. But history is written by the victors, and since Ruth's side—the side of South Dakota and farmers and the preconscription, pre-MTV America—lost, those Americans who stood for peace in 1940 have been calumnied and defaced beyond recognition.

We are told by apologists for the empire that every four years, Americans are given a choice, and thereby they ratify the consensus policies. It's a choice, yes, though it doesn't even rise to the level of Coke or Pepsi. Or Diet Faygo Grape versus RC Lite. And if one discounts the third-party candidates, handicapped as they are by restrictive ballot access laws and, latterly, enormous federal subsidies to the two parties (even their conventions are government-sponsored productions), when, since Bryan joined the communion of commoner saints—except possibly in 1972—have we had even the glimmer of a choice?

Let us consider that just-before-the-battle-mother year of 1940, which ranks with 1896 as the election year in which dies were cast most indelibly.

In her diary entry of June 28, 1940, Anne Morrow Lindbergh rejoiced at the news from the GOP convention in Philadelphia. "Willkie gets the Republican nomination! I don't know much about him but it seems wonderful that a man who is not a politician could get it, and also *not* a die-hard conservative. At least he knows we cannot turn backwards and has some conception of the forces of the future."[58] As the daughter of J. P. Morgan partner Dwight Morrow, Mrs. Lindbergh might be expected to mistake the banks for the ranks. But she was far from alone in hailing the nomination of Wendell Willkie, the barefoot boy from Wall Street, the fixture of the eastern establishment who was transmogrified, almost overnight, from a liberal utilities executive into a charismatic "outsider" who was "above politics."

The choleric Henry L. Mencken marveled that the nomination "was shot through with evidences of a miracle. At one time I actually saw an angel in the gallery . . . To be sure, the angel had on a palm beach suit, but nevertheless it was clearly an angel."[59] Even the queen of spleen herself, Ayn Rand, gushed that Willkie was "an outspoken and courageous defender of free enterprise."[60]

As Lou Reed would sing some years later, "It just goes to show how wrong you can be."

Wendell Willkie was a bright and ambitious lad from Elwood, Indiana, though he "hadn't been back since he was a pup," as the America Firster Alice Roosevelt Longworth cracked.[61] He became a corporation lawyer and then president of Commonwealth and Southern, the utility octopus. Until 1938 he was an FDR Democrat whose only serious disagreement with the New Deal came, not surprisingly, over the matter of public ownership of utilities.

As the 1940 Republican convention approached, the nomination seemed likely to go to one of two midwestern senators: Robert Taft of Ohio or Arthur Vandenberg of Michigan. Taft was of higher character and possessed an intellect superior to that of the skirt-chasing Vandenberg, but they were politically kindred. Both proposed to scale back the New Deal; each hewed to traditional U.S. neutrality and vowed to keep American boys out of the European war. They were "isolationists," which is to say they opposed U.S. involvement in foreign wars. They were peace candidates. And "whenever permitted to choose," as Felix Morley wrote, "between controlling their own government or extending its power overseas, Americans have shown disposition for the former."[62] It seemed that in the election of 1940 the Republican and Democratic candidates would offer starkly, or at least significantly, different visions of America's role in the world and the central state's role in everyday life. But then along came Tweedledee.

The media titans—the Henry Luce empire, the *New York Times*, the *Herald Tribune*—discovered amid the cornstalks of Manhattan a plainspoken man of the people with the alliterative moniker of Wendell Willkie. He was, according to *Fortune*, "the Mississippi Yankee, the clever bumpkin, the homespun, rail-splitting, cracker-barrel simplifier of national issues."[63] His luxury apartment on Fifth Avenue escaped mention, but *Fortune* smiles on cracker barrels.

This gush filled the national press for months, prompting the disgusted Representative Usher Burdick (R-ND) to say, "There is nothing to the Willkie boom for President except the artificial public opinion being created by newspapers, magazines, and the radio." Burdick pulled back the curtain on Oz: "We Republicans in the West want to know if Wall Street, the utilities, and the international bankers control our party and can select our candidate? I believe I am serving the best interests of the Republican Party by protesting in advance and exposing the machinations and attempts of J. P. Morgan and the New York utility bankers in forcing Wendell Willkie on the Republican Party."[64]

Tens of thousands of "We Want Willkie" telegrams—many sent by phantom names at nonexistent addresses—flooded the homes of Republican muck-a-mucks. "Willkie," jeered Mrs. Longworth, "sprung from the grass roots of a thousand country clubs."[65] And on the sixth ballot, the nomination was his.

(For those who like their history murky, much has been made of a dinner party of June 2, 1940, to which the hosts, House of Morgan chairman Thomas Lamont and Ogden Mills Reid, publisher of the *Herald Tribune,* invited Taft and Willkie and various Anglophiles. Talk turned to the European war, and "everybody began to scream at once," recalled the doughty—never dowdy— Martha Taft, wife of the senator.[66] Not for the last time, Taft, alone, stood on principle against the moneyed mob. And three weeks later the nomination slipped through his hands.)

As the campaign wore on and the magnitude of the Willkie fraud revealed itself, Republican jaws dropped. Willkie endorsed virtually the whole New Deal and the Roosevelt foreign policy. He offered an echo, not a choice. His appeal finally retreated unto the soft little shell of his nonpolitician pedigree and a vague promise of "a higher standard of life than we have ever dreamed of before."[67] As Norman Thomas remarked, "He agreed with Mr. Roosevelt's entire program . . . and said it was leading to disaster."[68]

"Where is the fellow who wants a change going to go?" plangently asked Representative Louis Ludlow (D-IN),[69] whose constitutional amendment requiring a national referendum upon a congressional declaration of war had been burked for good in 1937 by FDR, the *New York Times*, and Wall Street Republicans. Willkie won the endorsement of the *Times*—and just 82 electoral votes.

Even confirmed Roosevelt haters deserted the Republicans. John Dos Passos, who had earlier vowed, "I'll never vote for Mr. R . . . again, not if the devil himself runs against him," cast a reluctant ballot for FDR, explaining, "I felt that I did not have a proper choice."[70]

Within weeks of his November trouncing, Willkie took to the hustings to campaign for FDR's Lend-Lease bill. The president even offered him a position in the administration. He spent the rest of his short life (he died in 1944) castigating those mossback Republicans who didn't understand that "any national administration in a modern complex industrial society must exercise vast powers."[71] No small-is-beautiful hippie-dippy sap for the Double W! Willkie wrote a book, *One World* (1943), whose internationalism was so extreme as to make Woodrow Wilson look like Pat Buchanan. Barely a year after Anne Morrow Lindbergh's rhapsodies, Willkie was slandering her husband, Charles. Because when war comes down, home-front peacemongers are so much collateral damage.

Charles A. Lindbergh was a classic product of Upper Midwest populism: his congressman father, a fierce foe of U.S. involvement in World War I, was dubbed the "Gopher Bolshevik" by the *New York Times*. Lindbergh is easily understood in a Minnesota tradition that stretches from the Gopher Bolshevik and Senator Henrik Shipstead through Bob Dylan and Eugene McCarthy. He was no more a Nazi than FDR was.

But not since the Spanish-American War have honorable

Americans been permitted to criticize a foreign war without being slandered as traitorous lackeys for the enemy. Through his hatchet man Harold Ickes, who, as Clare Booth Luce memorably quipped, combined "the soul of a meat axe and the mind of a commissar,"[72] FDR smeared his opponents, especially Lindbergh, as Jap and Nazi symps.

Which brings us to the allegation of anti-Semitism that is occasionally directed at America First. The two scholarly deans of America First historiography, Professors Wayne S. Cole and Justus D. Doenecke, have cleared the AFC of this explosive charge. The committee expressly repudiated anti-Semitism and anti-Semites. Point-blank, General Wood told the followers of the Jew-baiting radio priest Father Charles Coughlin, "We don't want you people."[73] Undoubtedly, an organization of eight hundred thousand members contained a smattering of nuts, but they are hard to find, even in retrospect. The AFC made the big mistake of adding the anti-Semitic Henry Ford to its national committee (which had fifty-five members over its brief life), but he was swiftly and unceremoniously removed. Such Jewish staffers as James Lipsig and Sidney Hertzberg played key roles in the AFC. The former congresswoman Florence Kahn (R-CA) was a fairly inactive Jewish national committee member, as was the Sears, Roebuck director Lessing Rosenwald, who resigned on December 3, 1940, though stating that he was "still in accord with the Committee's basic principles."[74]

One passage in one speech by one orator is really the only stigma that the war party could ever affix to America First. The speech of September 11, 1941 (America First's 9/11) was delivered in Des Moines, Iowa, by Charles Lindbergh. No one in the AFC knew its contents beforehand; proud and independent men do not submit their remarks for the approval of censors. Lindbergh believed in "an independent destiny for America."[75] He favored hemispheric defense but opposed sending U.S. soldiers across the ocean because he did "not believe that our system of government in America, and our way of life, [could] survive our participation."[76] Through his father, he had seen the wholesale repression of speech and the regimentation of the economy in the First World War; he expected a replay on an even grander scale. The continental United States was impregnable against invasion; "history, and experience, and judgment, all showed that the destiny of America should not be tied to the outcome of European War."[77] If these views are traitorous, then American history is one long treasonous fugue.

In his Des Moines speech, which was broadcast over the Mutual Network, Lindbergh said, "The three most important groups who have been pressing this country toward war are the British, the Jewish and the Roosevelt administration." The only one of the trio for which he offered sympathetic exculpation were the Jews: "No person with a sense of the dignity of mankind can condone the persecution of the Jewish race in Germany." But American Jews, he said, should oppose war, for "tolerance is a virtue that depends upon peace and strength. History shows that it cannot survive war and devastation." He suggested that the "large ownership and presence" of Jews "in our motion pictures, our press, our radio, and our government" posed a "great danger" to our neutrality. He admired the British and Jewish people but concluded, "We cannot allow the natural passions and prejudices of other peoples to lead our country to destruction."[78]

Well, where to begin? Lindbergh spoke artlessly, to be sure: the British are "other peoples," but American Jews are American. The line about tolerance, while true, carries the hint of a threat. The Jewish "presence" in government was more significant than that of, say, Greeks, but less than the Irish. And while Hollywood was undeniably a heavily Jewish industry, the Jewish moguls shied from making pro-war films. (The English were another story. The muckraking North Dakota senator Gerald P. Nye, who in

1934–36 had led the investigation into the "merchants of death," those bankers and munitions makers who had profited from U.S. entry into the First World War, called movies "the most gigantic engines of propaganda in existence to rouse the war fever in America and plunge this Nation to her destruction."[79] Nye pointed to such films as *That Hamilton Woman* [1941], a romanticized account of the affair between Lord Horatio Nelson and Lady Emma Hamilton that had a pro-intervention message so thumpingly obvious that it could have been directed by Stanley Kramer. John T. Flynn called the Brits on their propaganda offensive: "Why is it that no picture is produced depicting the tyrannies and oppressions in India where at the moment there are 20,000 Indian patriots in jail? No, what we get are pictures . . . glorifying the magnificence, humanity, and democracy of the British Empire."[80] The extent of the British agitprop campaign was later revealed in works by Michael Korda and William Stephenson, among others.)

Reaction within America First to Lindbergh's speech flowed both ways. Flynn, the pugnacious liberal journalist and head of the New York City chapter, was incensed, but Norman Thomas, the Socialist Party leader who never formally joined the committee though he spoke at its events, wrote General Wood, "I know that Colonel Lindbergh is not anti-Semitic and that he meant good rather than evil by his address." But "what truth there was in [his address] with regard to the Jews, should have been put before a private conference with Jews, not a mass meeting and the radio public." Lindbergh, he said, needed to take "advice on public relations."[81]

Others defended him vigorously. In the *Cornell Daily Sun,* an Indiana-bred student named Kurt Vonnegut wrote:

> Charles A. Lindbergh is one helluva swell egg, and we're willing to fight for him in our own quaint way. Several sterling folk, *Sun* members

not excluded, have been taking journalistic pot-shots at the Lone Eagle, effectively, too . . .

The mud-slingers are good. They'd have to be to get people hating a loyal and sincere patriot. On second thought, Lindbergh is no patriot—to hell with the word, it lost it's [sic] meaning after the Revolutionary War . . .

Charles A. Lindbergh has had the courage at least to present the conservative side of a titanic problem, grant him that. The United States is a democracy, that's what they say we'll be fighting for. What a prize monument to that ideal is a cry to smother Lindy . . .

Lindy, you're a rat. We read that somewhere, so it must be so. They say you should be deported. In that event, leave room in the boat for us, our room-mate, Jane, mother, that barber with the moustache in Willard Straight, and those two guys down the hall—you make sense to us.[82]

There is a sense in which far too much has been made of Lindbergh. He was one man in the last broad peace movement in American history, almost a million strong. He was no more or less representative of the AFC than such speakers and directors as the pacifist novelist Kathleen Norris; Hanford MacNider, the Iowa banker who served as first national commander of the American Legion; or the astringently witty and amaranthine Alice Roosevelt Longworth.

Even if you find Lindbergh's Des Moines speech noxious, is the entire America First project to be written off for one intemperate act? Did Jane Fonda's gun cradling in North Vietnam discredit that peace movement? Do the juvenilities of the Bush haters in Hollywood define and stain the anti–Iraq War cause?

The Second World War was not an imperialist venture, but the America Firsters were heirs to the Anti-Imperialist League. They were Little Americans, fiercely loyal to their place and protective of their liberties. Home was big enough for them. "I come of British stock, with ten generations in New England behind me," wrote the Maine novelist Lincoln Colcord to General Wood in January 1941. "I personally should be heartsick to see totalitarianism triumph in Europe; every fibre of my being is democratic, everything I feel and know is opposed to autocracy in any form. But . . . I do not believe that it is the office of my nation to save the British Empire."[83]

Colcord and the America Firsters saw their country losing itself as it took the world stage. If America was everywhere, then it would be nowhere. To Colcord, home was Searsport, Maine, and his encomium upon it might stand as the true creed of America First and indeed the whole Little American tradition: "It's not a bad place, much like many others, but the secret of our love for it lies in what I have just said—we know it intimately. This is the lesson I get from Thoreau. Love your own pond. All are beautiful. Be contented where you are. Content!—a lost word in our America. This restless ambition—I cannot feel the truth of it. I cannot follow there."[84]

The America Firsters were not followers. They were content. They knew their places; they cherished their places. They were at odds, at antipodes, really, with the trend of U.S. foreign policy since 1898. But they deserve so much better than to be slandered by war lovers and undefended by career-cautious cowards and forgotten by amnesiacs.

In his own valediction, Professor Wayne S. Cole concluded:

After studying America First and its membership thoroughly over the course of more than three decades, I am increasingly impressed by how clean it was. Close scrutiny leaves an overall impression of loyalty, patriotism, good citizenship, courage, and devotion to the country. Its leaders and members used democratic methods responsibly to influence public opinion and government action on issues of vital importance to all Americans. If one were to balance negatives (that is, the morality of the "dirty tricks" used by opponents of America First versus the magnitude of unsavory or disloyal elements within the committee) the America First Committee comes off vastly better than its critics. The fact that one disagreed profoundly with the views of Lindbergh and believed him totally wrong did not justify accusing him of disloyalty and Nazi sympathies. Those charges simply were not true.[85]

Alas, the legend, or rather antilegend, has become printable fact. The committee, and Lindbergh in particular, are routinely smeared with the grossest lies: see, for an egregious example, Philip Roth's disgusting and defamatory novel *The Plot Against America* (2004).[86]

It is long past time to stop the smears and consider America First on its own terms, in its own words. The progressive pacifist Milton Mayer—one of the many antiwar Jews of 1940–41—characterized the "isolationists" as a mixture of "Anglophobic enemies of empire and imperialism in the best American spirit" and "tens of millions of genuinely neutralist Americans of purest patriotism who wanted no part of what Jefferson called 'the broils of Europe,' together with liberal internationalists . . . who all too clearly recalled the failure of the First World War to make the world safe for democracy and saw war, not Germany or Nazism but war itself, as the scourge of liberty." This "isolationist amalgam," wrote Mayer, was "much more representative of the country than the narrow interventionist movement, which was concentrated among the monied classes of the eastern seaboard."[87] (Much more representative than the war party were those favoring "aid short of war"—about half the public, according to opinion polls.)

Its contemporaries found the AFC to be an honorable organization, as American as Geronimo and George F. Babbitt. How else to explain the postwar careers of Stuart, Shriver, Ford, Kennedy, and its other youthful founders and adherents? They bore no shame; they had acted as citizens should act in a free republic.

Perhaps the United States, having renounced the policy of noninterference in European wars a quarter century earlier, would have been drawn ineluctably into any European conflict on so vast a scale. Certainly the kaiser's heavy-handedness was nothing compared to the evil of Adolf Hitler. Lest the U.S. intervention be interpreted solely as a second crusade for human rights, however, let us remember that the United States declared war first on Japan and then on Germany in response to Germany's declaration against us. And most America Firsters never could quite understand how our ally Stalin, whose toll of murders actually exceeded Hitler's, was any less repellent than the Nazi monster.

An America that had kept to the Anti-Federalist path of decentralized liberty, or to the Federalist-Whig acceptance of boundaries, of limits, could have remained, as Little Ruth Palmer sang, on this side of the sea. We cannot know what would have been the result: disaster almost beyond imagining (the triumph of Nazism or Stalinist communism over all of Europe) or, as Wayne S. Cole, for one, believes likely, "a bloody stalemate with both the Soviet Union and Nazi Germany and their people bled white and exhausted."[88]

The antiwar movement of 1940–41 was essentially libertarian: in favor of peace and civil liberties, opposed to conscription. Wartime repression of speech was considerably less severe than under President Wilson, but then Americans of 1917 were freer, more rural, less hemmed in by skyscrapers and time clocks and factory walls. They hadn't learned to watch their tongues. They didn't know yet that America was to be run by hall monitors and tattletales.

War and those who make it, however high-flown the speechifying, are ever and always curtailers of civil liberty, and there was one enormous blot on the Rooseveltian escutcheon: the internment of law-abiding Americans on racist grounds. When the Roosevelt administration issued Executive Order 9066 and thereby rounded up 110,000 Japanese Americans, the majority of them citizens, herding them into the concentration camps of the West, nary a peep was heard from the usual liberal champions of racial equality. In fact, John J. McCloy, FDR's assistant secretary of war, scoffed at pettifogging Constitution lovers: "If it is a question of safety of the country, [or] the Constitution of the United States, why the Constitution is just a scrap of paper to me"[89]—so much bumf.

The dissent came from the right, from Senator Robert Taft, who denounced the mass evacuations of Japanese Americans while liberal Democrats were whispering huskily about Jap perfidy. You don't hear about that because nothing can interfere with what John T. Flynn called "the Roosevelt Myth."

The Second World War completed the revocation of U.S. neutrality. Henceforth our garrisons would span the globe. Our soldiers would be so scattered to the dispersive winds of militarism that a World War II hero from South Dakota eventually would run for president on a platform pleading that we "Come Home, America." He would be trounced.

3

"ILL-FATED, UNNECESSARY, AND UN-AMERICAN": FOLLOWING A COLD WAR INTO ASIA

HAVING TWICE ESTABLISHED, in 1917 and again in 1941, that the founders' policy of neutrality vis-à-vis Europe was as outmoded as the peruke and the Tenth Amendment, the rulers of the postwar United States moved into a forty-year "twilight struggle" against our totalitarian ally of the Second World War, the Soviet Union. The Cold War was inevitable, given the interventionist premises of the modern American state. If the condition of Europe and Europeans was to be a central concern of the U.S. government, how could the legions of democracy not recross the Atlantic to defend the social democracies of western Europe against the barbed-wire socialism of the Soviet bloc?

Over twoscore years this policy would bleed U.S. taxpayers of up to $10 trillion and disorder American life in myriad ways, some to be recounted in chapter 5, but by the late 1940s to care more about Kansas than Budapest was the mark of a crabbed and calloused soul, an America First relict, an isolationist thought-criminal who had somehow escaped the bipartisan establishment dragnet. We were all interventionists now.

Whither the old isolationists in the Cold War? They have been written out of a triumphalist history, reduced to footnotes and then deleted by a Cold War historiography that finds the existence of anti–Cold War, anti–Truman Doctrine, anti–military-industrial-complex conservatives and Republicans too damned confounding for consensus history.

That Harry Truman's sharpest critics were on the antiwar "Right" satisfies no one—not the Cold War liberals, not leftist revisionists, not conservative hawks. They are inconvenient in the way that so many hale and red-blooded American dissenters have been inconvenient: think Mother Jones denouncing day care and woman suffrage; think Dorothy Day praising the church's teachings on abortion and sexuality; think Zora Neale Hurston reviling the *Brown v. Topeka Board of Education* ruling because it insulted African American schoolteachers; think William Appleman Williams defending Herbert Hoover and Gore Vidal praising the America First Committee.

Felix Morley, speaking in the diction of the old America, a lost language, reckoned the cost of the incipient Cold War in 1949. "What William Graham Sumner had called 'Blessed Isolation' was indeed abandoned. In its place, unwittingly and unwillingly, the American people had accepted imperial burdens that strongly imply the passing of their Republic."[1]

Morley, the son of distinguished Quaker stock (though he adopted his mother's Episcopalianism), had won a Pulitzer Prize for his *Washington Post* editorials. He stepped down after seven years (1933–40) as the *Post*'s editor because he understood what the forewinds of war portended: "newspaper writing in wartime can come close to intellectual prostitution."[2] Though he declined an invitation to join the America First Committee, Morley opposed U.S. intervention in the European war. He never recanted. Almost four decades later he wrote, "I could see no legal or moral reason for our involvement in the derivative hostilities, even with full realization of the Nazi tyranny. Equal disregard of 'human rights' was apparent in Soviet Russia, and the idea of an alliance with either regime seemed to me anathema."[3]

Having sowed his oats, he returned to his Quaker roots as president of Haverford College, his alma mater and as good a place as any to sit out a war. But Morley was a journalist, not a pompous dispenser of sententious advice to pustuled frat boys, and in February 1944, he and Frank Hanighen, a former *New York Times* correspondent, launched *Human Events* (appellation borrowed from the Declaration), a weekly newsletter of conservative politics—though Morley stubbornly called his philosophy "True Liberalism." Justus D. Doenecke describes *Human Events* as a mixture of "domestic conservatism with nonintervention."[4] It was anti–New Deal, antibureaucratic, and deeply skeptical of the projection of U.S. military might abroad. Backed financially by such old America Firsters as General Robert Wood, Charles Lindbergh, and Colonel McCormick, it welcomed pieces from the anti-intervention Left, even publishing the Socialist Party leader Norman Thomas.

It denounced Harry Truman's order to drop the atomic bomb on Hiroshima with a passion that one might expect to find in the *Catholic Worker.* In August 1945, Morley wrote: "Pearl Harbor was an indefensible and infamous act of aggression. But Hiroshima was an equally atrocious act of revenge . . . It was pure accident if a single person slain at Hiroshima had personal responsibility for the Pearl Harbor outrage." Those unctuous professional reassurers who tell us that God has blessed America were trying, reprehensibly, "to reconcile the mass murder of 'enemy children' with lip service to the doctrine that God created all men in his image."[5]

The Old Right, unlike the war-liberals, took no national pride in the vaporization of the women and children and even Tojo-kowtowing men of Hiroshima and Nagasaki.[6]

If the radioactive bomb-blast of Truman had scorched the American ground, his Cold War was freezing it to wasteland. With dismay, Felix Morley saw "conscript troops" from a once-free republic "on a frontier stretching from Korea to Bavaria."[7] And the cant was really too much. "With pronounced self-righteousness, at best not a lovable characteristic, we are rapidly establishing ourselves as the world's greatest moralizer on the subject of the conduct of other governments," Morley wrote in 1946.[8]

War, Felix Morley understood, was "the perfect device for replacing federalism with centralization."[9] National planning schemes beyond the wildest dreams of Rexford G. Tugwell were smuggled through the Congress because their authors cannily inserted "Defense" into the title. There was the National System of Interstate and Defense Highways, which scarified the land and contributed to the depopulation of rural America. The National Defense Education Act transferred a quondam local responsibility to the swelling federal leviathan.

Morley located the philosophical germ of totalitarian collectivism in Rousseau's concept of the *general will,* which amounted to a license to tyrannize individuals in the name of the mass. His own preference, as the historian Joseph R. Stromberg has written, was for "a Jeffersonian alternative consisting of republicanism, federalism, decentralization and nonintervention."[10] This is not merely the road less traveled (though the conservative Democrat Robert Lee Frost trod its path); it is the road plowed up and paved over with the asphalt of modern liberalism.

No beetle-browed xenophobe butchering foreign pronunciations, as interventionists like to imagine the straw-man "isolationists," the cosmopolitan Morley insisted that "there has never been a people whose natural instincts are less 'isolationist.' Mixed blood and mingled origins dispose Americans to think well of men as men. They are happily not disposed to think well of governments as governments. The fundamental American faith responds to associations of men—everywhere. It has no confidence in associations of governments—anywhere."[11]

Against all evidence, Morley was sanguine. He was confident, in the wake of the Second World War, of a coming "showdown between these advocates of Imperialism and those who intend to keep America a country in which men are raised as citizens instead of subjects."[12] He had faith that his landsmen would eventually rebuff the harlot of powerlust. "Americans mistrust empire," he wrote in 1949,[13] but while public opinion polls consistently found a strong minority of Americans favoring a withdrawal of U.S. troops from Europe, the bring-'em-home contingent in Congress would shrink within the decade from a feisty band of midwestern Republicans and Upper Midwest populists to an isolated ruderal few, who stuck out like roses pushing up through the concrete.

Within a year, Morley would be thrown out of *Human Events* on his ass. Not for another twoscore years would an avowedly conservative publication agree with Morley's profession in his memoir (which bore the hackneyed title *For the Record*): "I was, and continue to be, strongly opposed to centralization of political power, thinking that this process will eventually destroy our federal republic, if it has not already done so. The vestment of power in an HEW is demonstrably bad, but its concentration in the Pentagon and CIA is worse because the authority is concealed and covertly exercised. Failure to check either extreme means continuous deficit financing and consequent inflation, which in time can be fatal to the free enterprise system."

Human Events was a collateral casualty of the Cold War. Oh, it lived on, and publishes still today, with all the rhyme and reason of a Republican Party cheerleader. But the *Human Events* of Felix Morley, the weekly imbued with the spirit of 1776, died in February 1950, when Henry Regnery, who with Morley and Hanighen controlled one-third of the stock after incorporation, threw in with Hanighen. The issue was the Cold War. Let Morley tell the tale: "Hanighen and I had come to differ over its policy. He thought, correctly, that to achieve financial success we would have to push our paid circulation well above the 5,000 mark where it had seemed to settle. To do this, he wanted to exploit the popular mistrust of Russia that was daily becoming more apparent. I argued that this line could only encourage militarization and further centralization of power in Washington. It would run counter to our agreed purpose of seeking to reanimate the country's original political thought."[14]

Hanighen prevailed. When in the course of human events a conservative crosses the empire, that conservative is given a one-way ticket to his own Siberia.

Morley & Co. realized that by ratifying the North Atlantic Treaty Organization (NATO) on July 21, 1949, the U.S. Senate rejected decisively the "no entanglements or alliances" school of statecraft. Article 5 of the treaty begins, "The Parties agree that an armed attack against one or more of them in Europe or North America shall be considered an attack against them all; and consequently they agree that, if such an armed attack occurs, each of them, in exercise of the right of individual or collective self-defense recognized by Article 51 of the Charter of the United Nations, will assist the Party or Parties so attacked by taking forthwith, individually and in concert with the other Parties, such action as it deems necessary, including the use of armed force, to restore and maintain the security of the North Atlantic area."[15]

By a vote of 82–13, the Senate had incorporated Europe, that foul old whore from which the founders had adjured keeping a prudent distance, into the ambit of U.S. defense. The flag of the coiled rattlesnake that hissed "Don't Tread on Me" but implicitly pledged not to trespass against others had been furled. For an attack on Belgium was now an attack on the United States.

Those thirteen Senate dissenters, a baker's dozen in fealty to the pre-atom-bomb America, included only two Democrats: Edwin Carl Johnson of Colorado, most famous for denouncing the Ingrid Bergman–Roberto Rosellini affair from the Senate floor—if only he had instead condemned *Stromboli!*—and the leftist Glen Taylor of Idaho, who had been Henry Wallace's 1948 Progressive Party running mate. The other eleven comprised Taft conservatives (among them Mr. Republican himself), cantankerous nationalists (notably George "Molly" Malone of Nevada, who had predicted,

"If in our reaching to create a free world we find it necessary to associate ourselves with every blackguard, exploiter, cartelist and reactionary, we shall earn the hatred of peoples all over the world"),[16] and of course the entire Senate delegation of North Dakota ("Wild Bill" Langer and Milton Young), ever and always the most isolationist, antiwar, anti–Wall Street state in the Union.

("We believe in the Constitution out here," Langer once explained of his state, "and we bitterly resist any invasion by any group of war profiteers, corrupt politicians, so-called 100 percent self-loving hypocritical patriots, or by any other enemy of constitutional government."[17] In time, power would corrupt Langer, too, but in 1949 he spoke the Upper Midwest language of peace, branding NATO "a barren military alliance directed to plunge us deeply into the economic, military and political affairs of the other nations of Europe.")[18]

We were squandering our inheritance fooling around with the Eurotrash that great-great-grandfather had warned us against. Salty old America Firster Sterling Morton lamented of NATO that "should our country cross this Rubicon, we will . . . have taken the decisive step toward a complete change in our national way of life . . . and shall have embarked upon a path which can lead only to eventual bankruptcy, eventual dictatorship, and the end of that system of life known as 'the American Way.'"[19]

He was echoed by John T. Flynn, the erstwhile *New Republic* muckraker whose principled hatred of Franklin D. Roosevelt drove him into a kind of right-wing, libertarian McCarthyite exile: "Since 1945—nearly five years—we have been spending billions in what we are told is a 'cold war.' Unless we make an end of this it will bankrupt us. Even more appalling, it will lead us into another war at the end of which our liberties and our economic system will be ready for the scrap heap. The reason for all this is that the interests of America have been completely blotted out in this insane adventure in world salvation. We have saved nothing. We are contributing to the destruction of everything our civilization values."[20]

Reeling under the blows of hyperinterventionist, witch-hunting Cold War liberalism, the old isolationists gathered forces for one last campaign. It was dubbed the "Great Debate" at the time, but since it was a real debate over matters fundamental to the Republic, it has been utterly forgotten while the tawdry sideshow of Joe McCarthy has come to define the "Right" of the era. (A misrepresentation made all the more egregious by the fact that Tail-gunner Joe was elected in 1946 as a moderate Republican of interventionist stripe. He fustigated Robert La Follette Jr., the incumbent whom he whipped in the GOP primary, as an isolationist.)

The "Great Debate" sought and fought so desperately, so passionately, and with such resounding lack of success was kicked off by the unlikely duo of former president Herbert Hoover and ex-ambassador Joseph Kennedy. The Korean conflict, for which President Truman had never bothered to obtain a congressional declaration of war, relying instead on his asserted executive powers and a United Nations Security Council resolution, was going badly. Chinese troops had crossed the thirty-eighth parallel; General MacArthur's optimistic remark of November 1950—"I hope we can get the boys home by Christmas"[21]—was now a nullity. At the same time, Truman was denying that he needed congressional authorization before committing hundreds of thousands of troops to the occupation of Europe under NATO. The stage had been set: in the establishment corner were Democratic liberals, who supported the prosecution of the Korean War and the president's unilateral power to send troops thereto as well as to Europe. These troops were largely to be conscripts—a slave army. The Democrats were solidly behind the continuance of the draft, and many, Truman foremost among them, demanded universal military training (UMT) for all young American males.

In the other corner, weighing in at 120 pounds sopping wet

and with a record of 2–24, was the old Republic. Its cornermen were mostly "conservative" Republicans who opposed the draft, UMT, the commitment of troops to NATO, and Truman's possibly unconstitutional conduct in marching the nation off to war on the Korean peninsula.

Joseph P. Kennedy—bootlegger, paterfamilias, lobotomizer of Rosemary, Democrat, former ambassador to Great Britain, Gloria Swanson's boulevardier, and America First donor—threw the first punch on December 12, 1950, in a speech given, aptly, at the University of Virginia Law School Forum in Charlottesville. Jeffersonian echoes from an improbable source! For there was in old Joe Kennedy little of the agrarian, and his sons would help define a Democracy antithetical to that of the Sage of Monticello.

Kennedy's speech, and the sequel by Herbert Hoover, underline, capitalize, and exclaim the really astonishing extent to which surviving partisans of the Old Right and certain "conservatives" of both parties wished to sit out the Cold War. Clinging fast to Washingtonian neutrality and Jeffersonian abhorrence of entangling alliances, they whispered peace while the Truman Democrats chanted war.

"Our chief source of reliance must be ourselves," said Ambassador Kennedy, "and we cannot sacrifice ourselves to save those who do not seem to wish to save themselves."

The "first step" toward a sane foreign policy was "to get out of Korea." We must then "apply the same principle to Europe." After all, "what have we gained by staying in Berlin?" (His son John seems not to have absorbed this paternal lesson.) The proper U.S. sphere of defense, said Kennedy, included North America, the Caribbean, and Latin America. The rest of the world was on its own. To those ever ready to reach for the *a* word, he asked, "Is it appeasement to withdraw from unwise commitments, to arm yourself to the teeth and to make clear just exactly how and for what you will fight?"

The Cold War, or a potential World War III against the Soviets, was not worth it. For "if portions of Europe or Asia wish to go Communistic or even have Communism thrust upon them, we cannot stop it. Instead we must make sure of our strength and be certain not to fritter it away in battles that could not be won." This Kennedy would not pay any price, he would not bear any burden—nor would he accept garrisons, transatlantic deployments, or the demonization of Asiatic warlords as substitutes for constitutional governance.

There was a dour, saturnine, gloomy cast to Kennedy's speech. Joseph Kennedy's Uncle Sam was an "Atlas, whose back is bowed and whose hands are busy holding up the world." It was time for Atlas not to shirk, or even to shrug, but to mind his own place—"to conserve American lives for American ends, not waste them in the freezing hills of Korea or on the battle-scarred plains of Western Germany."

Kennedy appealed to ancestral memory, to the isolationist impulse that had been so sedulously suppressed for the last decade of carnage and parades: "We have never wanted a part of other peoples' scrapes. Today we have them and just why, nobody quite seems to know. What business is it of ours to support French colonial policy in Indo-China or to achieve Mr. Syngman Rhee's concepts of democracy in Korea? Shall we now send the marines into the mountains of Tibet to keep the Dalai Lama on his throne? [Richard Gere's pulse races.] We can do well to mind our business and interfere only where somebody threatens our business and our homes."[22]

Given the New Frontier imperialism of a decade later, a less Kennedyesque message is hard to imagine. (Perhaps a sermon condemning adultery?)

Herbert Hoover, the quasi-pacifist Iowan, was next in the ring. On December 20, 1950, he told a nationwide radio audience: "We must face the fact that to commit the sparse ground forces of the non-communist nations into a land war against this Communist land mass would be a war without victory, a war without a successful political terminal. Any attempt to make war on the Communist mass by land invasion through the quicksands of China, India, or Western Europe is sheer folly. That would be the graveyard of millions of American boys and would end in the exhaustion of this Gibraltar of western civilization."

Hoover counseled a hemispheric defense. Sounding notes discordant from the canorous melodies of the Society of Friends, the Quaker urged that we "arm our air and naval forces to the teeth." But their theater of operation would be the western hemisphere; by renouncing military intervention in Europe and Asia, we would "greatly reduce our expenditures, balance our budget, and free ourselves from the dangers of inflation and economic degradation."[23]

Hoover was roundly condemned by the voices of liberalism. *The Nation* announced that "world communism" had "in effect . . . captured for its purposes Herbert Hoover and a good section of the Republican Party." Hoover and his "sinister" allies, those "provincial little souls" of the beleaguered and "discredited forces of isolationism," were "super-appeasers" content to let the Russians "grab what they could get." "The line they are laying down for their country," pontificated the venerable organ of the Manhattan Left, "should set the bells ringing in the Kremlin as nothing has since the triumph of Stalingrad."[24]

The New Republic, under the editorship of the former Soviet spy turned Truman backer Michael Straight, engaged in its own soft-on-reds-baiting. If followed, Hoover's counsel against committing U.S. troops to NATO "may lead Stalin to attack Western Europe in 1951." Uncle Joe would take Asia forthwith and "move on until the Stalinist caucus in the *Tribune* tower would bring out in triumph the first Communist edition of the *Chicago Tribune*." (Recall, please, that within the next couple of years both

The Nation and *The New Republic* would fill endless and unreadable pages with hand-wringing over the bogey of McCarthyism.) The problem, as *The New Republic* saw it, was that Hoover, the conservative, was "appalled by the costs of mobilization." He would "greatly reduce our commitments" for niggling reasons of the purse. Parsimony = Appeasement. The liberal policy, insisted *TNR,* was "full-scale mobilization," which meant "tight controls" on the economy (and, inevitably, persons and liberties), universal military training, and the dispatch of U.S. troops to Europe, Asia, and the four corners of the world.[25]

Empire was serious business, and penny-pinching, Constitution-hugging conservatives were not up to the task. So grim was the mood that an effort to relaunch the Veterans of Future Wars sputtered and died. There was nothing funny about the empire.

Senator Robert A. Taft was next to lace up the gloves. On January 5, 1951, he spoke at considerable length (ten thousand words) to the new Eighty-second Congress. His subject was first things. "The principal purpose of the foreign policy of the United States is to maintain the liberty of our people," said Taft. "Its purpose is not to reform the entire world or spread sweetness and light and economic prosperity to peoples who have lived and worked out their own salvation for centuries, according to their customs, and to the best of their abilities."

The second goal of our foreign policy was peace, explained Taft. *Liberty* and *peace*; with those two words, he had placed himself as far outside postwar discourse as one could reasonably stand.

Taft denied that the Soviets coveted the world: "I myself do not see any conclusive evidence that they expect to start a war with the United States." War "promotes dictatorship and totalitarian government," he averred. "It is almost as disastrous for the victor as for the vanquished."

"The President claims the right without consultation with Congress to decide whether or not we should use the atomic bomb," complained Taft.[26] Since when did the executive become first branch among equals? Since long before yesterday. As far back as May 11, 1846, Senator John C. Calhoun had reproved the expansionist Democrat James K. Polk for provoking a border skirmish with the Mexican army and thus creating a casus belli for the war he desired. "The doctrine is monstrous," said Calhoun of the claim that the president possessed a coequal right with Congress to declare war.[27] A century later, the monster had been not slain but codified.

Like Hoover, Taft advised "superiority in air and sea forces" to ensure an impregnable United States.[28] But we ought not to fight ground wars in Asia or Europe, and we need not mobilize for war or conscript young men under the serfdom known as universal military training. All this war talk was encouraging panic and a disregard for the Bill of Rights. In casting suspicion upon honest dissenters, the Roosevelt and Truman administrations were imperiling the free exchange of ideas upon which our polity depended.

"During recent years a theory has developed," said Taft, with what I like to think of as a wink toward posterity, "that there shall be no criticism of the foreign policy of the administration, that any such criticism is an attack on the unity of the Nation, that it gives aid and comfort to the enemy . . . I venture to state that this proposition is a fallacy and a very dangerous fallacy threatening the very existence of the Nation."[29]

Senator Paul Douglas (D-IL), house pedant of the liberals, took the floor immediately after Taft's disquisition to deny that the president needed congressional authorization to send troops to Europe or Korea. Senator Douglas charged Taft with "defeatism," a line picked up by The New Republic, which ridiculed Taft for "telling the young men and the taxpayers and the mothers that it wasn't worthwhile, really, to employ big U.S. armies."[30] That the founders would agree, almost to a man, with Taft's antimilitarism mattered little to Paul Douglas, Michael Straight, and the party of Cold War liberalism.

The sophisticated eastern wing of the GOP was embarrassed by Taft. Thomas E. Dewey, the self-satisfied face of liberal Republicanism, the mustachioed neat freak and later boy toy of Kitty Carlisle, condemned the Hoover-Taft-Kennedy stance as "operation suicide."[31] To avoid war and preserve liberties is to commit hara-kiri—not to mention gaucheness.

Taft's ally Senator Kenneth Wherry (R-NE) offered a resolution on January 8, 1951, expressing the sense of the Senate that no ground forces should be assigned to NATO absent the congressional authorization thereof. Wherry's proposal went nowhere, and by March 1951 a string of last-ditch efforts by conservative Republicans to limit the deployment of U.S. troops to Europe and to assert the role of Congress in any such action went down to crashing defeats.

The Truman administration had been, well, untrue. Consider this colloquy between the Iowa Republican senator Bourke Hickenlooper and Secretary of State Dean Acheson from a hearing of the Senate Foreign Relations Committee:

SEN. HICKENLOOPER: I am interested in getting the answers as to whether or not we are expected to supply substantial numbers— by that, I do not mean a thousand or two, or 500, or anything of that kind, but very substantial numbers—of troops and troop organizations, of American troops, to implement the land power of Western Europe prior to aggression.

Is that contemplated . . . [under the NATO treaty] where we agree to maintain and develop the collective capacity to resist? In other words, are we going to be expected to send substantial numbers of troops over there as a more or less permanent contribution to the development of these countries' capacity to resist?

SEC. ACHESON: The answer to that question, Senator, is a clear and absolute "No."[32]

Secretary Acheson lied, but then that is what diplomats are paid to do. He was a Wise Man, after all.

President Truman lashed out at his critics. In his State of the Union address of January 8, 1951, he continued to scare the hell out of the American people, as the turncoat Republican senator Vandenberg had advised him to do when selling the Truman Doctrine. (Vandenberg was a pompous Michigander in love with the sound of his own voice. He was "the only Senator who can strut sitting down," as journalists joked,[33] and he had a roving eye that rarely lighted on Mrs. Vandenberg. As the diplomatic historian Thomas Mahl documents in his fascinating *Desperate Deception: British Covert Operations in the United States, 1939–1944,* Vandenberg fell under the spell of a series of beautiful British lady spies. By the time they had done with him, he had metamorphosed from an antiwar midwesterner to an interventionist Anglophile.)

"The threat of world conquest by Soviet Russia" lowered over Truman's State of the Union speech. We were in "peril" from this "total threat," which stretched from pole to pole. In contrast to Hoover, Taft & Co., Truman defined "the North Atlantic community" as an integral part of the "common defense," which constitutionalist pettifoggers heretofore had assumed was conterminous with the territorial United States. Truman also insisted that "Korea has tremendous significance for the world." Lest war-weary Americans slip into irresponsible dreams of peace, the president cautioned that "full wartime mobilization" was on deck. Congress might watch his acts, applaud them, or even pick at nits, but he was the commander in chief—the decider—and none would gainsay his right to send troops wherever he might wish.

And one last thing. Debate, said Truman, was all well and good, "but let every man among us weigh his words and deeds . . . If we are truly responsible as individuals, I am sure that we will be unified as a Government."[34]

We would hear that one again.

Representative Usher Burdick, the North Dakota Republican, spoke for the isolationists on Korea: "In my judgment, we had no business there in the first place and if we are to settle every row on the face of the earth we will be in continuous wars from now on. If we are in continuous wars, we will have to be regimented and controlled and our democracy will cease."[35]

Cue the Patriot Act, George.

The Rise of the Do Not Bend, Fold, Spindle, or Mutilate State

Conservative and classical liberal peaceniks might woolgather away a lazy summer day musing on what-might-have-been under a Taft presidency. Had he been elected in 1940, the United States may well have avoided war in Europe and the Pacific. Perhaps Hitler would have overrun Europe, catastrophically; or quite possibly Hitler and Stalin would have destroyed each other, a blessing to the world. Had he won the 1948 race, the United States would not have been a full participant in the Cold War. Had the 1952 election gone his way . . . well, he'd better have chosen wisely a running mate, for Senator Taft passed from this mortal coil on July 31, 1953, his last speech warning against the commitment of U.S. troops to the Asian mainland. Mr. Republican, forefeeling the Democratic Left.

Taft's midwestern campaign manager in 1952 was a Cornhusker member of Congress who'd have wanted to abolish almost any department a President Taft would have put under his charge. The name may be vaguely familiar: Howard Buffett. But man, did the apple ever fall far from this tree.

Warren Buffett, the legendary investor whose taste for hamburgers and life in Omaha, Nebraska, gives him a reputation for Middle American oddness in the world of high finance, is just another colorless gray-pinstriper when compared with his father: Representative Howard Buffett (R-NE), who half a century ago was perhaps the most radical and principled member of Congress.

The Buffetts were pillars of Omaha. Howard Buffett was a stockbroker, "gentle and sweet-natured," in the words of Warren's biographer Roger Lowenstein. His politics, though, were to "the right of God," cracked one local banker.[36]

Buffett was elected to Congress in 1942 with a pledge to keep FDR from "fasten[ing] the chains of political servitude around America's neck."[37] He marked himself a maverick by returning a pay raise to the Treasury and by subjecting each piece of legislation to a simple test: "Will this add to, or subtract from, human liberty?"

Very few H.R.s passed Howard Buffett's test.

In four nonconsecutive terms representing Omaha in the U.S. House of Representatives, the backbench Republican compiled an almost purely libertarian record. He opposed whatever New Deal alphabet-soup agencies and Fair Deal bureaucracies emerged from the black lagoon of the Potomac.

He was also a strict isolationist, denouncing NATO, conscription, the Marshall Plan ("Operation Rathole"),[38] and the Cold War, which he believed would enchain Americans in "the shackles of regimentation and coercion . . . in the name of stopping communism." He foresaw the reward for holding fast to the old ways: "Patriots who try to bring about economy would be branded as Stalin lovers."[39]

Foreign aid was a Buffett bugaboo. The story is told that as the family drove past the British Embassy late one night, Howard, seeing the lights still on, quipped, "They even stay up late to think of ways to get our money."[40]

Buffett summed up his views of America and the world in a speech on the House floor condemning the Truman Doctrine:

Even if it were desirable, America is not strong enough to police the world by military force. If that attempt is made, the blessings of liberty will be replaced by tyranny and coercion at home. Our Christian ideals cannot be exported to other lands by dollars and guns. Persuasion and example are the methods taught by the Carpenter of Nazareth, and if we believe in Christianity we should try to advance our ideals by his methods. We cannot practice might and force abroad and retain freedom at home. We cannot talk world cooperation and practice power politics.[41]

A leviathan of theretofore unimagined proportion was taking shape, its ravenous belly fed by the tax man. Buffett's colleague Representative George Bender (R-OH), a close ally of Senator Robert Taft, also foresaw a hemorrhage of tax dollars to the despots of the globe, once those despots learned how to sweet-talk Uncle Sam: "Every corrupt government in the world which has fastened itself on the backs of the people will raise the cry of communism to get money away from the United States to keep itself in power. This policy is one which can lead only to bankruptcy for the United States."[42]

Dissent must be its own reward; seldom does it bring promotion. Howard Buffett retired from politics after losing the 1954 Republican Senate nomination to Roman Hruska, who would achieve immortality in 1970, when he defended Nixon's doomed Supreme Court nominee G. Harrold Carswell from charges that he was a "mediocrity" with the immortal effusion, "Even if he were mediocre, there are a lot of mediocre judges and people and lawyers. They are entitled to a little representation, aren't they?"[43] Not to worry, Roman; they've got it now.

Even his critics conceded that Howard Buffett was no mediocrity. To *The Nation,* he was "an able young man whose ideas have tragically fossilized."[44] In retirement, he had the good fortune to befriend an energetic young economist named Murray Rothbard, who would in time become the Menckenian Happy

Warrior of the libertarian movement. For years, Rothbard touted the wisdom of Howard, the Buffett who was neither billionaire nor beach bum wasting away again in Margaritaville. After his death in 1964, Howard Buffett was revived as an unheeded prophet by such New Left critics of U.S. foreign policy as Carl Oglesby, the president of Students for a Democratic Society, who in his essay "Vietnamese Crucible" invited the libertarian Right to rediscover its Buffetts and join hands with "the Negro freedom movement and the student movement against Great Society–Free World imperialism"[45]—an invitation the Right never bothered to open, let alone accept.

Congressman Buffett's son, while revering Pop as a tower of integrity and honesty, seems not to have inherited the old man's libertarian streak. Warren Buffett is a liberal Democrat whose favorite political cause is legalized abortion.

But surely the father bequeathed the son a confident contrariety, for if Warren Buffett lacks Howard Buffett's politics, he shares his disdain for the eastern citadels of commerce and power, choosing to live in his hometown of Omaha: a decentralist act of which Representative Buffett would have heartily approved.

Howard Buffett was almost as radical as his young comrade Rothbard. In 1962, Buffett pointed out "An Opportunity for the Republican Party" to readers of the *New Individualist Review*. He was incredulous that his fellow Republicans could not see that "an issue of actual physical freedom, as vital and fundamental as the infamous Negro slavery, exists in America today. Its abolition awaits a political party courageous enough to champion liberty as the Republicans did a century ago. I refer, of course, to the Old World evil of conscription, carried out here under the soothing label of Selective Service."[46]

The military draft, argued Representative Buffett, was nothing less than slavery. And if Republicans did not rally to his emancipatory call, it is a little-remembered fact that a Republican president, Richard M. Nixon, oversaw the dismantling of the Democratic-erected draft (which Harry Truman had sought not to curtail but to expand under the label universal military training). The men who laid the philosophical foundation and devised the practical machinery for abolishing the draft were such free-market economists as Walter Oi—who as a Nisei child was interned in one of FDR's camps for Japanese Americans—and Milton Friedman.

As a key member of Nixon's Commission on an All-Volunteer Armed Force, Friedman challenged pro-draft witness General William Westmoreland. Friedman recalled, "In the course of [Westmoreland's] testimony, he made the statement that he did not want to command an army of mercenaries. I stopped him and said, 'General, would you rather command an army of slaves?' "[47]

Conservative economists had labored—opposed by such pro-draft liberals as Senators Ted Kennedy (D-MA) and Hubert Humphrey (D-MN)—to repeal the single most coercive program in the history of the U.S. government, an artifact of Democratic war-liberalism.

In kidnapping young men from their places and families and sending them to labor for the empire—or as Daniel Webster thundered, "tak[ing] children from their parents, and parents from their children, and compel[ling] them to fight the battles of any war in which the folly or the wickedness of government may engage it"—conscription was a profoundly anticonservative policy. It subverted—perverted—the most basic social institution, the family, and thereby leads us to the sociologist Robert Nisbet, who emphasized the importance of traditional social authorities as a bulwark of human liberty against the coercions and barbarities of the state.

Bred in a town south of Bakersfield (Maricopa), the son of a Christian Scientist mother and a father who managed a lumberyard,

Nisbet was a graduate and longtime faculty member at Berkeley who moved eastward, to Columbia, and then, improbably, incredibly, the American Enterprise Institute. For Nisbet hadn't a neocon bone in his body.[48]

"The modern release of the individual from traditional ties of class, religion, and kinship has made him free," wrote Nisbet in *The Quest for Community* (1953),[49] but it was a fool's freedom, the freedom of the unmoored, deracinated man, who henceforth would be "free" to be conscripted into mass armies, to purchase consumer products, and to have his cremated remains interred in a suburban cemetery alongside the ashes of ten thousand strangers. It was that easy elision from "free" to "free fallin'," as the song by a son of the working-class South goes.[50]

The state, Nisbet explained, seeks to undermine the family, the church, and the local community and to absorb functions otherwise performed by these human-scale entities.

The great beneficiary of the erosion of intermediate institutions—churches, civic organizations, unions, St. Vincent de Paul societies, lodges—is the state rampant, the state triumphant, the state as lord and master and savior of a disaggregated mass of anchorless men and women. It "is the pulverizing of society into a sandheap of individual particles," wrote Nisbet, "that makes the arrival of collectivist nationalism inevitable."[51] Rootless men, without loyalties or local attachments, make ductile subjects. Think of the suburban Limbaugh listener spooning up his Lean Cuisine and cheering as the smart missiles find their targets, and strangers die unseen deaths.

The proper words for this are *deracination* and *rootlessness*, though they are used with caution since a handful of hysterics regard them—indeed, regard any discussion of rootedness—as furtively anti-Semitic (the wandering Jew and all that). And so we are deprived of even the language to identify the problem. But mine is the America of Bob Dylan, Murray Rothbard, Emma

Goldman, Paul Goodman, Allen Ginsberg, Milton Friedman, and Norman "Power to the Neighborhoods!" Mailer, and if that's anti-Semitism then George W. Bush is Moses. The lack of roots is the single most disabling malady plaguing America, and we will never begin the long healing until we diagnose the illness.

Culture and personality, Nisbet believed, are rooted deeply in "neighborhood, family, and religion."[52] Undermine this trinity, set individuals adrift without their anchorage, and you reduce society to a faceless welter of listless and anomic consumers. The instruments of such dislocation are many—urban renewal, public education, the proletarianization of women in the industrial and service economies, the interstate highway system—but the most devastatingly powerful is war.

It makes perfect sense that those who most strongly resisted the state's usurpation and/or absorption of "community" were those whose lives were most enriched by the network of non-governmental institutions that compose a healthy society. "The solid and really formidable opposition to American entry [into the world wars] came from those closely linked to business, church, local community, family, and traditional morality," observed Nisbet.[53] This was very much a defensive effort by Americans at the grass roots, for "nothing has proved more destructive of kinship, religion, and local patriotisms than has war and the accompanying military mind."[54]

Recall that Nisbet was writing *The Quest for Community* in the early 1950s, the acme, or nadir, of the Cold War, when Americans herded docilely into fallout shelters whene'er the sirens blew like the noonday whistle of a waking nightmare.

Nisbet's prominence on the Right was something of a puzzle that owes, perhaps, to his kindness and decency. He was a resident scholar at the American Enterprise Institute from 1978 to 1980 and a contributor to *Commentary*—institutions not notable for their aversion to war.

Bizarrely, one scholar of the Right, William A. Schambra, actually claimed in 1990 that "Republican party doctrine through the Reagan and Bush years has come to reflect Nisbet's view that the yearning for community is most satisfactorily and safely accomplished through return of authority and function to intermediate institutions."[55] The evidence? A paragraph from a 1975 Ronald Reagan speech ghostwritten by the maverick Vermont Jeffersonian Republican John McClaughry (who quit his domestic policy position in the Reagan White House after serving for just a year) and Bush I's dim "Thousand Points of Light" speech, a vague call to voluntarism from a president whose proudest moment was the waging of the Gulf War, during which the visible points of light were oil field conflagrations.

Nisbet, in *Conservatism: Dream and Reality* (1986), wrote that "Reagan's passion for crusades, moral and military, is scarcely American-conservative. Conservatives dislike government on our backs, and Reagan echoes this dislike, but he echoes more enthusiastically the Moral Majority's crusade to put more government on our backs, i.e. a moral-inquisitorial government well-armed with constitutional amendments, laws and decrees . . . President Reagan's deepest soul is not Republican-conservative but New Deal–Second World War Democrat."[56]

"The state is the outgrowth of war," declared Nisbet.[57] He located the American derangement in the First World War. "Prior to 1917 we were the most decentralized, dispersed, regionalized, and localized government to be found among the great nations of Western society," he told a bemused audience of Reagan retainers in his 1988 National Endowment for the Humanities Jefferson Lecture. (How dare he make a Jeffersonian point in the Jefferson Lecture!) But then Parson Wilson broke into an imperative chorus of "Onward, American Soldiers," and "overnight America became a highly centralized, collectivized war state, virtually a total state."[58]

Wilson's domestic blitzkrieg moved Nisbet to asseverate, "I believe it is no exaggeration to say that the West's first real experience with totalitarianism—political absolutism extended into every possible area of culture and society, education, religion, industry, the arts, local community and family included, with a kind of terror always waiting in the wings—came with the American war state under Woodrow Wilson."[59]

American war state: imagine the fury of the yipping poodles of blogatory should a Cynthia McKinney or Russ Feingold utter such a Nisbetian locution today.

The sham "patriotism" of the television-land nationalists is one noxious legacy of Mr. Wilson's crusade. "There is nothing spontaneous or natural in the intense devotion we find given to a Germany or France or a United States in the nineteenth and early twentieth centuries," Nisbet wrote in *Twilight of Authority*. "To a given locality, region, or ethnic body, yes, but not to a vast expanse of territory that had had its boundaries and its actual component subjects or citizens so often altered by the exigencies of war, diplomacy, and sheer historical accident."[60]

"Liberals and social democrats like death and destruction no more than do conservatives," wrote Nisbet. "But they like some of the accompaniments of large-scale war: the opportunities created for central planning of the economy, for pre-emption of legislative functions, and other pursuits dear to the hearts of political rationalists and enthusiasts."[61] From day care to the metric system, from daylight saving time to summer school, the range and extent of militarism's intrusions into everyday American life has been staggering.

As Nisbet wrote in *The Quest for Community*, "It is in time of war that many of the reforms, first advocated by socialists, have been accepted by capitalist governments . . . Equalization of wealth, progressive taxation, nationalization of industries, the raising of wages and improvements in working conditions, worker-management councils, housing ventures, death taxes, unemployment insurance plans, pension systems, and the enfranchisement of formerly voteless elements of the population have all been, in one country or another, achieved or advanced under the impress of war."[62]

These reforms are not all pernicious, of course, but such "incidental benefits" have made war more palatable to certain liberal intellectuals. Indeed, the language of state violence would be employed to sell meliorative social welfare efforts (the War on Poverty) and behavior modification (the war on drugs). Nisbet estimated that "a good 75 percent of all the national programs which have been instituted in Western countries during the past two centuries to equalize income, property, education, working conditions, and other aspects of life have been in the first instance adjuncts of the war state and of the war economy."[63]

One might adduce as a positive adjunct Harry Truman's desegregation of the armed forces in 1948, though this example is complicated by the fact that the racist policy under correction was also an act of government. In our day, certain gay rights advocates viewed the second Gulf War as an opportunity to dress the cause of gay equality in camo; they want, it seems, an Audie Murphy of their own—as if skill in the state-sponsored murder of foreign strangers is a badge of honor.

Nisbet is as invisible as a modest patriotism in the conservative think tanks of post-9/11 America. His example reminds us, says the historian Thomas Woods, "that in the midst of the right-wing noise machine there still existed, if somewhat chastened and neglected, a humane and principled conservatism to which civilized men could repair."[64]

The great and learned reactionary historian John Lukacs, in a letter to Russell Kirk circa 1990, derided the neoconservatives for "wishing to pour cement all over the country and make the world safe for democracy, well beyond the dreams of Wilson." He continued, "A feeling for the land, for its conservation, and for the strong modesty of a traditional patriotism (as distinct from nationalism) none of them has."[65]

There is nothing modest about the degraded Right of Bush, Limbaugh, McCain, Kristol, and their ilk. They are boastful, puerile, and aggressively ignorant of American history. What they do know, or sense, is the usefulness of militarism in subordinating local, individual, or parochial pursuits to the demands of the expanding center.

Robert Nisbet observed that "the power of war to create a sense of moral meaning is one of the most frightening aspects of the twentieth century."[66] This was not a new development; Secretary of the Treasury Albert Gallatin remarked of the War of 1812 that it "renewed the national feeling which the Revolution had given . . . The people . . . are more Americans; they feel and act as a nation."[67]

Since the nation is always and forever the enemy of the local, the traditional, and the small, the conservative, if she wishes to "conserve" anything beyond Irving Berlin songs and Betty Grable DVDs, must "feel" not nationally but locally, on a scale that permits her to know her countrymen not as abstractions but as neighbors. And one does not send neighbors halfway 'round the world to kill and die for "democracy," "human rights," or "freedom."

Next Stop: Vietnam

The Vietnam War was designed, as Robert Nisbet wrote, by "the intellectuals—the Hillsmans, Bundys, Ellsbergs, Rostows, Schlesingers, Rusks, and McNamaras, and so many others like them, at all levels,"[68] though they cannily left conservatives holding the bag as they slipped into milquetoast dissent.

But not all conservatives. A remnant had not forgotten the counsel of Senator Robert Taft: "I have never felt that we should send American soldiers to the Continent of Asia, which, of course, included China proper and Indo-China, simply because we are so outnumbered in fighting a land war on the Continent of Asia that it would bring about complete exhaustion even if we were able to win. If the President can intervene in Korea without congressional approval, we can go to war in Malaya or Indonesia or Iran or South America."[69]

Take the already dour Taft, add two pinches asperity and a dash of verjuice, and you've got Harold Royce "H. R." Gross, who might have been played by Charles Lane (Potter's puckered parsimonious accountant in Frank Capra's *It's a Wonderful Life*) in an especially foul mood.

To discuss Gross one must begin on December 2, 1963, on the floor of the U.S. House of Representatives. The event: the single most heroically curmudgeonly act in the history of Congress.

Only ten days have passed since President Kennedy was killed in Dallas. Washington is draped in crepe. Mary McGrory is predicting "We'll never laugh again." The Kennedy impressionist Vaughn Meader is frantically trying to learn an LBJ drawl.

The House, heavy with mourning, is quickly disposing of grim business: emergency appropriations for JFK's funeral expenses. The Iowa Republican H. R. Gross rises. He is a wisp of a man, five foot six and 135 pounds, and he "wears loud neckties and a permanently worried expression," according to *Life*.[70] His self-proclaimed mission is "to save this country from national bankruptcy."[71]

Gross has already groused about the "around the clock" Secret Service protection for Widow Kennedy and her two children, but now he achieves the ne plus ultra of niggardliness: he protests that the American taxpayer should not be forced to foot the gas bill for the eternal flame at JFK's grave at Arlington National Cemetery.

Kennedy's obsequies and remembrance should be done "with restraint and in good taste," Gross observes,[72] implying that the eternal flame meets neither standard. House Speaker John W. McCormack immediately shuts off debate. The bill passes by voice vote, and the legend of H. R. Gross grows larger. He is the eternal flamethrower.

The American taxpayer never had a more colorfully ornery friend than Iowa cuss Harold Royce Gross. He had been a Des Moines and Waterloo reporter and newscaster billed as "the man with the fastest tongue in radio."[73] Among his employers was WHO, which had a slower-tongued baseball announcer named Reagan. But Dutch went west and Gross went east, after upsetting an incumbent Republican in a 1948 primary in which the anti–Cold War Gross was attacked as a "radical leftist."[74] He stalked congressional spendthrifts for thirteen terms until his retirement in 1975.

As a freshman he voted against the Marshall Plan; a quarter century later he opposed the bombing of Cambodia because it cost too much. In between he railed against the space program, foreign aid, congressional junkets abroad, and every post office and bridge he could find. Sometimes his targets merged: "Well, even if we don't get to the moon first, we'll be there first with foreign aid," he cracked.[75] A "determined isolationist," as *Current Biography* had him,[76] Gross later said that his only regret was voting "present" instead of "no" on the Gulf of Tonkin Resolution. Gross voted against the Eisenhower and Nixon administrations so often that Minority Leader Gerald Ford remarked, "There are three parties in the House: Democrats, Republicans, and H. R. Gross."[77]

He detested ostentatious wealth ("the mink-coat set")[78] and the celebrity-encrusted Kennedy administration in particular. He protested the provision of military drivers for Frank Sinatra and Peter Lawford at the inaugural ball; he hooted that White House police were guarding Caroline's ponies "Macaroni" and "Spaghetti." (The latter was actually named Tex.) One wall of his office was adorned with an aphorism: "There is always free cheese in a mousetrap."[79]

H. R. Gross was the bane of House leaders, constantly objecting to unanimous-consent requests and greeting each new piece of legislation by blurting, "Just what's in this turkey?" or "How much will this boondoggle cost?" His choleric barbs could fill a book, though he would no doubt fret over the expense of its publication. An overseas trip by a Truman underling was no mere junket but "a lush travel orgy." The Peace Corps was "a haven for draft dodgers."[80] A proposed national aquarium was "a glorified fish pond."[81]

Gross felt himself an utter alien in Washington. He was a Mason and an Elk and a husband to his wife, Hazel, for fifty-eight years, until his death in 1987. (Hazel died in 1999.) He avoided all parties and receptions and spent his evenings poring over government documents and watching wrestling on TV. When criticized for living in a cloister, he replied, "I just might take a trip one of these days, but it'll be at my own expense."[82]

H. R. Gross was buried in Arlington National Cemetery, without an eternal flame. No monument commemorates the flinty Iowan. His brand of penny-pinching peace loving is out of style. But it lingered until the late 1960s among a handful of anti–Vietnam War Republicans.

Consider Congressman Eugene Siler (R-KY), a Baptist lay preacher and attorney who "turned away all clients seeking divorces or accused of whiskey-related crimes." A proponent of "Christianism and Americanism" who announced himself "100 percent for Bible reading and the Lord's Prayer in our public schools," Siler, as the historians David and Linda Royster Beito note, "cast the lone vote in the U.S. House against the Gulf of Tonkin Resolution," though since he was absent and "paired against" the measure, his vote was not formally recorded in the negative.

Siler was moderator of the General Association of Baptists in Kentucky, and he drew from his faith the pacific implications that seem to have escaped a later generation of Christian conservatives. Unlike the Falwells and Robertsons of our day, he acted upon the New Testament. He was, as the Beitos write, a "Taft Republican who was averse to entangling alliances and foreign quagmires."[83] Representative Siler voted against the mobilization of reserves during the 1961 Berlin crisis and as early as 1964 was calling for the return of all U.S. troops from Vietnam. In June 1964, he declared on the House floor with tongue in cheek, perhaps, but heart in place, his own presidential candidacy: "I am running with the understanding that I will resign after 24 hours in the White House . . . What I propose to do in my one day as President is to call home our 15,000 troops in South Vietnam and cancel our part of that ill-fated, unnecessary, and un-American campaign in Southeast Asia."[84]

This was as radical an antiwar statement as one can find in 1964. While timid establishment men were soughing, sotto voce, tentative doubts about Vietnam, Eugene Siler was calling it a disaster in the making—an un-American disaster at that.

Representative Siler left office in 1965 after ten years in the House but ran for the Kentucky GOP Senate nomination in 1968 on a Christian antiwar platform calling for all troops to be home by Christmas. He lost. Hell, *we* lost.

By the fall of 1966 over a quarter of a million U.S. soldiers were in Vietnam. The GOP had its issue if it wanted it.

Thanks in part to public unease over the Democrats' war on Indochina, Republicans gained a total of forty-seven seats in the House and three in the Senate in the 1966 election. These pickups, as the Old Right historian Leonard Liggio notes, were centered on "the Farewell Address heartland circling 300 miles from the *Chicago Tribune* tower," which "returned to its isolationist roots," and on the "Upper Plains, Mountain, and Upper Pacific Coast," which "returned to the [antiwar] William Borah tradition." The new GOP senators included the forthrightly antiwar Mark Hatfield (OR) and Charles Percy (IL). The latter had defeated the warhorse liberal Paul Douglas, whom Liggio calls the Joe Lieberman of his time: "warmonger and extreme tool of unions."[85] Hatfield, who identified himself as a "Taft Republican" and was as close to a pacifist as has graced the postwar Senate, urged the GOP to become the "peace party" of 1968.[86] It could have happened. The Humphrey campaign, deep in hock to kingmaking war Democrats like Chicago mayor Richard Daley and AFL-CIO boss George Meany, provided an opening through which Richard Nixon, despite hints of a secret plan to end the war, did not fit.

In the Senate, Republican skeptics of the Vietnam War were led by two Kentuckians, John Sherman Cooper and Thruston B. Morton, and the Vermont icon George Aiken, who compared his country's rulers to the Romans, who were "so concerned with their own world prestige that they forgot what was going on at home."[87]

"[The peace Republicans'] dissent has been almost totally neglected by the same historians who laud the antiwar efforts of prominent Democrats," writes Andrew L. Johns of Brigham Young University.[88]

Senator Morton is an especially striking case. No barefoot Baptist he, the Yalie had been an assistant secretary of state under Eisenhower before winning a Senate seat in the Bluegrass State in 1956. He voted for the Gulf of Tonkin Resolution in 1964, but by 1967 he was suggesting that it was a fraud and that LBJ had deceived his countrymen into blundering into "one of the greatest tragedies in our history." Senator Morton's Republican Policy Committee produced a controversial 1967 report on Vietnam, whose dovish slant was immediately denounced by such GOP hawks as Texas senator John Tower. By April 1968, Morton was lacerating "wanton globalism" in the pages of the *Saturday Evening Post,* wherein he blamed Democratic "militarists and their civilian sycophants" for the Vietnam debacle.

Morton was no squishy John Lindsay liberal Republican turncoat nursing a secret desire to join the Democrats. "No war in this century has been conducted under a Republican Administration and the American people know it," he wrote.[89] Bob Dole would say the same thing in the 1976 vice presidential debate with Walter Mondale and be flayed for it. Dole learned his lesson and never again said an interesting thing. You can pitch boner medicine on TV and be a statesman in the fisheyes of the corporate media, but you can't knock FDR and Woodrow Wilson.

Republican men of business had bankrolled the two great transideological peace movements of our history, the Anti-Imperialist League and the America First Committee, and if most took a pass during Vietnam that does not mean they went all the way with LBJ. Echoing the pro-peace executives of the 1940s, Edward J. Hekman, president of the United Biscuit Company, warned that "our efforts in Vietnam to prevent a controlled economy from being imposed by force could easily result in a controlled economy being imposed on 200 million Americans."[90]

The anti-interventionist tendency has always been strongest among shopkeepers, corner store proprietors, and owners of small factories. The political scientist John Bunzel, in his classic study *The American Small Businessman* (1956), explained, "What particularly angers the small businessman about all of America's commitments around the world is that he can see no profitable ending for any of them." Rather than piss money down foreign ratholes, the American small merchant of that era believed that "America should devote her energies to strengthening her own free-enterprise economy at home and preserving the economic rights and liberties of Americans."[91]

That impulse has not vanished. Congressman Ron Paul (R-TX) once told me that "smaller businessmen are much better on foreign policy . . . They don't have big contracts from the government, they don't have military contracts, they're not into the military-industrial complex."[92]

Even big business, which historically has ranked behind only liberal intellectuals as the group most favorably disposed toward foreign interventions, shied from the Vietnamese horror show. A number of corporate chieftains, among them IBM's Thomas Watson, Allied Chemical's John Connor, and Bank of America's Louis Lundborg, outspokenly championed the antiwar cause. In March 1968, Newsweek's Kenneth Crawford hyperbolized only slightly when he wrote that "Wall Street, the symbol of American capitalism, is now a focus of peace sentiment rivalling the Berkeley campus." The gray-flannel peaceniks' spur, according to Crawford, was dollars and cents. War "threatens intensified inflation and this, in turn, puts pressure on government to impose wage-and-price controls, excess-profits taxes and other restraints onerous to free enterprise."[93] (As a Jeffersonian decentralist, I swallow hard at hearing IBM, Bank of America, and Allied Chemical described as creatures of "free enterprise," but there you are.)

The organizational umbrella for the antiwar businessmen was Business Executives Move for Vietnam Peace (BEM), founded in late 1966 by the Baltimore insurance executive and Quaker convert Henry Niles. BEM eventually grew to more than two thousand members, most of them "honchos," as an elderly CEO friend of mine used to say, at medium-sized and small companies. Like the bankrollers of the America First Committee, they were domestic manufacturers, "unburdened by oil wells, mines, and markets in far-off lands," as Steve Weissman wrote in the New Left monthly *Ramparts*.[94]

The antiwar Left never knew quite what to make of its buttoned-down allies. BEM advertisements emphasized the budgetary costs of war ("You've been spending $2.64 a day to keep the war going"), a gaucherie not endearing to some of the younger doves. That war is expensive as hell is beside the point, they would say, but then nineteen-year-old placard wavers don't file 1040s.

The influence of BEM specifically, and business generally, was assessed by the political scientist James Clotfelter in 1971 in *The Nation*: "The irony [is] that if and when the war is terminated, it may be as much because of pressure from business and financial elites (its presumed beneficiaries) as from The People."[95]

Okay—so the CEO of IBM and a snaky-haired, acid-dropping University of Montana sophomore listening to *Piper at the Gates of Dawn* were bummed over the Vietnam War for different reasons. Not all coalitionists can fit under one rainbow. But the words of Buffett, of Morley, of Taft could be discerned in the tunes of the New Left. When Felix Morley declared that the "lives of our youth are not the property of the State, to throw on a rubbish heap in Korea or Yugoslavia as some brass hat may ordain,"[96] he was anticipating the lament of a generation fifty years his junior that human beings were not to be bent, folded, spindled, or mutilated by the likes of the man Republican congressmen called Robert "Garbage In, Garbage Out" McNamara.

Old Right, Meet New Left

The essential kinship of the Old Right and the voluntaristic wing of the New Left was emphasized repeatedly by Murray Rothbard. In his charming memoir "Confessions of a Right-Wing Liberal" in *Ramparts*, Rothbard wrote:

I joined the right-wing movement—to give a formal name to a very loose and informal set of associations—as a young graduate student shortly after the end of World War II. There was no question as to where the intellectual right of that day stood on militarism and conscription: it opposed them as instruments of mass slavery and mass murder. Conscription, indeed, was thought far worse than other forms of statist controls and incursions, for while these only appropriated part of the individual's property, the draft, like slavery, took his most precious possession: his own person. Day after day the veteran publicist John T. Flynn—once praised as a liberal and then condemned as a reactionary, with little or no change in his views—inveighed implacably in print and over the radio against militarism and the draft. Even the Wall Street newspaper, the *Commercial and Financial Chronicle*, published a lengthy attack on the idea of conscription.

All of our political positions, from the free market in economics to opposing war and militarism, stemmed from our root belief in individual liberty and our opposition to the state. Simplistically, we adopted the standard view of the political spectrum: "left" meant socialism, or total power of the state; the further "right" one went the less government one favored. Hence, we called ourselves "extreme rightists."[97]

The "extreme rightist" Rothbard wended his way down a delightfully ambiguous political path that passed through the New Left, the Black Panthers, the Libertarian Party, and the 1992 campaign of Pat Buchanan. He had not changed, he insisted; his tactic was to align himself with the anti-imperialists, and by his lights the Peace and Freedom Party led quite naturally into the Buchanan Brigades.

If the Old Right appeared, wraithlike, in the tatterdemalion of the New Left, it was most emphatically rejected by the New Right of the late 1950s and 1960s. Centered on *National Review*, launched in 1955 by the ex-CIA operative William F. Buckley Jr. and a coterie of agency-tied publicists, *National Review*, wrote Rothbard,

"brought to the intellectual leadership of the right-wing a new coalition of traditionalist Catholics and of ex-Communists and ex-
radicals whose major concern was the destruction of the god that
had failed them, the Soviet Union and world communism. This
change of focus from isolationism to global anti-Communism had
been aided, in its early years, by the advent of Senator Joseph Mc-
Carthy, with whom Buckley had been allied. Before he launched
his crusade, incidentally, McCarthy had not been considered a
right-winger, but rather a middle-of-the-roader on domestic questions and an internationalist on foreign affairs."[98]

National Review would now and then throw off a spark of
life—Buckley's witty 1965 campaign for New York City mayor,
Russell Kirk's columns—but on one matter the magazine would
brook no discussion: empire. The journal of Manhattan conservatism was always for war and militarism, never for peace or "isolationism." The establishment Right dumped these twins into the
orphanage.

Left, right, liberal, conservative: of what use is a taxonomy
that pairs a militaristic war-waging centralizer (George W. Bush)
with a gentle tender of home and hearth (Russell Kirk) as "conservatives"? Or mates a bellicose internationalist who was the
house hawk during her husband's administration and outflanked
George W. Bush in calling for a hard line against Iran (Senator
Hillary Clinton) with a humanistic voice of the disarming Upper
Midwest (George McGovern)?

Why not acknowledge the kinship between Kirk and Mc-
Govern, Bush and Clinton, Nisbet and Eugene McCarthy, and Joe
Lieberman and John McCain?

I know, I know: What about abortion? Progressive taxation?
The films of Ang Lee? So much to divide us. But allow me to
make the case that after Bob Taft and Eugene McCarthy, the most
conservative of the serious presidential aspirants of the Cold War
era was a soft-spoken man of the prairies.

To the slanting wall above my desk is taped a large "Come
Home America/Vote McGovern Shriver '72" poster. Designed
by the artist Leonard R. Fuller, the collage fills an outline of the
United States with iconographic images, historic statuary, and
photos of unprepossessing but individuated Americans. The message is peace and brotherhood and a return to the ideals of the
founders. The mood is civics-class hippie, antiwar wife-of-
a-Rotarian, liberal community-college-professor-who-cries-at-
"America the Beautiful." Like George McGovern himself, the
poster suggests that a hopeful and patriotic mild radicalism resides
on Main Street America.

Even now, thirty-plus years after Senator George McGovern
of Mitchell, South Dakota, was buried by Richard M. Nixon
under an electoral vote landslide of 520–17–1 (Virginia elector
Roger MacBride, heir to the *Little House on the Prairie* gold mine,
bolted Nixon for the Libertarian John Hospers—my wife's college mentor, if we're playing six degrees of separation), "McGovernism" remains Beltway shorthand for a parodistic liberalism
that is, at once, ineffectual, licentious, and woolly-headed. It stands
for "acid, amnesty, and abortion," as the Humphrey-Jackson
Democrats put it.

But perhaps, as George McGovern ages gracefully while his
country does not, it is time to stop looking at McGovern through
the lenses of Scoop Jackson and those neoconservative publicists
who so often trace their disenchantment with the Democratic
Party to the 1972 campaign. What if we refocus the image and
see the George McGovern who doesn't fit the cartoon? Son of a
Wesleyan Methodist minister who had played second base in the
St. Louis Cardinals farm system, this other George McGovern
revered Charles Lindbergh as "our greatest American"[99] and
counted among his happiest memories those "joyous experiences" with his dad hunting pheasants.[100] He was voted "the
Most Representative Senior Boy" in his high school and went to

the college down the street, walking a mile each morning to Dakota Wesleyan and then coming home for lunch.

This other George McGovern was a bomber pilot who flew thirty-five B-24 missions in the *Dakota Queen,* named after his wife, Eleanor Stegeberg of Woonsocket, South Dakota, whom he had courted at the Mitchell Roller Rink. He grew up in and remains a congregant of the First United Methodist Church of Mitchell; he knows by heart the "old hymns" and sings them aloud "with the gusto of those devout congregations" that shaped his life "so many years ago."[101] This other George Mc-Govern is a lifelong St. Louis Cardinals fan and member in good standing of the Stan Musial Society. He lives most of the year in Mitchell, his hometown, and says, "There is a wholesomeness about life in a rural state that is a meaningful factor. It doesn't guarantee you are going to be a good guy simply because you grow up in an agricultural area, but I think the chances of it are better, because of the sense of well-being, the confidence in the decency of life that comes with working not only with the land but also with the kinds of people who live on the land. Life tends to be more authentic and less artificial than in urban areas. You have a sense of belonging to a community. You're closer to nature and you see the changing seasons."[102]

This George McGovern, dyed deeply in the American grain, is a hell of a lot more interesting than the burlesque that was framed by his neoconservative critics.

On a clement November morn in 2005, I chatted with Senator McGovern in his room at the Jefferson Hotel in Washington. He was in town for a memorial service for a friend of his, the late Senator Gaylord Nelson (D-WI), a casualty of the 1980 election, when a pack of liberal Senate Democratic lions were defeated by New Right "family values" Republicans, many of them with rather more unconventional domestic lives than the liberals.

Targeted by Terry Dolan and the National Conservative Political Action Committee (NCPAC), McGovern was trounced
58–39 percent by the ineloquent James Abdnor. McGovern can
laugh now about the perversity of the 1980 election. "It ticked
me off, and it was also kind of laughable. A group called American Family Index rated us. I came out with a zero, Jim Abdnor
got a perfect score. Here I am a guy who has been married to the
same woman for thirty-seven years with five children and ten
grandchildren and I'm running against Jim Abdnor, a fifty-eight-
year-old bachelor who gets a 100 percent rating. I'm not against
fifty-eight-year-old bachelors, not for one minute, but they're
hardly a symbol of what promotes the American family."[103]

McGovern, unlike his erstwhile Senate partner in peace,
Mark Hatfield, is an opponent of the Iraq War and the Bush administration, which he finds appallingly unconservative. "I like
conservatives," he says, citing Bob Dole and Barry Goldwater.
"Bob Taft I always admired." He grins. "But I don't like these
neoconservatives worth a damn! They have this view that we are
so much more powerful than any other country in the world that
we need to run the world—none of this business of coexistence.
I think that's just terrible. It's not conservatism, and it's not liberalism, either. It's a new doctrine that I find frightening. If Iraq
hadn't gone sour, there was a whole string of countries they were
gonna knock off. That's not conservatism to me."

I ask if Iraq is in Vietnam's class as a foreign-policy disaster.
"The casualty rate isn't nearly as high," he responds, "but the assumptions are just as misguided. Vietnam was a logical expression
of the Cold War ideology that we operated under for half a century. If you accepted the view that we had to confront communism wherever it raised its head, Vietnam became perfectly
logical." (McGovern quotes approvingly his pheasant-hunting
friend and University of South Dakota history professor Herbert
Schell, who told a reporter in 1972, "He is the only nominee of

either major party since World War II who has not accepted the assumptions of the Cold War."[104] Taft would have been on the list, too, had he been the GOP nominee in 1948 or '52.)

What advice does McGovern, one of the first Democrats to dissent from a Democratic war in the 1960s, have for antiwar Republicans? "Make a little more noise," he says. He points to the House Republicans who voted against the Iraq War. "They're the kind of Republicans I've always admired. They're close to where my father would have been. He was a lifelong Republican. My dad was a big admirer of old Bob La Follette and voted for him when he ran for president. It's an honorable tradition to be a dissenting Republican."[105] (One of McGovern's early enthusiasms as a senator was a war profits tax, which came straight out of the La Follette playbook.)

With the Oregon Republican and neo-Taftie Mark Hatfield, McGovern sponsored the 1970 McGovern-Hatfield Amendment to End the War, which called for the withdrawal of U.S. troops from Vietnam and "an end to all U.S. military operations in or over Vietnam, Cambodia and Laos no later than December 31, 1971."[106]

Impatient with the chronically cautious, with the kind of eunuchs who tell you behind closed doors that they're against a war but don't want to risk their position by taking a public stand, McGovern told his colleagues, "Every Senator in this Chamber is partly responsible for sending 50,000 young Americans to an early grave. This Chamber reeks of blood."[107]

It still does, Senator. It still does.

Robert Sam Anson wrote in *McGovern* (1972), his fine biography: "To the extent that his vision of life is bounded by certain, immutable values—the importance of family, the dependence on nature, the strength of community, the worth of living things—he is a conservative. He seeks not so much to change America as to restore it, to return it to the earliest days of the Republic, which he believes, naively or not, were fundamentally decent, humane, and just. Like the Populists, he is willing to gamble with radical means to accomplish his end. There remains in him, though, as it remained in the Populists, a lingering distrust of government, a suspicion of bigness in all its forms."[108] I read that to McGovern. Was there a "conservative" side to him that people somehow missed?

"Absolutely," he replies. "I remember that observation. I'm a confirmed liberal, but I think there's a conservative aspect to liberalism at its best": an awareness of limits, a respect for tradition, a love of the familiar.[109] For instance, McGovern writes in his autobiography, "I prefer old houses or churches or public buildings that are built for the ages rather than modern-style structures that quickly deteriorate. I am uncomfortable with any translation of the Bible other than the magnificent King James version." He traces this "sense of stability and permanence" to his thrifty family of Dakota Methodists.[110]

"Throughout his congressional career, George McGovern won elections by conceptualizing his constituents as peaceful Christian agriculturalists," wrote the South Dakota State political scientist Gary Aguiar.[111] He spoke South Dakotan as fluently as he spoke liberalese, and when he asked, in 1972, "Who really appointed us to play God for people elsewhere around the globe?"[112] he was grounded in plains soil as surely as Scoop Jackson was riding first-class aboard Boeing.

For sharing his father's skepticism about military crusades, McGovern, holder of the Distinguished Flying Cross, was mocked for being "weak on defense." Stephen Ambrose, who wrote up McGovern's military career in *The Wild Blue* (2001), thought that he ought to have used his bomber pilot experience "to more effect in his 1972 presidential campaign."[113]

"I think it was a political error," McGovern tells me, "but I always felt kind of foolish talking about my war record—what a hero I was. How do you do that?"[114]

Well, you don't if you're a polite, decent fellow from Mitchell, South Dakota—even when you're being pilloried as a Nervous Nellie by think-tank commanders who wouldn't know an M-1 Garand from a grenade. LBJ had urged McGovern to sell himself as an avenging angel of the air, but McGovern demurred, saying, "It was not in my nature to turn the campaign into a constant exercise in self-congratulatory autobiography."[115]

I suppose no Democrat could have defeated Nixon in 1972. The incumbent's popularity was buoyed by a fairly strong economy, détente with the USSR, the opening to China, and rumors of peace in Vietnam. But still, imagine George McGovern running not as an ultraliberal caricature but rather as the small-town midwestern Methodist, a war hero too modest to boast of his bravery, a liberal with a sympathetic understanding of conservative rural America.

That George McGovern might have given Nixon a run for Maurice Stans's money.

In his autobiography *Grassroots* (1977), McGovern wrote, "To this day I remain addicted to movies and those who act in them."[116] He was a bit starstruck, and the stars reciprocated: his 1972 campaign prominently featured Warren Beatty, Shirley MacLaine, Dennis Weaver, and other stellar eminences of varying magnitudes. Alas, their presence lent the McGovern campaign a taint of Hollywoodish decadence that partly erased the South Dakota Methodist McGovern, who would have played so much better in Middle America.

"I've wondered about that myself," McGovern says. "I still treasure their endorsement, but it may have offset the South Dakota image."[117]

As for acid, amnesty, and abortion, McGovern's positions now seem positively temperate: he favored decriminalizing marijuana; he argued against "the intrusion of the federal government" into abortion law,[118] which should be left to the states; and, as he told me, "I couldn't favor amnesty as long as the war was in progress, but once it was over I'd grant amnesty both to those who planned the war and those who refused to participate. I think that's a somewhat conservative position."[119]

In the home stretch of the 1972 campaign, McGovern was groping toward truths that exist far beyond the veal crates of Left and Right. "Government has become so vast and impersonal that its interests diverge more and more from the interests of ordinary citizens," he said two days before the election. "For a generation and more, the government has sought to meet our needs by multiplying its bureaucracy. Washington has taken too much in taxes from Main Street, and Main Street has received too little in return. It is not necessary to centralize power in order to solve our problems." Charging that Nixon "uncritically clings to bloated bureaucracies, both civilian and military," McGovern promised to "decentralize our system."[120]

In the clutter and chaos of the campaign, one discerns themes that place McGovern on a whole other plane from that drab anteroom of Democratic losers, the Mondales and Dukakises and Humphreys and Kerrys. George McGovern had convictions; like Barry Goldwater in 1964, he stood for a set of ideals rooted in the American past. He spoke of open government, peace, the defense of the individual and the community against corporate power, a Congress that reasserts the power to declare war. After the petulant departure of his mentally ill running mate, Thomas Eagleton, McGovern chose as his veep the undervalued Sargent Shriver, founding member of the America First Committee, a pro-life Catholic who admired Dorothy Day.[121]

Unlike the bilious Ed Muskie, who dismissed George Wallace's Florida primary victory as a triumph of racism, McGovern credited Wallace's appeal to "a sense of powerlessness in the face of big government, big corporations, and big labor unions."[122] He asked Wallace for his endorsement, though as he recalls with a smile, "He said, 'Sena-tah, if I endorsed you I'd lose about half of my following and you'd lose half of yours.' "[123] Well, maybe, Guv-nah—but just think of the coalescent possibilities of the remaining halves.

"It is not prejudice to fear for your family's safety or to resent tax inequities . . . It is time to recognize this and to stop labeling people 'racist' or 'militant,' to stop putting people in different camps, to stop inciting one American against another," said McGovern, who called the Wallace vote "an angry cry from the guts of ordinary Americans against a system which doesn't seem to give a damn about what is really bothering people in this country today."[124] Yet McGovern defended busing, in which children were uprooted, sent away from neighborhoods, and a pitiless war was waged upon working-class urban Catholics.

Look: George McGovern was a liberal Democrat. He voted for social welfare programs of every shape and size; his philosophy then and now was a product, he says, of the social gospel movement, which translates Christianity into an interventionist welfare state.

But at its not-frequent-enough best, McGovernism combined New Left participatory democracy with the small-town populism of the Upper Midwest to create, if fleetingly, a conservatism that might have actually conserved something worthwhile. In a couple of April 1972 speeches, he seemed to second Barry Goldwater's 1968 remark to aide Karl Hess that "when the histories are written, I'll bet that the Old Right and the New Left are put down as having a lot in common and that the people in the middle will be the enemy."[125]

"Most Americans see the establishment center as an empty, decaying void that commands neither their confidence nor their love," McGovern asserted in one of the great unknown campaign speeches in American history. "It is the establishment center that has led us into the stupidest and cruelest war in all history. That

war is a moral and political disaster—a terrible cancer eating away
the soul of the nation . . . It was not the American worker who
designed the Vietnam war or our military machine. It was the establishment wise men, the academicians of the center. As Walter
Lippmann once observed, 'There is nothing worse than a belligerent professor.' "[126]

Try to imagine a Democratic backbencher, let alone a presidential candidate, saying as much today. No wonder the scriven-
ers of the Suffocating Center have no more potent imprecation
in their thesauri than "McGovernism."

Candidate McGovern called for a U.S. withdrawal from Vietnam and South Korea and a partial pullout of troops from Europe.
In his acceptance speech, which with exquisitely bad planning was
delivered at 3:00 A.M. eastern time, or prime time in Guam, Mc-
Govern declared, "This is also the time to turn away from excessive preoccupation overseas to rebuilding our own nation."[127]
Close your eyes and you can hear McGovern's prairie drawl back-
ing Merle Haggard's anti–Iraq War II single: "Let's get out of Iraq
and get back on the track / And let's rebuild America first."

"Come home, America," McGovern implored in that 1972
campaign. "Come home from the wilderness of needless war and
excessive militarism."[128]

"Come home, America," the most moving, the most reso-
nant, the truest political slogan in the history of our Republic,
was suggested by Eleanor McGovern after she saw the phrase in a
speech by Martin Luther King Jr. Because it echoed the peaceful
dreams of the old Middle American isolationists, and because it
drew a sharp contrast between the vision of the founders and the
condition of modern America, McGovern was roasted for the
slogan by the Vital Centurions.

"Late in the campaign I was having a visit with Clark Clifford," remembers McGovern, "and I said, 'Clark, just out of cu-
riosity, what do you think of my slogan, Come Home, America?'

He said, 'Well, George, to be honest with you, I don't know what it means.' "[129]

Of course he didn't! No bumper sticker that Clark Clifford understood would have been worth the vinyl it was printed on.

"Food, farmers and his fellow man—those are the foundation stones upon which George McGovern has built his philosophy of life,"[130] ran a flattering press account early in the senator's career, and in his retirement he returned to that trinity. Appointed U.S. ambassador to the UN Agencies for Food and Agriculture by President Clinton, McGovern lobbied for a universal school lunch program funded partly by a $1.2 billion annual U.S. contribution. As an isolationist skeptical of foreign aid, I am able to restrain my huzzahs, but I'd sure as hell rather spend a billion buying lunch for kids in Bangladesh than $400 billion occupying Iraq.

In his Bush-era book *The Essential America* (2004), McGovern kept the faith of '72. "Let's support our troops by keeping them safely at home with their families rather than dispatching them abroad under the cockeyed notion of what our president has called 'preemptive war,' " he advises. The petty tyrannies and indignities of the War on Terror infuriate him: "I have no fear of doing battle with some character threatening me with a box cutter. What sets my teeth on edge is seeing a frail little aging woman trying to get her shoes off to be searched, lest she slip by with some trinket that could endanger the republic."[131]

He quotes Dwight Eisenhower at greater length than any other political figure in *The Essential America*. Eisenhower's Farewell Address warning of the dangers of the military-industrial complex is samizdat in the age of Homeland Security; while McGovern remains fond of Adlai Stevenson, he admits that in the postwar era, Ike "was the best president at recognizing the dangers of excessive military outlays. And he showed great courage in stopping the Israeli move against Egypt over the Suez Canal."[132]

He calls the Patriot Act "completely unnecessary . . . a contradiction of the Bill of Rights" and counsels resistance if and when the federal police come for our library cards: "I'll go to jail rather than accept such an invasion of my freedom as an American."[133] In 2006, he and foreign-policy analyst William R. Polk published *Out of Iraq: A Practical Plan for Withdrawal Now*, which the Democrats, poltroonish as ever, ignored as, well, McGovernite.

The octogenarian George McGovern remains a voice for peace and freedom in a party more comfortable with the militaristic schoolmarm Hillary Clinton. Oh, how the Democrats could use a bracing shot of McGovernism.

In "Vietnamese Crucible: An Essay on the Meanings of the Cold War" (1967), Carl Oglesby, the president of Students for a Democratic Society who hailed, fittingly, from that cradle of presidents, Ohio, averred that "it would be a piece of great and good fortune for America and the world if the libertarian right could be reminded that besides the debased Republicanism of the Knowlands and the Judds [substitute today the Bushes and McCains] there is another tradition available to them—their own."[134]

The linkage of Old Right and New Left was embodied also in the revisionist historian William Appleman Williams, who rescued that wise critic of the Korean War, Herbert Hoover, from the ash heap of Vital Center historiography. Williams, Oglesby noted, was very much "in the grain of the American libertarian right."[135] Was he ever.

Bill Williams was an Eagle Scout, basketball star, paperboy, and jazz drummer in the Atlantic, Iowa, of the Depression. He was a wholesome mixture of small-town bohemian and Jimmy Stewart: he shared bottomless ice cream sodas with his girlfriend and read Hemingway; he played piano and made a soapbox derby racer. The Atlantic he lived in and would carry with him always was a place, in the words of Paul M. Buhle and Edward Rice-Maximin, authors of the excellent biography *William Appleman Williams: The Tragedy of Empire*, of "judges handing down suspended sentences for theft of food, theater managers looking away when kids opened the back door for their poorer friends, and storekeepers keeping a 'tab' that they rightly suspected would never be repaid."[136] Bill Williams grew into William Appleman Williams, the brave and idiosyncratic historian of United States diplomacy, and it is the genius of Buhle and Rice-Maximin to locate Williams's "patriotic anti-imperialism"[137] in "his roots in the small-town America of the Depression."[138]

"Attacked frequently as an America-hater," they write, "Williams cared about the nation passionately, even obsessively, as if from a sense of family responsibility."[139] Like Gore Vidal and Edmund Wilson, he was a proprietary patriot. The country belonged to him (both sides of his family traced their lineage to Revolutionary War soldiers); imperialism sullied his birthright, and he'd be damned if the liberal interventionists would bully him into silence. Williams believed his Atlantic (an ironically named hometown for a Beardian isolationist) to be virtually classless. Like so many of our best Americans—Sinclair Lewis revisiting Sauk Centre, Jack Kerouac ever on the road back to Lowell—Williams's life can be read as an attempt first to escape, then make peace with his hometown. Williams's mother was a melancholy teacher, his father a barnstorming pilot who was killed in a plane crash when the boy was eight. Charles Lindbergh once flew over the Williams home as a gesture of friendship; the historian later wrote of the Lone Eagle as a "last national hero from the past" who personified the "nineteenth-century dream that the individual could become one with his tools and his work."[140]

Young Williams won appointment to the Naval Academy. He wore his "Annapolis ring the rest of his life," write Buhle and Rice-Maximin, "sometimes consciously fingering it to unnerve his left-wing graduate students."[141] His classmates informally voted him most likely to join the Joint Chiefs of Staff, but he got his fill of war in the Pacific in 1944–45. So he traveled as far inland as he could go, ending up at the University of Wisconsin, where he studied for his doctorate with the storied Progressive Americanists of Madison: Fred Harvey Harrington, William B. Hesseltine, and Merrill Jensen (who, like Williams, preferred the Articles of Confederation to the Constitution). American independents all, "defenders of free thought and of resistance against the national juggernaut state," the "Madisonians seemed at once quaintly outdated and yet almost recklessly courageous in the face of cold-war pressures."[142] Madison fit Williams; he would return as a professor, a citizen-scholar, and spend his most productive years in the state of La Follettian isolationism. He can be viewed as one of the last of the retroprogressives of the Upper Midwest: those Sons of the Wild Jackass, as Williams's hero William Borah and his brethren were known. Williams was reviled in the early 1960s for the same reason that Bob La Follette would have been execrated in an age of Nixon and McNamara: as small-town midwesterners operating from a set of radically different assumptions from those prevailing, they were rooted in an America that had been marked for extermination by the ruling class and its smug publicists. Atlantic had been swallowed by the Atlanticists.

Williams, whose ardent wish it was to return to the loosely binding and gentle Articles of Confederation, wrote that "the core radical ideas and values of community, equality, democracy, and humaneness . . . can most nearly be realized through decentralization . . . Our humanity is being pounded and squeezed out of us by the consolidated power of a nationalist corporate welfare capitalism."[143]

Williams viewed "Open Door imperialism" as the propellant of U.S. foreign policy: markets were to be pried open with crowbars and gunboats, and this expansion "denies and subverts American ideas and ideals."[144] The corporate state that developed at home to administer this imperialism was choking the last breaths out of the ten thousand Atlantics that made up America. And the villains, in Williams's view, were the pantheon dwellers: Presidents Roosevelt, Wilson, and Truman. The wiser men were "the people who lost"—the "Enlightened conservatives," most famously Herbert Hoover, who sought to "evolve a way of having and eating the expansionist cake without paying for it by imperial wars."[145]

Williams the solid radical defended Hoover the thoughtful conservative, perhaps because the socialism of small communities that Williams endorsed bore similarities to the "corporatist decentralism" that Williams and his students found in Hoover. (See especially Joan Hoff Wilson's *Herbert Hoover: Forgotten Progressive.*) But something even finer pushed Williams toward Hoover: Iowa patriotism. His was a praiseworthy attempt to stick up for the much-maligned Hawkeye president, in the same way that John Updike has devoted a play and a novel to the great postponer, his fellow Pennsylvanian James Buchanan.

Hoover stood outside the "bipartisan imperialism" to which both parties are devoted. Williams shrewdly noted that when a corporate boss like Averell Harriman can run for governor of New York using "the rhetoric of left-liberals,"[146] the rule book must be a lie.

The bipartisans are always looking for bright young men who know that we're living in the "real world," as the snake hisses when he offers you the apple. Adolf Berle sought to bring Williams—who voted for Nixon as the lesser evil in 1960—into the Kennedy administration and the Council on Foreign Relations. Williams suspected that he was being neutered, made "ready to join the system," and he refused. He preferred Madison to Georgetown, and as he said of the Kennedys, "Don't ask me why, I just don't trust them."[147]

Williams maintained a distance from the New Left. His biographers note his "socially conservative sensibilities,"[148] his consistent belief that the middle class was the American marrow, and his disdain for feminism. Surely Williams was the only hero of the antiwar movement who subjected his children to "Annapolis rituals such as shining their shoes and holding them up for inspection when he came home."[149] At the apex of his reputation, he packed his family off to the Pacific coast, where he took a sharp pay cut to teach at Oregon State and live near the ocean in one of the small, working-class, pool-hall towns he so loved and idealized. He fished and built model airplanes—including replicas of the *Spirit of St. Louis.*

Williams was an old-fashioned American village dissenter, contentious and refractory and sentimental to the core, and either you dig the type or you don't.

A boy never forgets a visit from Charles Lindbergh, and if you can understand why Lindbergh's father was called "the Gopher Bolshevik," Williams the patriotic decentralist-socialist Iowan makes perfect sense. His prescriptions may have been wrong, but what the hell, he wasn't a druggist, he was an American. He closed *Empire as a Way of Life* with a story about stealing "a very fine and expensive knife from the best hardware store in town."

My maternal grandmother, Maude Hammond Appleman, discovered what I had done. She confronted me with the question: did you steal the knife? Yes, I stole the knife. Why? Because I wanted it, because I liked it, because I can use it.

She said: the knife is not yours. You have not earned it. You will take it back.

I said: I *can't* do that.

She said: You *will* do that. *Now.*

Oh, my: the moral force of the declarative sentence.

And so I walked back along those long and lonely blocks to the store. And in through the door. And up, face to face, with the member of that small community who owned the store. And I said: I stole this knife and I am sorry and I am bringing it back.

And he said: Thank you. The knife is not very important, but you coming down here and saying that to me is very important.

Remembering all that, I know why I do not want the empire. There are better ways to live and there are better ways to die.[150]

Williams was not the only son of the American Middle to idolize the Lone Eagle. Minnesota's Bob Dylan was also very much in the Upper Midwest populist grain. In *Chronicles* (2004), the first volume of his memoirs, he throws Charles Lindbergh in with F. Scott Fitzgerald, Eddie Cochran, Sinclair Lewis, and Roger Maris as sons of the North Country who "followed their own vision, didn't care what the pictures showed them."[151]

Greenwich stakes its claim, but Hibbing is a village, too, you know, and it took a Norwegian academic, Tor Egil Forland, to place Dylan within his native milieu. In "Bringing It All Back Home *or* Another Side of Bob Dylan: Midwestern Isolationist," Forland made a convincing case that "Dylan's *foreign policy* views are best characterized as 'isolationist.'"[152] His excoriations of the "Masters of War" are very much in the Gerald Nye tradition of Upper Midwestern agrarian-populism. Though he was born in 1941, the year isolationism died as a potent political force, Dylan helps bridge the gap between the Henrik Shipsteads and the Eugene McCarthys—between the peace party of 1940 and the peace party of 1968.

(So, for that matter, does Neil Young, child of the Canadian prairie and patriotic American in the Dylan-Haggard mold. His manager, Elliot Roberts, told the biographer Jimmy McDonough: "Neil's an isolationist. I mean, if it were up to him, we'd have no foreign aid, we'd talk to no one, we'd really deal with no one else—'If they can't cut it, fuck 'em.' Neil is extreme. I don't know where it comes from. One minute he's a leftist Democrat, and the next minute he's a conservative."[153] Where "it comes from" is that same place that produced Bob Dylan and Little Ruth Palmer: the conjunction of "Don't Tread on Me" American contumacy and an unexpectedly gentle windswept pacifism. Home, sweet home—the only place worth fighting for, and the one place for which the U.S. military never fights.)

The likes of Dylan and Young, cultural rather than political figures, were where the old isolationism went to rejuvenate.

By the 1980s, conservative skeptics of empire were as common as new schools being named for Williams's hero Herbert Hoover. President Ronald Reagan, an erstwhile Cold War liberal who had objected to the confiscatory tax rates applied to movie stars and moved rightward in response, authorized his subalterns to overthrow the elected Marxist government of Nicaragua and to engage the Soviet Union in a series of proxy wars in the Third World. Angola, Mozambique, Nicaragua, El Salvador, Cambodia, Afghanistan—no firefight between rival gangs of thugs was too insignificant to fit within the Reagan Doctrine.

The American Left, ever ready to romanticize dark-skinned peasants even while deriding the white American poor as "trailer trash" and crypto-Klansmen, rallied to the anti-imperialist cause, especially in Central America, where U.S. tax dollars bought the guns and knives that slayed Salvadoran revolutionaries and Nicaraguan Sandinista soldiers. The Right, in turn, idealized problematic figures such as the charismatic Angolan rebel Jonas Savimbi and the Afghan mujahideen, whose handheld rockets could be aimed just as surely at American invaders as at Russians.

The isolationist, even semipacifist tincture of the American Right had long faded. Few if any Reagan Republicans questioned the subversion of Nicaragua, even when it was revealed that the administration had flouted the Boland Amendment, which barred the federal government from expending funds to overthrow the Sandinista regime. Constitutional conservatives might have called for Reagan's impeachment over his Central American skullduggery. Article 1, Section 8 of the U.S. Constitution vests Congress with the sole power to declare war. But there were no more Taft Republicans, jealous guardians of congressional prerogatives. Conservatives had grown to love the strong executive, the imperial presidency. Libertarians such as Murray Rothbard might condemn the Reagan Doctrine, but they were blind, said the Reaganites, to the unique world-historical challenge of Soviet communism.

When pressed, some conservatives admitted that if the Soviet Union should disappear, the United States might shed its burdensome alliances, pare back its military establishment, and return to what Warren G. Harding neologistically called "normalcy." But verily, the Soviet Union would never disappear.

4

"MEDDLERS IN THE AFFAIRS
OF DISTANT NATIONS"; OR, SINCE
WHEN DID IRAQ DEFINE CONSERVATISM?

THE EMPIRE NEEDS an enemy. So Felix Morley diagnosed in his essay "American Republic or American Empire?" in the Summer 1957 maiden issue of *Modern Age:* "We seem to have reached a stage, in our national evolution, where we have a vested interest in preparation for war. It has become necessary for us to have a powerful enemy . . . Russia could revert to free enterprise; or restore an hereditary Czardom, tomorrow; and still our Secretary of State would be compelled to question her bona fides . . . because our economy apparently needs the constant stimulus of a threat of large-scale war."[1]

By 1991, as the Soviet Union dissolved and Yakov Smirnov's career came a-cropper, auditions were held for Russia's successor as Public Enemy Number One. Would it be South American narco-terrorists? Manuel Noriega? Islamic jihadists? Saddam Hussein?

The spinner stopped at Hussein, and then a dozen years later the terrorist-homicides of September 11, 2001, set the wider Islamic world as the empire's idée fixe.

Only two Republican senators opposed the first Bush's war on Iraq: Charles Grassley, the inarticulate Iowan who has fitfully—far too fitfully—partaken of H. R. Grossian cheapness, and Senator Mark O. Hatfield of Oregon, who in 1970–71 took to calling himself a "Taft Republican" and consistently voted against military appropriations and foreign wars, whether in Vietnam, Bosnia, or the Middle East. (Shockingly, in retirement, and perhaps senescence, Hatfield—who had been plagued by ethical problems toward the end of his Senate career—turned his coat and became a shill for the second Bush and his war. His reasoning? That "our world changed on September 11, 2001."[2] Like Daniel Webster's astonished New England countrymen who could not quite believe that the godlike Daniel had endorsed the Compromise of 1850, including the Fugitive Slave Act, Hatfield's quondam admirers, of whom I am one, simply avert their eyes. I'm sorry, Mark; I missed that. You were saying?)

Libertarians and traditionalists, led by Murray Rothbard and Pat Buchanan, echoed Old Right themes in opposing Bush 41's Mesopotamian crusade. As the pugnacious Buchanan—who metamorphosed in the Cold War's wake from fierce hawk to a combatively eloquent voice for peace—described it, "Saddam Hussein's invasion of Kuwait briefly gave us a new Hitler and George Bush an opportunity to smash Iraq and declare the building of a New World Order to be America's next crusade."[3]

Unlike his Reaganite confreres, Buchanan reassessed everything in the peaceful light of the Cold War's end. He was content to see the United States withdraw from its role as world cop, defender of the Free World. He proposed that the United States leave NATO. And South Korea. And Japan. He urged a reduction in the defense budget. He wanted no part of the restoration of the Kuwaiti monarchy. Saddam Hussein, however vile a character, was no enemy of ours. So Buchanan launched a feisty campaign against the incumbent president George H. W. Bush for the 1992 Republican presidential nomination, and for his troubles he was mocked as a born-again McGovernite and smeared as an anti-Semite.

Buchanan was not alone on the newly recovered Peace Right. He was joined by a stylist just as distinctive, a *National Review* editor who had remained his own man in a milieu of kept men. If most conservatives lost sight of home in the tenebrific darkness of an America perpetually at war, those who stayed home did not. Witness Russell Kirk: the Bohemian Tory of Mecosta, Michigan, author of badly underrated ghost stories (pick up *Ancestral Shadows* and tell me if you don't agree), isolationist boy grown to traditionalist scourge of the neocons.

Born in the resonantly named Plymouth, Michigan, and raised amid ancestral shadows in Mecosta, Kirk was a conscript in the Second World War. Instead of composing odes to the Greatest Generation, he came home convinced that "for the mass of men there is no tyranny more onerous than that of military life." Paroled from military servitude in the brief peace following the long war, Kirk denied that he or any other man was a mere "unit of human energy, a cog in the wheel of the state."

He penned a classic attack on the draft in the July 1946 *South Atlantic Quarterly.* "Abstract humanitarianism has come to regard servitude—so long as it be to the state—as a privilege," he wrote. The army was said to be a substitute family, an alternative avenue for disciplining young men, but Kirk argued that "if parental authority failed of beneficial effect, impersonal military authority could not be expected to accomplish more. It is a curious notion, that teaching a boy to make a bed and fire a Garand under compulsion will make him sober, self-reliant, and sane." By loosing ties of kinship and severing the boy from his place, the army debilitates and enfeebles young men. "In military life, distant from home and most of the forces of social opinion, there is every inducement for an average young man to sink into indolence and indulgence and every reason for him to rely increasingly upon the state for very existence."

Certain Kirk readers several years hence, among them Ronald Reagan, might melt at the sight of a man in a uniform, but the Mecostan would have none of it: "The writer, who has been on the inside of conscription looking out, has not found himself ennobled, strengthened, or educated thereby. He is not aware that being ordered about has made him tread the earth more proudly or even, alas, more highly valued by the women."[4]

Repatriated to the rural heart of Michigan, Kirk carved out a singular career as a grounded man of letters: part Anglophilic dandy, part eccentric hick defending "the permanent things" from the highway wideners and standardized testers and IBM and the AFL-CIO and any other institution large enough so that the janitor and president do not know each other by name. He glossed the life and thought of the great *Randolph of Roanoke* (1951). He made the cover of *Time* (yikes!) with *The Conservative Mind* (1953), and for the next four decades, from his Mecostan redoubt, the preciously tagged "Piety Hill," from which "he once threw a television set out of a second-story window in a fury against its invasion of his household,"[5] he explicated a traditionalist Anglo-American conservatism that was saved from a hopeless fuddy-duddyism by Kirk's delightfully esoteric vocabulary, his respect for oddballs and mavericks, and his profound rootedness. More than one nascent conservative intellectual found his thrill on Piety Hill.

The ghost story, of which he was a modern master, was his métier, perhaps because of his environs. As Washington Irving wrote of Sleepy Hollow, "Local tales and superstitions thrive best in these long-settled retreats, but are trampled under foot by the shifting throng that forms the population of most of our country places."[6] Mecosta made Sleepy Hollow look like Myrtle Beach.

Russell Kirk was a man you don't meet every day—the *National Review* editor Jeffrey Hart recalls him as "a plump fellow with a kindly face wearing a cape, a black, wide-brimmed, floppy felt hat, a gold stick-pin in his necktie, and carrying a sword cane."[7] But Kirk was not immune to the flattery of powerful men. He oft told the tale of April 4, 1972, when for forty minutes he met privately in the Oval Office with President Nixon while outside shabby scads of what Kirk called "militant pacifists" and "young persons in jeans or stranger attire" were demonstrating against Nixon's escalation of the bombing of North Vietnam. "Dr. Kirk," beseeched the president, "have we any hope? Have we any hope?"[8] (Do not be fooled by Nixon's plaintive tone. In that same week he was boasting to more incult men that "the bastards have never been bombed like they're going to be bombed this time.")[9]

Kirk replied with recondite references to the Byzantine Empire and T. S. Eliot's *Notes Towards the Definition of Culture*. There would be no gentle urgings to peace, no voices of isolationist Michigan, no echoes of John Randolph. Whatever his private reservations about the war, Kirk stood publicly with the president, with the Republicans. (His wife, Annette, whom he fondly dubbed the Mistress of the Faux Pas, almost rescued the day when, after receiving several trinkets and souvenirs from Mr. Nixon, she spiritedly replied, "At the devil's booth, all things are sold!")[10]

Russell Kirk caught his second wind in the backdraft of Bush I's Iraq War.

In *The Politics of Prudence* (1993), the last of his books to appear during his lifetime, Kirk scorned "meddlers in the affairs of distant nations"[11] and the stationing of "garrisons throughout the world."[12] He denounced "zealots for global democracy—that is, of course, American-directed democracy"[13]—as imperialists who had no decent claim upon the title "conservative."

Libertarians, whom he had disparaged not infrequently as "chirping sectaries,"[14] he now lauded for having an "understanding of foreign policy that the elder Robert Taft represented."[15] Neoconservatives, he jested, sometimes "mistook Tel Aviv for the capital of the United States,"[16] a one-liner for which he was flayed by those same neoconservatives as an anti-Semite. Never make jokes at the expense of the humorless. And if Kirk had nary a kind word for anti-imperialists of the Left (Eugene McCarthy, for whom he voted in 1976, excepted) and praised the banana-boat diplomacy of the Grenada invasion, well, old habits die hard.

The lectures in *The Politics of Prudence* were delivered at the Heritage Foundation, the Capitol Hill headquarters of the sound and fury and facile position-paper wing of Reagan Republicanism. Never before or after, I venture to say, had Taftite noises disturbed the slumber within the Heritage mausoleum. In the mid-1980s I had asked a closeted isolationist then resident at Heritage how much space the Taft view was allotted therein. "Zero," he replied, and I half wanted to exit by the back door, lest my peacenik cooties stigmatize him in the dead eyes of the zombies.

I wonder that the building didn't collapse when Kirk unburdened himself of the lecture "Toward a Prudent Foreign Policy," but then seldom have a conservative elder's words been so thoroughly repudiated by the movement. The Soviet Union was gone; the possibility that America might yet return to being a "normal country," in former UN ambassador Jeane Kirkpatrick's words, beckoned. Kirk warned the assembled that "Soviet hegemony ought not to be succeeded by American hegemony."[17] Diversity, he reminded them, was a core principle of the legitimate Right, and it was the worst kind of folly to undertake "the mission of recasting every nation and every culture in the American image."[18]

"Why engage in wars halfway around the world, at incalculable expense in men and money?" he asked, as his predecessors had asked in 1900, in 1917, in 1941, in 1950, in 1966, and as his heirs would ask in 2003.

Kirk's peroration was as powerful as it was unwelcome and unheeded by its intended audience. For the first time in half a century, he followed his traditionalist principles into opposition:

> A war for Kuwait? A war for an oil-can! The rest is vanity; the rest is crime.
>
> A Republican administration in Washington contrived American

entry into the Spanish-American War. Since then, until 1991, it was Democratic governments of the United States that propelled the United States to war, if sometimes through the back door: the First World War, the Second World War, the Korean War, the Indo-Chinese wars. But an unimaginative, "democratic capitalist" Republican regime, early in 1991, committed the United States, very possibly, to a new imperialism.

For Mr. Bush's "New World Order" may make the United States detested—beginning with the Arab peoples—more than even the Soviet empire was. Mr. Bush's people hinted at their intention of stationing an American military "presence" permanently on the Persian Gulf, to insure the steady flow of petroleum to the consumers of the United States. Increasingly, the states of Europe and the Levant may suspect that in rejecting Russian domination, they exchanged King Log for King Stork.

President Bush's assembling of half a million men in the deserts of Arabia, and then bullying and enticing Congress into authorizing him to make war, sufficiently suggests that conservative views are not identical with the measures of the Republican party. We learn from the saturation-bombing in Iraq that genuine conservatives—as distinguished from arrogant nationalists—have a hard row to hoe when they endeavor to teach the American democracy prudence in foreign relations; and that the exercise of foreign politics, as of domestic politics, is the art of the possible.[19]

Kirk accepted the honorary position of Michigan chairman of the 1992 Buchanan campaign. The leading intellectual of the traditionalist Right had joined hands, politically, with its leading polemicist, but instead of leading a short and happy march out of the GOP Buchanan and Kirk found themselves traduced by a new establishment Right for which war, empire, and militarism were a holy trinity. (Kirk, in a letter to libertarian Lew Rockwell, called for hanging the "war criminal Bush" from gallows on the White House lawn.[20] What punishment might he have devised for the war criminal's dense offspring?)

Russell Kirk, insists Jeremy Beer, the coeditor of *American Conservatism: An Encyclopedia* (2006), "ought to be remembered not as 'the principal architect of the postwar conservative movement,' as the quasi-official adulation has it, but because he went home. There he restored an old house, planted trees, and became a justice of the peace; took a wife (and kept her) and had four children; wrote ghost stories about census-takers and other bureaucrats getting it in the neck; took in boatpeople and bums; and denounced every war in which the U.S. became involved—especially the first Gulf War, which he detested. And he also denounced abstractions because he knew they were drugs deployed to distract us from the infinitely more important work of the Brandywine Conservancies of the world."[21]

Kirk's conservatism was rooted in his little hometown in Michigan. It was Mecosta or the empire, and Russell Kirk chose the former. It was not the sort of move a savvy careerist would make, but then Russell Kirk was no Bill Bennett.

George W. Bush had pledged a "humble" foreign policy in his 2000 campaign against the liberal interventionist vice president, Albert Gore, leading anti-imperialist conservatives to believe that he might be a domestic president, unlike his father.

Wrong again.

The Bush-led invasion and messy occupation of Iraq revealed a Republican Party that has forsworn the mind-your-own-business mind-set of Main Street as thoroughly as the Democrats have renounced the agrarianism of Thomas Jefferson. If the McGoverns are strangers in the craven Democratic Party of Iraq II, then the specter of Bob Taft would no more be welcome at the banquet table of the Bush-McCain-Giuliani GOP.

But Mr. Republican would not be wholly without prandial companionship.

John J. "Jimmy" Duncan Jr. of Tennessee was one of the noble sextet of House Republicans who voted on October 11, 2002, against authorizing (but not declaring—that's never done anymore) a war upon Iraq. The others were Ron Paul of Texas, John Hostettler of Indiana, Amory Houghton of New York, Jim Leach of Iowa, and Connie Morella of Maryland. By 2007, only Paul and Duncan were left in the House.

In the summer of 2005 I interviewed Jimmy Duncan, who had, in turn, interviewed me several years earlier on his Knoxville radio program. I am, perhaps, the least influential political writer since Wavy Gravy, but Duncan has been a good and appreciative reader. Oh, to play the anarchist Clark Clifford.

His antiwar vote, Duncan says as we chat in his Capitol Hill office, "was a tough one" for him. "I have a very conservative Republican district. My Uncle Joe is one of the most respected judges in Tennessee: when I get in a really serious bind I go to him for advice. I had breakfast with him and my two closest friends and all three told me that I had to vote for the war. It's the only time in my life that I've ever gone against my Uncle Joe's advice. When I pushed that button to vote against the war back in 2002 I thought I might be ending my political career."[22]

He wasn't. Representative Duncan has won almost 80 percent of the vote in the three elections subsequent to his vote against Mr. Bush's war. Not all acts of political courage are suicide.

On the wall of Jimmy Duncan's Knoxville office hangs a framed quotation from Janet Ayer Fairbank's political novel *The Lions' Den* (1930): "No matter how the espousal of a lost cause might hurt his prestige in the House, Zimmer had never hesitated to identify himself with it if it seemed to him to be right. He knew only two ways: the right one and the wrong, and if he made a mistake, it was never one of honor: He voted as he believed he should, and although sometimes his voice was raised alone on one side of a question, it was never stifled."[23]

It is a principled maverick's credo, though Duncan's own

maverick streak is really an adherence to pre-imperial conservative principles. He is a Robert Taft Republican in a party whose
profligate and bellicose foreign policy today melds the worst features of Nelson Rockefeller and Wendell Willkie.

Jimmy Duncan's paternal grandparents were small farmers in
Scott County, which in 1861 left Tennessee, refusing to follow
the Volunteer State into the Confederacy, and declared itself "the
Free and Independent state of Scott."

Duncan is a free and independent member of Congress as
well as that even rarer specimen in modern American politics: a
man who knows his place. Which in this case is Knoxville, Tennessee. His father, John Duncan Sr., "hitchhiked into Knoxville
with five dollars in his pocket," and after an education at the
University of Tennessee he was elected mayor of Knoxville and
then congressman.

Duncan's father was also co-owner of the Knoxville Smokies
of minor league baseball's Sally (South Atlantic) League, and
Jimmy grew up breathing the invigorating American air of pine
tar and resin bags and concession-stand hot dogs. He was a bat-
boy, a ball shagger, scoreboard operator, and, as a freshman at the
University of Tennessee, the Smokies' public address announcer.

Perhaps a boyhood spent in the minors equipped Duncan
with the valuable faculty to discern the insidious way in which
this war, like all wars, is making our country less neighborly,
less American, less minor league. It is the minors, after all, with
their communal atmosphere, grassroots base, and good-natured
acceptance of eccentricity, that represent the best of America.
The major leagues—TV-driven, impersonal, corporate, and
arrogant—are a sport suitable for American Empire.

This congressional district has been represented by a Duncan
since his father's election in 1964, the year Jimmy, a teenage Goldwater enthusiast, rode a train for seventy-seven hours to the San
Francisco convention to serve as an "honorary assistant sergeant

at arms." "My Dad was the hardest-working and kindest man I have ever known," he states. "I was very close to him, and very proud of him, but I am sure he has rolled over in his grave at some of my votes, because he went straight down the line with the Republican leadership."

I ask Jimmy Duncan how his views on war, peace, and military intervention have changed since he was elected to Congress in that Mourning-in-America year of 1984.

"I've become convinced that most of these wars have been brought about because of a desire for money and power and prestige," he says. "I supported the first Gulf War because I went to all those briefings and heard Colin Powell and all of 'em say that Saddam Hussein was a threat to the entire Middle East. I saw his troops surrendering to CNN camera crews, and I became convinced that the threat had been greatly exaggerated."

Duncan was not going to be fooled again. As Bush II readied his war, "I was called down to the White House for a briefing with Condoleezza Rice and George Tenet and John McLaughlin. I asked, 'How much is Saddam Hussein's total military budget?' It was a little over two-tenths of one percent of ours. He was no threat to us whatsoever. He hadn't attacked us. He hadn't threatened to attack us. He wasn't capable of attacking us."

The U.S. invasion, he says, was "like the University of Tennessee football team taking on a second-grade football team—it's unbelievable."

The war has enshrined foreign aid—once a conservative bête noire—as a virtual sacrament of the twenty-first-century Washington Republican. Duncan notes that the United States is draining its treasury into Iraq to "rebuild roads, sewers, power plants, railroads," and subsidize a "small business loan program, prisons, a witness protection program, free medical care . . . I've said all along that the war in Iraq was going to mean massive foreign aid and huge deficit spending."

"When I was called down to that briefing at the White House," recalls Duncan, "Lawrence Lindsey had just said a war would cost between $100 and $200 billion. I asked about that. Condoleezza Rice said no, it wouldn't cost anywhere close to that—and now we're going to be at $300 billion by the end of September." (By late 2007 the cost of the war was approaching $500 billion.)

Echoing like a voice from conservatism past—he has observed that "we need more Calvin Coolidges in our government today"—Duncan says, "There is no one I talk to on either side who can tell me how we're going to be able to pay all the Social Security, Medicare, Medicaid, military pensions, civil service pensions, the trillion-dollar prescription drug benefit . . . the money's just not there."

Duncan rejects the cant and tripe that served as the rhetorical fig leaves for shock and awe: "It's ridiculous to say they're a threat to us because they 'hate our freedom.' They don't hate our freedom. They hate our policies in the Middle East. They hate our foreign policy. I believe very strongly in national defense, I just don't believe in international defense. I don't believe we can take on the defense problems of the whole world."

"I'm pro-military," he says, "but you can't give any department or agency in the federal government a blank check. Eisenhower warned us against the military-industrial complex. He would be astounded by how far we've gone down that path. My goodness, we're spending as much as all other countries of the world combined on defense spending—and they always want more."

Duncan reckons that the defense budget could be cut by $100 billion. But then by *defense* he means *defense*. Consider, by contrast, the unintentionally illuminating remark of Representative Dan Burton (R–IN), chairman of the House Government Reform Committee, who called the Department of Homeland

Security "a Defense Department for the United States, if you will."[24]

Think on that one for a while—or at least until the Thought Police start knocking at your door.

Duncan ascribes Republican support for the war to the strait-jacketing exigencies of party loyalty—that is, the subordination of one's critical judgment to the demands of Team Red and Team Blue. (As if the spectrum contained no other colors! And since when do we allow television networks to paint our lovely land in only two hues?)

"Eighty percent of the House Republicans voted against the bombings in Bosnia, Kosovo, and all that," he points out. "I'm absolutely convinced that if Gore or Clinton had been in the White House, 80 percent of the Republicans would have been against this, too."

Jimmy Duncan has that quality that is drained out of most politicians, whose characteristic trimming induces a catatonic timidity. That is to say he has guts. He speaks his mind and he votes his conscience.

"I've had a lot of members privately tell me they wish they had voted against the war, but they don't want to vocally oppose the president," says Duncan, who adds, "I like President Bush. But whoever is president, there is great pressure to get involved in all these situations around the world. A president always gets more credit than he deserves for a good economy and more blame than he deserves for a bad economy. So with each passing year, all presidents gravitate more toward foreign policy. They all want to go down in history as World Statesmen."

"I hate for this to be considered a 'conservative war,' " grieves Duncan, whose credentials date back forty years, to when he sent his "first paycheck as a bagboy at the A&P grocery store to the Barry Goldwater campaign." For "the traditional conservative position is against this war." He dismisses the war's neoconservative instigators as "big-government conservatives" who "keep wanting to expand federal power and put Big Brother into an even more powerful position."

Duncan concedes that the Republicans have become a party of Big Government, but he sees no sign that the flaccid party of putative opposition is about to undergo a Jeffersonian metamorphosis. "The Democrats almost without exception want us to spend more money on everything," he says, adding that "the Democrats would have supported the war" had it been waged by Gore or Clinton.

The three leading House Republican voices for withdrawal—Duncan, Ron Paul, and Walter Jones of North Carolina—are all southerners, oddly, and if they are not a GOP antiwar caucus, they are the harbingers—one hopes—of an eventual debate within the Republican Party between the imperialists and those who love America for its own sake.

If Jimmy Duncan is a throwback, a Taft Republican in search of a party of peace and frugality, he is, even more, a glorious anachronism as a representative of a place and a people.

Unlike almost every other member of Congress, Duncan writes his own newsletters—"every word"—and he writes them on legal pads in longhand, for he proudly admits to being a "holdout" from the mousy tyranny of Microsoft. "I do not use, and do not worship, the computer," he says. "One of my goals is to get to the end of my career without ever learning how to turn on a computer."

Duncan's newsletters contain none of the usual taxpayer-funded self-aggrandizement. They are, at once, chatty, ruminative, and informative: letters to the folks back home from a small-*r* republican. Instead of vapid happy talk, he writes: "I hope more of my fellow conservatives will soon wake up and realize that an unnecessary war and a greatly exaggerated threat of terrorism are being used to expand government at a faster rate than any time in our history."[25] In his newsletters he muses about the ways in which computers sever people from their communities; he criticizes the Patriot Act and No Child Left Behind; he praises the Tenth Amendment and the civic-minded citizens of Knoxville. He urges the University of Tennessee to hire professors who are able to speak recognizable English. He is, in short, an intelligent, patriotic small-city American who finds himself in Congress during a topsy-turvy age when down is up, imperialist bullies masquerade as "conservatives," and dissent is treason.

Duncan operates from a base of principles—rooted, localist, old-fashioned American—that gives his views a freshness, a vitality. What others accept without a second thought he sees for its underlying wickedness. He has, for instance, criticized the fetish for "national searches" to fill "key government jobs" in Tennessee. He sounds just the right note of pissed-off local pride: "I think possibly that some people in East Tennessee have been teased so much that they have developed unjustified inferiority complexes. There are good, well-qualified people for every job living right in East Tennessee. We should not fall for the old myth that an expert is someone with a briefcase 500 miles from home."[26]

His brand of conservative Republicanism is straight out of Robert Taft, with a dollop of La Follettian populism. "Traditionally, conservatives have been for small government; they've been supported by small farmers, small business," he says to me. "Now what you have is this big government–big business duopoly" wherethrough "big business gets government contracts, favorable tax rules, and all these things small businesses don't get."

Thus he is a vocal critic of corporate welfare ranging from the space station ("the biggest boondoggle in the history of Congress") to the imposition of the metric system (a project of "multinational companies"[27] scornful of American uniqueness).

Duncan annually rates among the most parsimonious House

members in the report cards of the National Taxpayers Union. A fair-minded chairman of the Water Resources and Environment Subcommittee until the House flipped in the 2006 election, he is liked and respected by the Democrats even though he routinely votes against welfare-state programs they believe to be incised in biblical stone.

He is an antiwar conservative, a Tennessee decentralist, a Republican critic of globalization because, to reclaim a fine word, he cherishes *diversity*: "I do not favor one-world solutions to our problems, in part because I hope this world never becomes a dull, bland, homogenized place where everyone has to be and think and act alike."[28]

This belief in human-scale institutions, in the blooming of a thousand flowers, motivates Duncan's promotion of small schools and his sharp criticism of the consolidation movement, which herded children into the anonymity of the centralized super-school, which has plenty of computers but no heart or soul. He cosponsored the Smaller Schools Initiative, an attempt to break large schools into manageable pieces, for as he says—and these words should be spray-painted upon the Department of Education building just moments before it is blasted, metaphorically, to that white elephants' graveyard in the sky—"Children are better off going to a small school in an old building, as long as it is clean and safe, than to a brand-new, gigantic school where few people know who they are."[29]

Again, Duncan acts as the voice of the truer, more honorable, organic conservatism. Just because the Bush Republicans have rejected the Middle American conservatism of Robert Taft doesn't mean that Jimmy Duncan forgets.

I suggest to Duncan that he would make a fine antiwar candidate for the 2008 GOP presidential nomination. Surely there are still Republicans who care about limited, decentralized governance within a constitutional republic and who would rally to Duncan's blend of front-porch antiwar patriotism, Scots-Irish Presbyterian rectitude, East Tennessee pride, and taxpayer-watchdog populism. He laughs. "I'm not going to get in any race that I don't have a good chance of winning. I would certainly be one of the most unusual candidates," he allows, "but I would get slaughtered."

When it comes time to retire, Jimmy Duncan will not whore himself out as a lobbyist, one of those pathetic specters who haunt the halls of Congress dunning favors from colleagues who will cross the street to avoid them.

"I don't want to be a lobbyist," he says. "I want to go home to Knoxville and play with my grandkids." Wanna bet that he follows through?

Jimmy Duncan is a great American because he is a great Tennessean. Healthy patriotism is rooted in the love of the local, of the small, of the particular, be it East Tennessee, West Kansas, or Greenwich Village.

Thus Duncan eschews think-tank clichés and offers, in one sentence, the most concise analysis I have ever heard of Al Gore's malady: "None of his four kids went to school one day of their lives in Tennessee." Adds Duncan: "One thing I'm proud of is all of our four kids have gone to school every day of their lives in Tennessee."

This kind of regional patriotism, this feeling for one's home state, is so far outside the experience of the Washington neoconservatives as to make a man like Jimmy Duncan seem as foreign to them as minor league baseball and small farms.

But you know what? Jimmy Duncan's America is still out here. And some of those boys in the minors can hit.

Duncan and McGovern. The Taft Republican and McGovernite Democrat. Will ever the twain meet? It hasn't for sixty years now, so I suppose the switchman can be excused for dozing off. But I wonder. How much longer can our useless—nay, pernicious because they are so damned misleading—political taxonomies endure? At what point do we adopt new polarities: localist vs. globalist. Placeless vs. placeist. Empire lover vs. holy parochialist. Yeah, I know, my genera are slanted, invidious, tendentious as all get-out. Tough. Much as I like the Jefferson Airplane singing, screw-you-ishly, "Everything you say we are, we are," it's about time our side—the Little American side—started naming things. We know enough to call an imperialist an imperialist.

The Republicans in the age of George W. Bush have become a war party, nothing less and certainly nothing more. Dissident GOP voices are rare and unwelcome echoes. Among the Democrats, it is the most culturally conservative national figures (Senators Robert Byrd of West Virginia and James Webb of Virginia) who have the guts and the convictions to take on the Bush policy of hyperinterventionism. The liberals dither, and apologize whenever an errant brother or sister of the Congressional Black Caucus speaks in too straightforwardly antiwar a fashion. The senior member of that caucus, alas, the marcelled Harlem congressman Charles Rangel, kicked off the new Democratic Congress of 2007 with a proposal to revive the military draft. Just what war-weary voters weren't asking for! Leave it to the Democracy to fumble an intercepted pass, to mishear the signals, to jump offside just when the end zone is within sight. As if to dot and cross their interventionist *i*'s and *t*'s, House Democrats chose as the new majority leader the oleaginous pro-war operative Steny Hoyer of Maryland and rejected Speaker Nancy Pelosi's candidate, the crusty Iraq War critic Jack Murtha of Pennsylvania.

If, as Felix Morley averred, one "characteristic of empire is to dilate in grandiose terms about its blessings for mankind,"[30] then the Bush imperialists dilated like anacondas after swallowing Iraq.

The secular war hawks promoted the invasion of Iraq as an act of Wilsonian magnanimity. The "United States," claimed the neoconservative columnist Charles Krauthammer in the *Washing-*

ton Post, "is in a position to bring about a unique and potentially revolutionary development in the Arab world: a genuinely pluralistic, open and free society."[31] Uncle Sam had sought to civilize the Hun in 1917; now he would teach the Arab democracy. We were to "rid the world of evil," exulted the president's speechwriters. Now, one might think that the Christians who are said to be Bush's core nonoil constituency would act as a brake on such political messianism, but the activist Christian Right has chosen Revelations over the Sermon on the Mount as its canonical text. The defense of Israel is its paramount foreign-policy concern; there is even an influential organization called Christians United for Israel, which its founder, the Texas televangelist John Hagee, calls "a Christian version" of the American Israel Public Affairs Committee (AIPAC).[32] Its board has included the usual pharisees of televised Christianity, among them the late Jerry Falwell and the Washington weasel Gary Bauer, whose commitment to a foreign policy of perpetual war is so overweening that in 2000, after he dropped his voteless campaign in the GOP presidential primaries, he endorsed Senator John McCain (who was blasting Bauer's ostensible constituency on the Christian Right) because McCain promised more war, more military spending, and endless interventions.

The gulf separating Christian practices from Christian profession is not new to the Iraq War. Theodore Parker, the minister and transcendentalist, said in protesting the Mexican War, "If war be right, then Christianity is wrong."[33] The poet William G. Eggleston commented sardonically on Christian support of the conquest of the Philippines. Pointedly, he used the tune of Julia Ward Howe's grapy anthemic tribute to an earlier war of conquest:

We are marching on to glory with the Bible in our hands,
We are carrying the gospel to the lost in foreign lands;
We are marching on to glory, we are going forth to save

With the zeal of ancient pirate, with the prayer of modern knave;
We are robbing Christian churches in our missionary zeal,
And we carry Christ's own message in our shells and bloody steel.
By the light of burning roof-trees they may read the Word of Life,
In the mangled forms of children they may see the Christian strife.
We are healing with the Gatling, we are blessing with the sword;
For the Honor of the Nation and the Glory of the Lord.[34]

The Christian conservatives who have supplied Bush with an indispensable, almost blasphemously enthusiastic following might consider alternative Christian political traditions: that of William Jennings Bryan, for instance, or the anti-Vietnam Republican Kentucky Baptist Eugene Siler. Or, if I am not being too much of an originalist, a biblical fundamentalist, that of Jesus Christ.

But no, the Christian Right, marching onward as if to virtual war, combined with the secular (if often Jewish by cultural background) imperialists known as neoconservatives. Seldom has ecumenism been put to such nefarious purposes. Together, the Christian Right and the neoconservatives dedicated the GOP—exiled from Main Street—to war and empire. Iraq II was only the beginning—or so they prayed.

For instance, a mere six Republicans were among the twenty-one House members who voted against the Orwellian-titled "Iran Freedom Support Act" on April 26, 2006. The measure, which contained sanctions aimed at "support[ing] a transition to democracy in Iran," that is, regime change, was the legislative prelude to the Iran war that was so grimly promoted by the neoconservatives. Jimmy Duncan and the libertarian Ron Paul were among the anti-war GOP stalwarts; they were joined by Jim Leach the liberal Iowa Republican, Walter Jones the North Carolina patriot, the family-values conservative John Hostettler of Indiana, and Arizona's free-market-oriented Jeff Flake. (Gene Taylor of Mississippi, one of the fifteen Democratic dissidents, is regarded as far and away the most conservative Democrat in the House.)

The Republican Party of the Bush wars was so remote from the Old Right Republicans as to defy the diction of distance. "Today, we are all Israelis!" chirped then–Republican National Committee chairman Ken Mehlman to a July 2006 crowd of thirty-four hundred delegates at a Washington rally of Christians United for Israel. Mehlman was flanked at the rally by such stalwarts of the Republican Right as Senators Sam Brownback (R-KS) and Rick Santorum (R-PA). As if to confirm Russell Kirk's 1988 remark that neoconservatives mistake Tel Aviv for the capital of the United States, Mehlman pledged GOP solidarity with Israel's attack on Lebanon, which the conservative publicist Lawrence Kudlow had called "doing the Lord's work" and *The Weekly Standard* editor Bill Kristol had claimed as "our war."

Pat Buchanan, the only isolationist permitted a voice in the national discourse, was having none of it: "No; Kenny boy, we are not 'all Israelis.' Some of us still think of ourselves as Americans, first, last, and always. And, no, Mr. Kristol, this is not 'our war.' It's your war."[35] Buchanan was asking why the U.S. taxpayer should subsidize what Gore Vidal once called "the theological and territorial quarrels of Israel and Islam."[36]

Few conservatives echoed Buchanan, and in fact only Ron Paul and seven leftist and Lebanese-American Democrats voted against a July 20, 2006, House resolution affirming U.S. support of the Israeli attack on Lebanon. (Congressman Duncan was absent.) Pundits, publicists, and politicos on the right had learned long ago that discretion is not only the better part of valor; when the subject is U.S. policy in the Middle East, discretion (in practice, silence) is the price of keeping one's job.

There were brave exceptions: the writers gathered around *The American Conservative* magazine, for instance, and the popular Web site antiwar.com, whose gifted chief polemicist, Justin Raimondo, had provided one of the great unreported man-bites-dog political stories of recent years when this openly gay San Franciscan delivered the nominating speech for Pat Buchanan at the 2000 Reform Party convention. The wit, the fervor, and the welcome burdens of history and justice were on the side of the small band of antiwar conservatives, but they were outliers, men and women without any real institutional base of support, despised as un-American traitors by the broader conservative movement.

When in February 2007 the new Democratic majority timidly put forth its "nonbinding" resolution criticizing President Bush's escalation (which his press agents called a *surge*—a stronger word, with a sexual fillip) but expressing the de rigueur "support for the troops," the party's leaders, not exactly Bryanesque orators in the best of circumstances, tripped over their tongues in issuing halting, paltering, equivocal, and captious strictures not so much upon the war as upon President Bush.

By contrast, several of the seventeen Republican supporters of the resolution spoke with that plain sternness one finds in independents who have stepped away from the pack. Howard Coble (R–NC), striking Gross notes, said, "I insist that we do not maintain an eternal presence in Iraq if for no other reason than the cost to taxpayers, which has been astronomically unbelievable." Jimmy Duncan, a Republican conscious of the historical echoes, said, "We need to tell all these defense contractors that the time for this Iraqi gravy train, with their obscene profits, is over. It certainly is no criticism of our troops to say that this was a very unnecessary war. This war went against every conservative position I have ever known."[37]

But so bedazzled were conservative Republicans by the contrails of the bombs bursting in air that few bothered even to protect a basic link in the party coalition: small-town America. A disproportionate number (46 percent) of the American dead in the Iraq War have hailed from towns, villages, and human-scale cities with populations under twenty-five thousand. The states with the highest per capita death rates are Vermont, South Dakota, Alaska, North Dakota, Nebraska, Wyoming, Delaware, Montana, Louisiana, and Oregon.[38] The dead are rural kids whom the think-tank commanders regard as mere fodder, saps who often enlist out of a genuine patriotism and find out, too late, that the last thing they are fighting for is the security of their neighbors back home.

Mr. Republican of 1950 would have been read out of the twenty-first-century GOP. Republicans now venerate the executive branch, distended almost beyond recognition, and pronounce members of Congress who take a constitutional interest in foreign policy "micromanagers." Thus the Moral Majority flak turned hawkish columnist Cal Thomas decried "meddling by Congress in foreign policy" and said of senators who spoke out on matters of war and peace that they had "disrupted the apparatus [of foreign policy] as effectively as a family would be disrupted if the children began making all the decisions."[39]

As if Fulbright, Moynihan, Byrd, and Webb had been petulant children in a national family ruled with patriarchal wisdom by the likes of LBJ, Nixon, Clinton, and George W. Bush!

"Conservative" mouthpieces parrot the foreign-policy slogans of previous generations of liberal Democrats and are either too stupid or too cynical to acknowledge the reversal. FDR and Truman are heroes (and Harding and Hoover zeros) at the Heritage Foundation. Meanwhile, Cal Thomas huffed that the Democrats during the 2006 election wished "to pervert John F. Kennedy's vision and instead say that the United States will pay no price, bear no burden and go nowhere in the defense of liberty."[40] (In fact, Cal Thomas and Ted Sorenson were perverting John Quincy Adams's famous adage that the United States is a friend and well-wisher to freedom everywhere but a guarantor only of its own.)

By the second term of George W. Bush, conservatism had

shrunk to the size of a warhead. It had but one definiens: support for the Iraq War and the neoconservative project to remake the world. The Ohio Whig Thomas Corwin had in 1847 derided "the heathen, barbarian notion, that our true national glory is to be won, or retained, by military prowess or skill in the art of destroying life."[41] But Corwin did not anticipate the rise of neoconservatism. Or "national greatness" conservatism, as its young votaries dubbed it. When the editor Bill Kristol of Rupert Murdoch's *Weekly Standard* suggested the Connecticut senator Joe Lieberman as a possible running mate for John McCain or Rudy Giuliani in 2008, Pat Buchanan noted the Democrat Lieberman's standard-issue liberal support of abortion rights, gay rights, and gun control, and charged that "as long as you support war in Lebanon, war in Iraq and a 'war-fighting Republican Party,' in the *Weekly Standard*'s phrase, you get a pass on everything else. Beat the drum for permanent war for global democracy and against Islamo-fascism, and all other sins are forgiven you."[42]

Was the junior Bush a dupe of the neocons?

Moorfield Storey entertained no such illusions about an earlier Republican who came to the White House eschewing jingoism but who soon launched a global crusade. "For some reason there is a disposition to treat McKinley as if he was a very well-meaning man who is deceived by wicked subordinates," wrote Storey in 1899. "I am satisfied that he knows exactly what is going on." McKinley's Spanish-American War set the table for empire, and we are still feeding on its putrid scraps. Said Storey: "I deny that Mr. McKinley, Mr. Hanna, Mr. Lodge, or any other politician for the day in office, or all together, are my country. I deny that they may commit us to a bloody and needless war, and then insist that those who oppose their policy are not patriots."[43]

True conservatives—if such rarae aves even exist anymore, outside the musty archives of moldering old periodicals—pronounce the same anathema upon the George W. Bush presidency. The cockeyed militarism of the Bush administration, and the historical ignorance and cowardice of the subsidized Right that has cheered him on, have poisoned the word *conservative* for years, if not wars, to come. Whether the word ever regains its luster, and loses its blood-crust, is up to Morleys and Tafts and Storeys yet unknown, maybe even unborn.

5

BLOOD, TREASURE, TIME, FAMILY:
THE COSTS OF AMERICAN EMPIRE

WAR: WHAT IS it good for? No one ever answered Edwin Starr's question. Well, Edwin, I'll tell you what it's good for. It's good for taxes; it's good for day care; it's good for year-round schooling; it's good for the metric system; it's good for daylight saving time; it's good for the Interstate Highway System; it's good for divorce; it's good for school consolidation and the space program and the IRS. In short, it's good for nothing that a genuine conservative might cherish.

I might quote James Madison, who wrote in 1795 that "of all the enemies to public liberty, war is, perhaps, the most to be dreaded, because it comprises and develops the germ of every other [enemy],"[1] but who would listen? We have long since lost the founders.

Yet Edwin Starr's question is a distinguishing characteristic of "conservative" critics of empire: they ask what will be the effects at home. What are the domestic consequences of foreign intervention?

Empire is the engine of Big Government. Libertarians and conservatives from the early Republic through Herbert Hoover and Russell Kirk have contended that empire drains the Treasury and requires a vast expansion of government powers. Even in the Stygian black of the Cold War, when Vital Centurions typed their calls to anticommunist arms with fury and befogged spectacles, the libertarian Right kept its eyes on the disprize. Wrote Dean Russell of the free-market Foundation for Economic Education (a kind of musty proto–think tank for radicalized Kiwanians) in 1955: "Those who advocate the 'temporary loss' of our freedom in order to preserve it permanently are advocating only one thing: the abolition of liberty. In order to fight a form of slavery abroad, they advocate a form of bondage at home! However good their intentions may be, these people are enemies of your freedom and my freedom; and I fear them more than I fear any potential Russian threat to my liberty. These sincere but highly emotional patriots are clear and present threats to freedom; the Russians are still thousands of miles away."[2]

Imagine reading that in your dentist's office, in Olathe, Kansas, which—contra *The New Yorker*'s Harold Ross and the little old lady in Dubuque he mocked (while being not half so well-read as she)—is where the gentle souls at FEE wanted their mustard seeds to fall. Not quite *Reader's Digest,* eh? Or *Time,* for that matter, which under its founder, the silly son of Chinese missionaries, promoted a militarized "American Century," a hubristic goal to which no modest Yankee, let alone Kansan with a toothache, would agree.

The "Right," at its best, has always cherished the small, the familiar, the everyday. It has been animated by G. K. Chesterton's truth that "the supreme psychological fact about patriotism" is "that the patriot never under any circumstances boasts of the largeness of his country, but always, and of necessity, boasts of the smallness of it."[3] This would be news to Fox News, of course, but then the neoconservatives of our time are distinguished by their placelessness, their lack of attachment to anything that cannot be fitted into a television screen or a defense budget.

Wars for expansion and conquest and even "human rights" rob a country of its soul. "We have changed our birthright for a gourd," as the conservative William Vaughn Moody wrote in "An

Ode in the Time of Hesitation," his classic anti-imperialist poem. They also rob us of our property, our tax dollars, and our Bill of Rights. Or as the Arkansas senator J. William Fulbright, a Tory Confederate often mistaken for a liberal, remarked in 1967, "The price of empire is America's soul, and that price is too high."[4]

The Fulbrights and Moodys tend not to idealize foreign foes of the empire. Republican critics of the Vietnam War never mistook Ho Chi Minh for Thomas Jefferson, and Robert Taft, in dissenting from U.S. involvement in the Second World War and the Cold War, harbored no roseate illusions about Adolf Hitler and Joseph Stalin. Their concern, rather, was with the home front. (*Not* the "homeland," Nazispeak unfit for American tongues.)

The overquoted French tourist Alexis de Tocqueville might provide the epigraph for Bush II's war in the Levant: "All those who seek to destroy the liberties of a democratic nation ought to know that war is the surest and the shortest means to accomplish it."[5]

Conservatives once understood such truths.

"We will come out of this war without a Constitution," predicted John Randolph of the War of 1812,[6] and if he was, per usual, too pessimistic—the Constitution is fragile but not friable—his prophecy hits closer to the mark in modern times.

To the impatient progressive ready for war and its attendant modernizations, the Bill of Rights—indeed, our whole "horse and buggy Constitution," as some New Dealers called it—is a damned nuisance. President Franklin D. Roosevelt's designated jailer of the Japanese, John J. McCloy, sneered that in times of trouble "the Constitution is just a scrap of paper to me." So it is to former GOP House Speaker Newt Gingrich, who in November 2006 called for replacing the Bill of Rights with "a different set of rules."[7] The War on Terror shan't be hobbled by such trivialities as habeas corpus and the First Amendment.

As Felix Morley wrote of the Cold War, "National security was defined in terms that meant the loss of individual freedom."[8]

The freeborn American was, to the architects of war, just another brick in the wall. His liberties were impediments to mobilization. Indeed, in permitting stateside Communists, socialists, and pacifists the freedom of speech and petition, the Bill of Rights undermined juggernaut.

(The proper attitude toward Communism had been expressed by that states'-rights Democrat, Governor Al Smith of New York, who frequently referred to Communists as "crackpots" and denied that they were worth bothering about, let alone repressing.)

Come the Cold War, the Smithian view survived only in lonely farmhouses and mountain redoubts, rather like the refuges for normal human beings in the *Night of the Living Dead* movies. Few anatomized the zombies with the mournful cogency of Iowa-bred Edward Peter Garrett, an odd duck who shaved off the redundant consonants and restyled himself Garet Garrett.

Garrett wrote short stories and editorials for the *Saturday Evening Post* for a quarter century (1917–42) before that erstwhile magazine of the Middle American reading class stumbled in the fog of war, losing its way and its isolationist editors. Garrett, once a popular novelist and stock analyst, found himself in the common condition of principled men who fail to bend with the prevailing ideological breezes: his literary markets dried up, his readership shrank, and he would publish his final books with small but stalwart right-wing presses (Caxton in Caldwell, Idaho, and Regnery in Chicago).

Garrett was unreconstructed. The New Deal, he wrote, was a revolution whose purpose was fastening the "executive power over the social and economic life of the nation."[9] The office of the president had broken its (admittedly lax) constitutional fetters; a nation consecrated to personal liberties now exalted "the leader principle."[10]

Reflecting his readership, Garrett had editorialized against U.S. entry into the Second World War. The people, he later wrote, "did not vote for getting into World War II. So far as they could they voted against it."[11] Ah, but "so far" wasn't far at all. 'Twas, perhaps, the distance that FDR could throw Wendell Willkie.

Out of Garrett's despair came poetic elegy. In 1952, he declared, "We have crossed the boundary that lies between Republic and Empire. If you ask when, the answer is that you cannot make a single stroke between day and night; the precise moment does not matter. There was no painted sign to say: 'You are now entering Imperium.' Yet it was a very old road and the voice of history was saying: 'Whether you know it or not, the act of crossing may be irreversible.' And now, not far ahead, is a sign that reads: 'No U-turns.' "[12]

American Cassandras from John Randolph to Henry Adams to Gore Vidal have been spotting that boundary for nigh unto two hundred years. Or we can stretch it back even further, to the Anti-Federalists, who warned that in scrapping the Articles of Confederation for the centralizing Constitution drawn up behind locked doors in Philadelphia, Americans were exchanging their libertarian birthright for consolidation and, inevitably, empire. And the wages of empire, sooner or later, are paid in blood.

Withhold Nothing!

In republican days of yore conservatives had the wit, withal the courage, to ask about the domestic consequences of war. The dead are the first and most obvious costs: 116,516 American lives lost in the First World War, 405,399 in the Second, 36,000 or more in Korea, 58,000 plus in Vietnam, and the diabolical meter is still running on the Bush wars in the Middle East. The legless and armless and blind and insane locked away in veterans' hospitals are the costs from which we avert our eyes. The social costs, in forms ranging from the nationalization of child care to booming divorce rates, of which more anon, are monuments to the hypocrisy of conservatives. (Dissolution at home—of the home—is a small price to pay for vanquishing the Hun, the Nazis, the Soviets, the Korean Communists, the North Vietnamese, Saddam Hussein, Islamofascism, et cetera, et cetera, and so on unto the final conflagration, say the propagandists for war.)

But if there was once a single distinguishing characteristic of American conservatives, a common bond linking traditionalists of the Russell Kirk stripe, Robert Taft constitutionalists, Edward Atkinson libertarians, Moorfield Storey Brahmins, and Main Street America Firsters, it was the conviction that government spending ought to be strictly limited. If the power to tax is the power to destroy, that power ought to be exercised with an almost paralytic caution. The revenues raised therefrom might be eyed covetously by spendthrift liberals, but conservatives would do their damndest to turn off the spigot.

Empire means confiscatory taxes. Empire means exorbitant spending. Conservatives opposed both.

As the economic historian Robert Higgs, a partisan of laissez-faire, has written, "Before [World War I], federal revenues had never exceeded $762 million in a fiscal year; during the 1920s they were never less than $3,640 million . . . Before [World War II], fewer than 15 million individuals had to file an income-tax return; in 1945, approximately 50 million had to do so."[13]

"In one mighty wartime push," notes Higgs, "the government had completed the transformation of the income tax from a 'class tax' to a 'mass tax.'"[14]

War is the health of the state. Randolph Bourne's truism may have long since hardened into cliché, but it remains true. In June 1945, Department of War employees constituted a whopping 21 percent of the total U.S. labor force. The number of federal employees skyrocketed from 950,000 in the New Deal–fattened

Washington of 1939 to 3.8 million in 1945; over that same time federal expenditures swelled from less than $9 billion to $98 billion.

Leviathan was here. The New Deal eidolon—Every Man a Government Employee or Government Dependent—was realized in the war that ended the New Deal.

In his fierce polemic *The Cold War and the Income Tax: A Protest* (1963), Edmund Wilson, my upstate landsman, made explicit the link the between the IRS and empire. Wilson, an old republican in the fashion of Gore Vidal, had violated Vital Center etiquette the previous year when in his brilliant introduction to *Patriotic Gore* he compared Lincoln to Lenin and cast a doubting eye on the American imperial project, observing, as if gazing into an Iraqi crystal ball, "Whenever we engage in a war or move in on some other country, it is always to liberate somebody."[15]

In *The Cold War and the Income Tax,* Wilson admits, "Between the year 1946 and the year 1955, I did not file any income tax returns."[16] This may strike the reader as a case of absentminded professorhood in extremis, but you must remember that Wilson was a citizen of the old Republic and as such paid a Thoreau-like no mind to the petty rules and harassments that bound and restricted the Cold War American.

Wilson saw, with his Argus eye, that the pelf raised by the income tax went not to the indigent or the distressed. Rather, the tax, which made its first appearance in 1862 in order to finance the Union during the War Between the States and its reappearance in the teens, just in time for Mr. Wilson's War to End All Wars, was imposed "due to the commitments of Washington to civil or foreign wars or to its conviction of the imminence of a foreign one."[17] To Wilson, this was a distinction without a difference: the Civil War had enabled the United States to fill its "Treasury of Virtue," which we had drawn upon time and again in the subsequent century to support the "insufferable moral attitudes" with which we justify our wars.[18] (Bryan and many of the Populists had supported an income tax not as war-fuel but as a substitute for regressive and anti-agrarian tariffs.)

In his late-blooming role as taxpayers' friend, the splenetic Bunny outdid even Barry Goldwater as a critic of government spending. Like Edith Wharton plunging into a manure pile, he actually read the fiscal year 1964 Budget in Brief and was astonished by the profligacy with which the federal bureaucracy spends money on the weaponry and equipage of war.

Wilson, like so many independent bourgeois Americans, voted regularly for Norman Thomas, the America First Socialist. I daresay Thomas attracted more "conservative" votes than any left-winger until Ralph Nader. Thomas in the 1940s had emphasized peace and civil liberties, themes that in the first half of that dingy decade guaranteed that the intrepid American would be subjected to the "pro-Nazi" libel and in the second half the "pro-Soviet" slander. The interventionists refused to admit that a patriot might wish his nation to remain neutral in foreign quarrels.

The empire, as Edmund Wilson realized in his dotage, was indurate and impersonal and very much like the monster against which the anti–New Deal conservatives had warned. The tax collectors were omnipresent and omnipotent. "People often become panic-stricken, it seems," wrote Wilson, "in the presence of IRS agents, and have sometimes been know to faint. They feel that they are up against an official police which possesses unlimited power and from which there is no appeal."[19] Freewheeling political conversations and pointed dissent were going the way of Sunday dinner; Americans were struck dumb by fear and helplessness, ground down into a television-assuaged torpor. The United States of Acedia was hurtling toward "a blind dead end,"[20] the path to which was littered with war casualties and the tax dollars of an acquiescent and dispirited populace. The empire, according to this patriotic son of upstate New York, was "self-intoxicated, homicidal and menacing."[21]

"We have taken many leaves from the Soviets' book,"[22] concluded Wilson, who in *Patriotic Gore* lamented "the Russians emulating America in their frantic industrializing and we imitating them in our persecution of non-conformist political opinion, while both, to achieve their ends, were building up huge government bureaucracies in the hands of which the people have seemed helpless."[23]

The nepenthe that numbed Americans to the extractions of the revenue service was withholding, that insidious practice by which the national government seizes a portion of one's wages in transit between employer and employee. Withholding was a wartime innovation of 1943. Its father was none other than Milton Friedman, the free-market economist, Nobel laureate, and avuncular spirit of the libertarian movement. As Friedman later explained to Brian Doherty of *Reason,* "I was an employee at the Treasury Department. We were in a wartime situation. How do you raise the enormous amount of taxes you need for wartime? . . . I think it's a great mistake for peacetime, but in 1941–43, all of us were concentrating on the war. I have no apologies for it, but I wish we hadn't found it necessary and I wish there were some way of abolishing withholding now."[24]

Ah, but you see, there never is. The martial necessity becomes the peacetime convention. Withholding was one of those wartime emergency measures that never seem to expire when peace breaks out. In time, it became an uncontroversial, of-course-we've-always-done-it-this-way institution that—like the Interstate Highway System and television—changed our daily lives and relationships in ways that no seer might have predicted. But not everyone was reconciled to withholding . . .

The Rotary Club of Los Angeles seems an outrageously staid audience before which to declare a revolution, but the woman who did so, Vivien Kellems, was an outrageous individualist beside whom Ayn Rand looks like an unchurched mouse.

Vivien Kellems was born in Des Moines in the great state of Iowa, manger of so many American originals, to a Disciples of Christ minister who was working his way through college. "None of this G.I. Bill of Rights paternalism rot for *him*," she later boasted of the old man. Her mother would succeed her father in the pulpit, but as for Vivien, "I suppose in my case shouting about all that stinking, rotten business going on in Washington simply takes the place of shouting at the devil."[25]

Young Vivien, a looker who was not unaware of the fact, became a booker for the West Coast Chautauqua lecture circuit before pursuing a graduate degree in economics. But fate soon had her in its grip, as it were. Her brother Edgar invented the "endless-weave grip" by which cables and wires can be pulled through conduits. Vivien—who admitted, "[I] didn't even know there were underground cables; I thought you merely turned the switch and the light came on"[26]—sensed profit. Armed with her brother's grips, she waltzed into the offices of New York City's electric utilities, demanding to speak to "the head man," and within weeks she had secured enough orders to necessitate the building of a factory. She would become president of the Kellems Company; her grips pulled the wires for the Boulder Dam, the George Washington Bridge, and other monuments to uncivilly large Engineering and gargantuan government.

But on February 13, 1948, as Harry Truman's Cold War was freezing the once ardently antistatist hearts of the Old Right, Vivien Kellems almost threw it all away—on principle. Declaring herself heiress to the founders, Thoreau, and the conductors along the Underground Railroad, she told the Los Angeles Rotarians that the Kellems Company would no longer deduct and pay the federal withholding tax.

Withholding was "a monstrous invasion of the rights of a

free people,"[27] charged Kellems. Its object "was to lull the tax-payer to sleep, to deceive him and make him believe that not he, but someone else was paying the tax. This was an insidious tax narcotic, and the men who framed the law knew well that if the taxes were taken from the envelope each week, the individual would soon disregard the tax entirely. He would consider only the amount of money in his envelope as his pay."[28]

Henceforth, announced Kellems, if "High Tax Harry" Truman wanted her to collect taxes, he must appoint her an Internal Revenue agent, pay her a salary, reimburse her expenses, and give her a badge, too. The Rotarians erupted in thunderous ovation.

For almost the next three years, the Kellems Company paid its workers every last cent they earned. Each quarter, the company supplied money orders and registered mail envelopes to its employees, who paid their estimated tax directly to Uncle Sam. (As do we serfs of the self-employed class.) Vivien begged the secretary of the Treasury to arrest her so that the constitutionality of withholding might be tested, but he refused. "Like all bullies and bloodsucking parasites, those mangy little bureaucrats down in Washington are, at heart, yellow cowards," she said with typical demureness.[29]

Instead, revenue agents seized almost eight thousand dollars from the Kellems Company's bank account. She eventually won almost a full refund in court, but Vivien never got the chance to challenge withholding's constitutionality. Nor did she convince her countrymen that "the most un-American phrase in our modern vocabulary is 'Take-Home Pay.' "[30]

Nonetheless, Vivien Kellems became a folk hero. Her naughty debutante style—she descended into a Chicago manhole while wearing a mink coat; she flouted the zoning laws of Westport, Connecticut, and then when the city fathers complained she simply moved her factory—won her mostly affectionate press coverage. Emboldened, she broadened her crusade. Having failed to repeal withholding, she now failed to repeal the Sixteenth Amendment. A *New Yorker* profile called her "the most persistent, articulate, and controversial opponent of the income tax, both state and federal, that the nation has ever known."[31]

She ran for office twice, unsuccessfully, losing to Clare Booth Luce in 1942 (and mustn't *that* have been a catfight?) and Prescott Bush in 1950. She wrote a feisty account of her legal battle, which she titled *Toil, Taxes, and Trouble* (1952).

Perhaps because she made her refusal to withhold so public a matter, Vivien Kellems captured the hearts of America's Rotarians. As the Indianapolis chapter serenaded her:

Lady, lady you've bewitched us,
Lady, lady just betwixt us,
We'll follow every precept that you left us,
But we'd rather follow you.[32]

They didn't follow her, alas. "So much pressure is put on nonconformists," lamented Kellems.[33] Or as a later band of hippie Kellemsites were to sing, "They just won't let you be."

In best Old Right fashion, Vivien Kellems denounced the "'Defense' rackets,"[34] with their complex interlacings and iron grips. If she scorned the GI Bill, she also scorned the process by which Bills were turned into GIs.

"Many people lack an understanding of the real meaning of patriotism," explained Kellems. "They confuse love of government with love of country. The true patriot may love his country and utterly despise his government."[35]

The head cheerleader of the first Iraq War, editor Bill Kristol, supplied the twenty-first-century riposte to Kellems in a piece he wrote with David Brooks: "How can Americans love their nation if they hate its government?"[36] (Ask a Russian, circa 1951.)

Pre-Kristol, conservatives wished to abolish the income tax as a means, in part, of ensuring peace and defanging the empire.

Take T. Coleman Andrews, the most radical inductee of the Accounting Hall of Fame at Ohio State University—a shrine that is visited, perhaps, less than the nearby Pro Football Hall of Fame in Canton, but just wait until the interactive depreciation games are installed.

Andrews, a Virginia Democrat who sang barbershop quartet, was the first accountant to serve as U.S. commissioner of internal revenue until, in the Washington version of a Damascene epiphany, the nation's head tax collector denounced the very taxes he was collecting.

Born in 1899, Thomas Coleman Andrews became the youngest CPA in America at age twenty-one. He served in a variety of private and public positions, including comptroller of Richmond, where he "dramatically increased the collection rate on delinquent property taxes"[37]—not quite the mark of a Taxation Is Theft libertarian.

After a stint as president of the American Institute of Accountants, Andrews was appointed commissioner of the Federal Bureau of Internal Revenue by President Eisenhower in 1953. The new commissioner promptly renamed his fiefdom the Internal Revenue Service and went about cleaning up the corrupt mess left by the Democrats, for the bureau had been racked by scandals during the Truman administration. Andrews was "a blunt and hard-driving" bulldog who had "trod on many a toe" in previous jobs, noted an admiring *Time*.[38] In his new job, Andrews gave greater power to IRS field offices and launched "Operation Snoop," under which revenue agents went door-to-door sniffing out tax evaders.

Andrews was widely lauded for his efficiency at the head of the IRS, but at some point during his thirty-three months in Washington he began to wonder if Efficiency was the alpha and omega of governance. And so on Halloween 1955 he quit the IRS. (As Thoreau wrote in "Resistance to Civil Government," which after his death was slapped with the milksop title "On the Duty of Civil Disobedience," "If the tax-gatherer, or any other public officer, asks me, as one has done, 'But what shall I do?' my answer is, 'If you really wish to do any thing, resign your office.' "[39] T. Coleman Andrews: the accountant as Thoreauvian.)

Four months after quitting, having observed what he deemed a decent interval of silence, Andrews came out swinging. The income tax was a "devouring evil" that is "slowly but surely destroying the middle class," he declared to a disbelieving press. Unless repealed, it would "penalize outstanding ability and success until the will to achieve has been destroyed throughout the nation and we've all been reduced to the aimless status of an indifferent conglomerate of bone, tissue, and blood."[40] Fodder fit for the army, perhaps, but not for American citizenship.

Having walked away from power, T. Coleman Andrews was now a crusader. Whereas IRS Commissioner Andrews had instructed the agency to send income-tax kits to every school in the country so that teens could learn the basics of tribute paying between gym and social studies, Citizen Andrews suggested that "every person who gets a tax return receives a copy of the *Communist Manifesto* with it so he can see what's happening to him."[41]

Why hadn't he spoken up earlier? "My job was to enforce the law, not philosophize," he said. "I was happy as far as doing a challenging management job was concerned," but "I was constantly unhappy about what I saw the income tax doing to us."[42]

Andrews liked to quote Elbert Hubbard's description of accountants: "spare, wrinkled, intelligent, cold, passive, non-committal, with eyes like a codfish . . . Happily they never reproduce and all of them finally go to Hell."[43]

But once he saw the light, the renegade IRS commissioner was about as passionate and committal as they come. In a truly

quixotic act that added up only in the ledger of the heart, he announced his candidacy for president in 1956 on the Independent
States Rights ticket. The Republicans and Democrats, he said,
"have converged on their common highway to one-doctrine,
one-party dictatorship, under which . . . the people are permitted
only a choice of men, never a choice of political philosophies."[44]

I know what you're thinking: Independent States Rights. A
Virginian. 1956. Surely this campaign was *really* about maintain-
ing segregation in the South.

Well, not really. An earlier States Rights Party, the Dixiecrat
movement of 1948, had nominated South Carolina governor
Strom Thurmond, an interventionist who had endorsed the Cold
War foreign policy of President Harry S. Truman just a year earlier. The States Rights Party of 1956 did follow the lead of the
Dixiecrats in declaring itself in favor of local control of schools, a
noble principle that was being used to defend an ignoble racist
system, and at its hastily convened convention the choir of the
Grove Avenue Baptist Church of Richmond did sing a politically
charged hymn written by eighty-year-old Amanda Worthington
of Greenville, Mississippi, that contained the lines:

Let no thoughtless court decree
What our way of life shall be[45]

But Andrews never let the income tax out of his sight, and he
also emphasized such eye-opening positions as the repeal of the
draft. The makeshift party's chief theoretician, as it were, was
John T. Flynn, warhorse of the 1930s antimonopolist Left and the
New York City chapter of the America First Committee. Flynn
urged the party to defy "that old and hated European curse—
universal military training. Along with this," he added, "goes the
continuance of government spending on militarism in America."
Flynn, like Andrews, saw the income tax as the sponsor of "the

un-American institution of militarism." Repeal the tax and we might restore a limited constitutional government that refrains from foreign adventuring. Otherwise we were in for endless iterations of "the oldest racket in history for creating prosperity and silencing criticism—war."[46]

According to the historian Justus D. Doenecke, Andrews's nomination was engineered primarily by a right-wing organization called For America. Founded by Colonel Robert McCormick, the irrepressible publisher of the *Chicago Tribune,* For America stood for a minimal state at home and peace abroad. Its manifesto denounced "our costly, imperialistic foreign policy of tragic super-interventionism, and policing the world single-handed with American blood and treasure." Sounding pacific notes that would have harmonized at a Berkeley rally a dozen years later, For America declared, "If our sons and daughters are to be saved from compulsory military service and death in the rice paddies of Asia or the bloody plains of Europe, we—today—will have to save them."[47]

They didn't save them. Fifty thousand would die in an Asian war against which Robert Taft, Douglas MacArthur, and Colonel McCormick warned. The income tax that fed the war machine kept pumping, quite undisturbed by the taxing campaign of T. Coleman Andrews. The accountant won just 167,000 votes in the fourteen states in which he made the ballot. He ended his career in a business rather cleaner than politics: insurance.

As IRS commissioner, T. Coleman Andrews liked to joke about the time he was getting a trim in an airport barbershop. Tonsor, ignorant of the identity of his client, was bragging about how he never declared his tips on his income tax. When the haircut was done, Andrews rose and said, "For your information, I'm the collector of Internal Revenue." To which the quick-thinking barber replied, "Shake hands with the biggest liar you ever met."[48]

The longer T. Coleman Andrews ran the IRS, the less funny the joke seemed to him.

The Andrews campaign would be the last political gasp of right-wing isolationism until its populist revival in the campaigns of Patrick J. Buchanan. Abolishing the draft, rebuking militarism, bringing the troops home—somehow these positions slipped through the cracks of the Nixon, Kennedy, Goldwater, and Humphrey platforms. Not until the South Dakota Methodist and World War II bomber pilot George McGovern's 1972 campaign did a presidential nominee break, Andrews-like, with the Cold War consensus.

Among the handful of prominent politicos to support the ticket of Andrews and his running mate, former Bakersfield congressman Thomas Werdel, was Utah governor J. Bracken Lee. Governor Lee was a Utah Republican, but no one has ever mistaken him for Orrin Hatch.

A congenital politician, Lee served twelve years as the mayor of Price, eight years as governor of the Beehive State, and finally another dozen years as mayor of Salt Lake City. He was the kind of noisy right-winger whom eastern liberals find tacky and disturbingly exotic, until the keener of their children's children take another look and find that Lee could fit into the decentralist wing of the twenty-first-century Green Party.

J. Bracken Lee took special delight in smashing to smithereens the "untouchable" pieces of a budget. Confronted with an "education crisis" as governor, he snapped, "If it's necessary to close every school in the U.S. for a year to save the government, close them." Besides, "I would rather have a son with only an elementary school education than a son with a college degree and no freedom."[49]

To Lee, foreign aid and the income tax were Washington's most brackish concoctions. He refused to declare United Nations Day in Utah; he wrote the foreword to the anarchist Frank Chodorov's charmingly titled book *The Income Tax: Root of All Evil* (1954). He deplored the expanding American Empire and what he saw as its possible concomitant, a police state: "I do not believe you can fight a dictatorship—and that's all Communism is—by setting up another dictatorship."[50]

Perhaps Lee's wisest act came in 1965, when as mayor of Salt Lake City he led the No forces in a citywide referendum on whether to participate in the federal urban renewal program, which devastated so many cities and displaced so many of the urban poor and working class in 1960s America. Salt Lake City's residents voted 29,119 to 4,900 against letting Uncle Sam raze their town; the city was the largest in America to follow the sage advice of Jane Jacobs and refuse the federally subsidized wrecking ball. (The *New York Times*, ever willing to stick its nose into things that are not Gotham's business, whined that Lee's triumph was "painful proof that a scare campaign centering around fear of 'the Federal Bulldozer backed by eminent domain' can easily defeat city planners and civic organizations.")[51]

Mayor Lee was frequently criticized for his laxity in stamping out vice, particularly prostitution and libationary acts. Salt Lake City public safety commissioner James L. Barker told Lee biographer Dennis L. Lythgoe that Lee's attitude was "if you wanted to do those things, you did them. He didn't enjoy them himself. I never knew a guy who was quite as dedicated to his wife as Brack Lee." Barker added that Lee could have been "one of the great men of this country if you could have added a couple of attributes to him. He was always AGIN'."[52] Which is not a bad place to be in a government filled with Fors.

The Moon Is a Harsh Mistress

Edmund Wilson, in *The Cold War and the Income Tax,* objected to "the cost of a trip to the moon." No panderer to Demos, he asked, "What is this breakneck competition between us and the Soviet Union for planting a flag on the moon and for the navigation of space, when our big cities are dark unhealthy horrors, so crowded, impeded and chaotic that they have hardly the dignity of the anthills to which they used to be compared, and when our mountains and countrysides are partly inhabited by human mammals who do not really differ much in intelligence from the vermin with which they contend?"[53]

Ouch, Bunny! That qualifier—"partly" inhabited—is not much of an analgesic.

Wilson was not alone, though we have flushed the sizable, often poetical, anti-space-program partisans down the memory hole. Bob Dylan, Jim Morrison, and even the less hirsute dawdlers on the American Parnassus have objected to the empire's designs on the empyrean. Oliver Wendell Holmes, the autocrat of the breakfast table, wrote, as if anticipating Percival Lowell and Carl Sagan and NASA:

> *The snows that glittered on the disk of Mars*
> *Have melted, and the planet's fiery orb*
> *Rolls in the crimson summer of its year;*
> *But what to me the summer or the snow*
> *Of worlds that throb with life in forms unknown,*
> *If life indeed be theirs; I heed not these.*
> *My heart is simply human; all my care*
> *For them whose dust is fashioned like my own;*
> *These ache with cold and hunger, live in pain,*
> *And shake with fear of worlds more full of woe;*
> *There may be others worthier of my love,*
> *But such I know not save through these I know.*[54]

Charity, begins Holmes, ends at home. Beyond the range of one's love lies abstraction. Imagining Martians is one step shy of conquering Martians.

Not all of the sublunary agitators for invading Mars and the moon have had militaristic motivations, but if you scratch a ter-rene Martian you'll like as not find an earthling of martial bent, or at least a world remolder. (As J. G. Ballard said of the moon landing, "If I were a Martian I'd start running.")[55]

Consider Percival Lowell, the blue-blooded astronomer who a century ago fired imaginations with his peremptory assertion that "we may consider as certain" that "Mars is inhabited by beings."[56]

Mars, in Lowell's telling, was populated by a race of superior, if always thirsty, engineers whose curious social organization coin-cided precisely with the political prescriptions of Percival Lowell.

Lowell was born in 1855 into the Boston Brahminate. Brother A. Lawrence was president of Harvard; sister Amy wrote poems. Percival's early life was a whirl of French boarding school and independent study in the Orient—constant travel of the sort that unhinges a man, and indeed, Lowell suffered bouts of neuras-thenia, that chronic fatigue syndrome of nineteenth-century aris-tocrats.

Percival instructed Amy, "You had much better be honest with yourself even if wrong, than dishonest in forcing yourself to agree with the multitude."[57] Say this for Percy: he walked it like he talked it. He was not afraid to be wrong.

In 1877, the Italian astronomer Giovanni Schiaparelli had claimed to see *canali*, or channels, on Mars. These eerie canals be-came Lowell's magnificent obsession. He led an observing expe-dition in the Southwest during the great Mars opposition of 1894; so impressed was he by the "steady air" of Arizona that he built Lowell Observatory near Flagstaff.

With his twenty-four-inch refractor telescope, Lowell saw Schiaparelli's *canali* and more—much more than any human eye has seen or is ever likely to see. He watched "the turning of the leaf under autumnal frosts." Conceding that "in observations of minute detail, the psychic element insensibly creeps in,"[58] Percival produced meticulous sketches of a cobwebbed Mars. The lines exhibited a draftsmanslike uniformity that moved Lowell to declare, in his blockbuster *Mars* (1895) and the lyrical sequel *Mars and Its Canals* (1906), that beyond question Mars was inhabited by intelligent beings whose history, which was as plain as the lines on the planet's face, proved the folly of isolationism.

The local intelligentsia, it seems, possessed civil engineering degrees. For the Martian water supply was drying up, Lowell asserted, and so the Martians had constructed a planet-wide network of irrigation canals. This, Lowell modestly told his readers, was "the most startling discovery of modern times."[59]

"Not everybody can see these delicate features at first sight," admitted the lynx-eyed Lowell.[60] In fact, few astronomers not on Lowell's payroll could descry them. You see, Percival's sight was colored by ideology: think of him as a premature World Federalist at the eyepiece, an interventionist internationalist under the dome. In his fantastic telescope he saw a "cosmopolitan" Mars. "Girdling their globe and stretching from pole to pole, the Martian canal system not only embraces their whole world, but is an organized entity." This "continuity of construction" provided a lesson for parochial earth dwellers: thanks to the water shortage, "arctic and equatorial peoples are at one . . . Isolated communities cannot be therefore sufficient unto themselves; they must combine to solidarity or perish."[61]

Martians, like Lowellian liberals, had a sense of the "common good." In fact, "party politics" had been banished from the Red Planet. (If I'm not mistaken, Phobos had an early chapter of Common Cause.) Lowell invited us to marvel at "the necessarily intelligent and non-bellicose character of the community which could thus act as a unit throughout the globe."[62] If only tribal earthlings could emulate our universalist canal-building planetary neighbors! Interdependence, not independence, was the creed that saved Mars.

This was nonsense of a high order, sheer hokum, but Lowell

dismissed skeptics as hidebound Earth exceptionalists, remarking that "conservatism sounds finely, and covers any amount of ignorance and fear."[63]

The eccentric Lowell is worlds more charming than later propagandists for global uniformity, and his batty benevolence bore fruit when in 1930 the Kansas farmboy Clyde Tombaugh, whose father had counseled him, before the son boarded the train to Flagstaff, "Clyde, make yourself useful, and beware of easy women,"[64] discovered Pluto at the Lowell Observatory. (The planet's first two letters honor Percival Lowell. The debate over Pluto's status may seem nongermane here, but then as a non-German—well, mostly—I abhor regimentation and relish divagations. The best paths always wend. So allow me to frame the Pluto question thus: Clyde Tombaugh, the Kansas amateur without formal credentials, discovers a planet in the most laborious way possible, using a crude device called a blink comparator, in a triumph of sheer stick-to-itiveness at the American original Lowell's private observatory. The astronomers of 2006 whose discoveries knocked Pluto from the elect were credentialed professors using computers in government-subsidized facilities. No man born with a living soul can fail to take Pluto's side.)

Percival Lowell foreshadowed the later debate, or what little we had of debate, over the space program. The advocates were sometimes internationalists, à la Lowell, and more often militarists (as Lowell was not); they caricatured their opponents as earthbound clodhoppers, conservative sticks-in-the-mud who lacked the soaring imagination and willingness to spend taxpayers' money that are essential to the exploration of space. The space skeptic, harrumphed Arthur C. Clarke in *The Exploration of Space* (1959), was an isolationist with a "narrow, limited type of mind which is interested in nothing beyond its town or village."[65] The would-be tyrant in *Good News* (1980), Edward Abbey's novel of postapocalypse America, is given to magniloquent orations on the majesty of space travel; his tellurian critics are crippled by their "Proudhonian libertarianism," their "shopkeeper's anarchism," their "Jeffersonian mediocrity."[66] The mossbound rocks, the stay-at-homes, members of the family-dinner party, do not yearn for new worlds to conquer, moondust in which to plant the flag, alien faces to trample underboot.

In a 1996 PBS documentary titled *Mars: The Red Planet,* Dr. Carol Stoker of NASA testified, "We are, after all, one planet . . . Once we get off our planet, especially once there's a colony on another planet, national boundaries start to become really insignificant because I really think the new world order isn't going to be America *uber alles,* it's going to be maybe Earth *uber alles.* It's going to be an order where nations don't actually mean anything anymore and what means something is what planet you're from."

So this is the future: the faceless billions of the third planet chanting "Earth! Earth! Earth!" as the TV screen reveals Mars being bombarded by nuclear missiles like so many Comet Shoemaker-Levys, and all because a Martian Zapata got cheeky with the bosses. In the background we hear Lee Greenwood croaking, "I'm proud to be an earthling . . ."

The early rocket societies from which the U.S. space program grew were dominated by "German expatriates and science fiction fans," writes Howard E. McCurdy in *Space and the American Imagination* (1997).[67] Wernher von Braun and the popular science writer Willy Ley gave the American rocketeers a distinctly Teutonic accent. *Uber alles,* indeed. Space-flight advocacy has always been the realm of exiles, émigrés, and misfits—the unmoored.

The visionaries, the dreamy Lowells, may have planted the seed, but this beanstalk didn't reach to the skies without assiduous, if not acidulous, watering by scare-mongering Cold Warriors. Neil Armstrong took his small step because enough politicians agreed with Senator Lyndon B. Johnson, who said in 1958: "Control of space means control of the world . . . Whoever gains that ultimate position gains control, total control, over the earth, for purposes of tyranny or for the service of freedom."[68]

Earth's natural satellite was presented, absurdly, as an outpost of military significance. Mars, it seems, had taken up residence on the moon. As one missile man advised in *Collier's*, "Control of the moon . . . could mean military control of our whole portion of the solar system."[69] Venusians, lock and load.

In the inert movie *Destination Moon* (1950), a general explains: "The first country that can use the moon for the launching of missiles will control the earth. That, gentlemen, is the most important military fact of our century." Sorry, General. As Howard E. McCurdy notes, "In retrospect, few of the early warnings about the military significance of space turned out to be true."[70] The anarchomilitarist Robert Heinlein coscripted *Destination Moon* and its far more entertaining and campily feminist sequel *Project Moonbase* (1953), in which a general explains why a civilian has been invited aboard a lunar mission: "If we hadn't played the science angle, we wouldn't have gotten the authorization." Taking pictures of the dark side of the moon was the facade; the real reason for invading Earth's satellite was military—for "the safety of the Free World."

On the screen and in the Congress, the fright worked. Between 1960 and 1965, NASA's budget increased tenfold. Eventually, several men bounded around on the moon. We may expect that several years and trillions of dollars from now, a few government employees may wind up on Mars.

The Apollo voyages to the moon marked the triumph of the thirty-fifth president over the thirty-fourth. Dwight D. Eisenhower was something of a space doubter who was "not about to hock [his] jewels"[71] for sidereal vainglory. And besides, Ike was busy with his own massive public-works program, the Interstate and Defense Highway System.

Democratic hawks attacked Eisenhower for his indifference

to their dreams of interstellar dominion. When Ike left to play golf the week of the *Sputnik 1* launch, the Cold War liberal Henry Jackson (D-WA) called it "a week of shame and danger."[72] Senate majority leader Lyndon B. Johnson panicked, saying, "Soon, they will be dropping bombs on us from space like kids dropping rocks onto cars from freeway overpasses."[73] What a brutal cast of mind it takes to produce such a perversely homey image!

In his extraordinary Farewell Address, Eisenhower warned of the "danger that public policy could itself become a captive of a scientific-technological elite." He viewed the rise of Big Science with republican alarm: "The prospect of domination of this nation's scholars by Federal employment, project allocations, and the power of money is ever present—and is gravely to be regarded."[74]

President Kennedy, by contrast, seemed to welcome such domination. State and science were natural partners; JFK assured Americans that "every scientist, every engineer, every technician, contractor, and civil servant gives his personal pledge that this nation will move forward" into space.[75]

And so it did.

Congressional foes of the space program consisted mostly of a few liberals who wished the money might instead be wasted on the Great Society, and a handful of parsimonious conservatives who objected to the astronomical expense. The incomparable H. R. Gross grumbled, "I hope that if we do get to the moon we find a gold mine up there because we will certainly need it."[76]

Among maverick Democrats, the Senate gadfly William Proxmire of Wisconsin denounced Apollo as just another instance of "corporate socialism,"[77] while Senator Fulbright called the moon landing a "9-day wonder of history, a gaudy sideshow in the real work of the world."[78]

The social critic Lewis Mumford found the space program "anti-human."[79] Space travel, he argued, requires "the total mobilization of the megamachine, commanding to the point of exhaustion all the resources of the state: it is both a symbol of total control and a means of popularizing it and extending it as an ineffable symbol of progress."[80]

Russell Kirk, imagining fairy castles on the moon threatened by "grim military uses of 'space' research," proposed "to allow the fairies to dwell peacefully in them to the end of time."[81] You can imagine how well that one went over at the Pentagon. Damned hippie conservatives!

Robert Lee Frost, the reactionary radical from New England who read the night sky as well as any poet who has ever written, imagined himself exiled from modern America.

> *They may end by banishing me*
> *To the penal colony*
> *They are thinking of pretty soon*
> *Establishing on the moon*[82]

Liberal Apollonians took from the moon landing a boundless faith in the efficacy of a centralized state. As the *New York Times* columnist Tom Wicker mused, "If the same concentration of effort and control were applied to some useful earthly project, a similar success might be obtained."[83]

But such government-directed "concentration of effort and control" struck truer Americans as potentially nightmarish. The poet of the American Middle, Bob Dylan of Hibbing, Minnesota, said darkly, "Man has invented his doom/First step was touching the moon."[84]

Conscientious objectors to this first step into solar systemic empire were accused of possessing crabbed souls, of lacking even the most rudimentary imaginations. The bombastic if often stirring astronomer Carl Sagan wrote, "For all its material advantages, the sedentary life has left us edgy, unfulfilled."[85] To take the edge off, the lethargic masses are urged to turn on the TV and watch the fortunate ones float weightlessly in their capsules. We can be vicarious explorers—contributors, too, every April 15!—to this grand expression of the human urge to reach out and molest someone. We gaze, starstruck, as billions and billions of dollars burn up upon reentry.

This alleged American restlessness may define those who hold the levers of power, but it does not explain the lives of the millions who, unedgily, stay put. Most scientists, unlike most blue-collar workers, are willing to sacrifice place for career; recall the incomprehension of Reaganites and neoliberals when in the early 1980s laid-off Rust Belt workers didn't just move to Arizona and learn computer programming.

In a centralized state and economy, the mobile rule the immobile. The grocery bagger pays for the physics Ph.D.'s education, his federally funded job, perhaps even the space colony in which the boffin will frolic in that happy future. We, the muckbound, can enjoy the stunning images sent back by the planetary probes, but we know our place: on the couch. City dwellers can call up pictures of Mars on their laptops, but they can't even see the Red Planet in the night sky, so turbid is the light pollution.

I write, by the way, as an astronomy buff who believes that there is, indeed, magic in the moon's mild ray. Why, tonight I'll set up my eight-inch Dobsonian and gaze upon the crescent moon. The greatest amateur astronomer in American history was Leslie Peltier of Delphos, Ohio. From his native ground Peltier commanded a view of the universe. He didn't need the aerospace industry for "fulfillment"; Mars was no farther than the telescope in his backyard. But then he had a backyard, unlike the intrepid heroes of TRW. Peltier was from Delphos, which was not an insignificant speck in the cosmos, as the mobile men of science so often tell the immobile payers of taxes, but the center of his universe.

In his beautiful memoir *Starlight Nights* (1965), which describes astronomy's lure better than anything ever written, Leslie Peltier wrote, "I know that someday man will reach the moon but I sincerely hope this will not happen for a long, long time . . . If [man] must conquer something let it be himself." The word *conquest* is a favorite of space boosters. The conquest of space. The conquest of Mars. The conquest of the solar system. Leslie Peltier concluded his book, "The moon and I have been firm friends all these many years."[86] Does one conquer a friend? Just what on earth are we doing up there?

Riving Riveting Rosie's Family

And just what are we doing down here? Empire makes war upon the family and upon traditional marriages. The founders understood this: in 1792, Benjamin Rush proposed that "over the portals of the Department of War" be painted the mottoes "An office for butchering the human species" and "A Widow and Orphan making office."[87] Rush was right. We might add "The Great Cuckold Maker," since no government agency separates husbands from wives quite like the mendaciously renamed Department of Defense.

Speaking of a proposed draft, Daniel Webster made the case in his classic 1814 speech with a wholly fitting, almost novelistic, lachrymosity:

> Anticipate the scene, sir, when the class shall assemble to stand its draft, and to throw the dice for blood. What a group of wives and mothers and sisters, of helpless age and helpless infancy, shall gather round the theatre of this horrible lottery, as if the stroke of death were to fall from heaven before their eyes on a father, a brother, a son, or a husband . . . Does the lot fall on the father of a family? His children, already orphans, shall see his face no more. When they behold

him for the last time, they shall see him lashed and fettered, and dragged away from his own threshold, like a felon and an outlaw. Does it fall on a son, the hope and the staff of aged parents? That hope shall fail them. On that staff they shall lean no longer. They shall not enjoy the happiness of dying before their children. They shall totter to their grave, bereft of their offspring and unwept by any who inherit their blood. Does it fall on a husband? The eyes which watch his parting steps may swim in tears forever. She is a wife no longer. There is no relation so tender or so sacred that by these accursed measures you do not propose to violate it. There is no happiness so perfect that you do not propose to destroy it. In the paradise of domestic life you enter, not indeed by temptations and sorceries, but by open force and violence.[88]

Empire subverts families and social life. This essential point seldom has been made, except by the most percipient and honest figures on the "family values" right, e.g., Iowa-bred Allan Carlson, the wise and courageous president of the Rockford, Illinois–based Howard Center on the Family, Religion, and Society. Most conservative bunco artists are too guileful or too grant-conscious to acknowledge what sociologists have known since the 1940s.

Given that any reconsideration of the wisdom of U.S. involvement in the Second World War is virtually proscribed (see the two-minute hate directed at Pat Buchanan upon publication of his *A Republic, Not an Empire,* perhaps the most sweepingly antiwar book ever written by a candidate for the presidency), we are hard-pressed even to reckon the familial losses from that war. But let's try.

In one striking World War II propaganda poster, a Veronica Lake look-alike with ruby lips and an air of remediable loneliness— of the sort Gary Grimes sensed in Jennifer O'Neill in *The Summer of '42*—superposes the message *"Longing won't bring him back sooner . . .* GET A WAR JOB! SEE YOUR U.S EMPLOY-

MENT SERVICE." Allan Carlson sent me a copy of the ad with
the note "Get thee out of the home, woman, & *into the defense/war
plant.*"

Rosie the Riveter had nice biceps, but you can't raise a child
on the shop floor. The social worker Josephine D. Abbott repined
in 1943 that women were "repudiating their children in their
newly found freedom."[89] Good War nostalgia merchants may idealize assembly-line women turning out instruments of mass
death, but Mrs. J. Russell Henderson, chairwoman of the Youth
Advisory Association of the Arkansas Council for Social Agencies, said, "This war is directly responsible for the boom in bad-
ness because children's fathers go off to war and their mothers go
to work, and thus the interest of parents is diverted from the
home and the children."[90]

Mrs. Henderson's observation was borne out by statistics
from around the country. The FBI reported a 55.7 percent increase in arrests of female minors in 1942. In Portland, Oregon,
juvenile delinquency cases skyrocketed by 500 percent between
1940–41 and 1942–43. "Many mothers apparently prefer $60
a week now to good health and behavior for their children
later," remarked Dr. Thomas Meador, a Portland public-health
officer.[91]

Agnes E. Meyer, wife of the publisher of the *Washington Post,*
reported in 1943 that "From Buffalo to Wichita, it is the children
who are suffering most from mass migration, easy money, unac-
customed hours of work, and the fact that mama has become a
welder on the graveyard shift."[92]

The children, like the fathers, were fodder. Replaceable parts
in a machine.

I am going on here, piling quote upon quote, because war ef-
faces and perverts everything that traditionalist conservatives pro-
fess. Every damn thing, from motherhood to the country church.
And yet postwar conservatives, and especially the scowling ninnies

of the Bush Right, revere war above all other values. It trumps the First Amendment; it razes the home; it decks the decalogue. And they don't care.

The Lanham Act of 1940 allocated $50 million for the supervision of Rosie the Riveter's kids. At its peak in July 1944, the act was subsidizing 3,102 day-care centers incarcerating 129,357 children. Between 550,000 and 600,000 American tots were turned over to stranger-care in Lanham centers during the course of the war.

The war ended, but government-sponsored day care had only just begun. War-contorted California, which had 7 percent of the nation's population but supplied almost 25 percent of Uncle Sam's day-care inmates, was the harbinger of the revolution.[93] In 1946, the California legislature and Governor Earl Warren launched their own day-care program, prodded by lobbying from those workers who had been employed under the Lanham Act.

The war hurled unprecedented numbers of mothers into the paid workforce: by 1945, women constituted more than one-third of the civilian labor force. Yet many resisted government day care, for as one official conceded, "There is a positive aversion to group care of children in the minds of working women. To some it connotes an inability to care for one's own; to some it has a vague incompatibility with the traditional idea of the American home; to others it has the taint of socialism."[94]

Today, Hillary Clinton and the corporate feminists point to the U.S. Army as the model day-care provider. And yet many conservatives who froth at the merest hint of the carpetbagger's name are quiet, muted by their worship of the widow-making bureaucracy.

Authentic conservatives—those who defend the near and dear against remote and abstract powers—used to understand the iniquity of militarism. In July 1945, Mrs. Cecil Norton Broy, representing a ladies study club in Arlington, Virginia, told a roomful of heedless U.S. senators that universal military training and an interventionist foreign policy would lead to "the further disruption of normal American family life . . . Our men would be like hired mercenary soldiers going forth to protect the commercial interests of greed and power. Our men thus forced into foreign service would see little if any of their native soil again. We would be working on the principle of scattering the most virile of our men over the face of the globe."[95]

Tens of thousands of abandoned Amerasians who grew up without fathers shake their heads in assent. Mrs. Broy was no hag but a sibylline prophetess. Yet in the unlikely event that a contemporary Mrs. Broy made it past the thought-crime detectors and into a Senate hearing room today, I expect that she'd be given a stern lecture by a GOP family-values fraud and be sent on her way with a minatory copy of the Patriot Act.

War separates men from women, husbands from wives. Divorce flourishes in the ruins. The divorce rate more than doubled between 1940 and 1946. It fell in the postwar years, as husbands and wives were reunited, though of course it never again approached prewar rates.

The Second World War, by removing men from households and removing many of those households from the rural South into the unwelcoming urban North, waged its own miniwar upon the American family.

The farms were depleted of more than 2 million men between April 1940 and July 1942. As John W. Jeffries wrote in *Wartime America: The World War II Home Front* (1996), "Expecting jobs and a better life, people left declining mining towns, ethnic and racial urban enclaves, depressed mountain areas, and struggling farms in the South and the Midwest for booming war communities where new opportunities beckoned."[96]

Soulless hellholes like San Diego emerged as major cities. Just as the exigencies of the First World War crowned Los Angeles as the motion picture capital, so did the Second World War irrigate public monies westward. Government supplied nine of every ten dollars in new investment capital to California during the war.

The country withered as the city grew, and no place grew faster than those towns hooked to the federal pipeline.

A majority (2.7 million) of the 4 million Americans wearing the fibers of servility in World War I were draftees; the same was true in the Second World War, as 10 million of the 16 million Americans who served in the armed forces were there under compulsion. Each was his own story, his own song, a being made in God's image, a person belonging to a place, a creature of ubiety. Each, in an unduplicable way, was missed.

The sociologist James H. S. Bossard likened the removal of a family member to "an amputation."[97]

Bossard would have no glib talk about relocated children adapting easily to new surroundings: "Extensive studies which I have made convince me that the security which the growing child obtains from living under circumstances and with persons which are familiar and established is of tremendous importance to his normal development." The transient, the military brat, the child, whether of Okies or Manhattan Project engineers, who is dragged from town to town, faces a "pervasive social isolation." For the "adolescent who does not know his community and its leading personnel, who feels a sense of isolation in it, who has not taken and cannot take satisfactory root in it, is missing many of the indispensable requisites for normal, wholesome development."[98]

More than half (58.2 percent) of fathers aged 18–25 were on active duty in the summer of 1945. Their little ones, too, were casualties of war. Accounts by social workers of the loneliness of children and siblings of soldiers can sluice even the tightest tear duct. One boy described in a 1944 paper in the *American Journal of Orthopsychiatry* sits "with tears streaming down his face, utterly lost in his misery."[99] At the mention of his absent brother the tears begin again. Other children "repeatedly asked when their father or brother would come home again." As Leona L. Gustafson recalled of her father's departure for war, "I asked Dad when he would be home and for the first time in my life I saw tears in his eyes as he answered that he didn't know."[100] But the empire does not believe in tears.

Writing in the November 1971 *Journal of Marriage and the Family,* E. James Lieberman of the Howard University School of Medicine speculated on the ways that the Vietnam War, by removing more than 2 million young men from "the arena of normal courtship,"[101] might alter marriage patterns. There is a difference, after all, between taking the girl next door to the Sadie Hawkins Dance and paying a Saigon whore three chocolate bars for a blow job. (Once the United States has secured permanent bases in Iraq, I expect the going rate will be an iPod for each crack at a chador-clad magdalen.)

Standing armies, as our forebears understood, were instruments of rape as well as rapine, of carnality as well as carnage. In 1788, the Anti-Federalist writer known as "Federal Republican" warned that a standing army "will inevitably sow the seeds of corruption and depravity of manners. Indolence will increase, as with it crimes cannot but increase. The springs of honesty will gradually grow lax, and chaste and severe manners will be succeeded by those that are dissolute and vicious. When a standing army is kept, virtue never thrives."[102]

VD does, though. An army, whether mercenary or conscript, that consists of men garrisoned far from home is a pack of swordsmen loosed from the usual conventions of courtship. Young men, dissevered from the bonds of their homeplace, are going to get drunk and get laid.

The dauntless Edward Atkinson, the Boston cotton mill and fire insurance mogul who cofounded the Anti-Imperialist League, wrote President McKinley what Robert L. Beisner calls "a remarkable letter which, in tasteless detail, predicted the wholesale decimation of American forces in the Philippines by the ravages of venereal disease."[103] Atkinson later charged that U.S. occupation forces maintained a whorehouse in Manila "guarded by United States soldiers, and under the supervision of United States army surgeons, over whom Wm. McKinley is Commander-in-Chief."[104]

The warmasters, it seems, were also whoremasters.

Another Masters, the poet Edgar Lee, knew of such things. Over in the Spoon River cemetery the stele of Harry Wilmans, a Spanish-American War casualty, concludes:

> And there were whores who followed us, full of syphilis;
> And beastly acts between ourselves or alone,
> With bullying, hatred, degradation among us,
> And days of loathing and nights of fear
> To the hour of the charge through the steaming swamp,
> Following the flag,
> Till I fell with a scream, shot through the guts.
> Now there's a flag over me in Spoon River!
> A flag! A flag![105]

The moral decay of the American serviceman, spreading clap as he spreads democracy, was a frequent theme of anti–imperialist literature. The Chicago Liberty League published as an appendix to Henry Hooker Van Meter's *The Truth About the Philippines from Official Records and Official Sources* a map of Manila's "1,109 licensed liquor saloons" and hinted scandalously at the "200 houses of ill fame or the 600 opium dens."[106] And this was only the beginning of the debauch: rates of venereal disease would spread with a licentious celerity in future wars, particularly those fought on the ground in the Orient, reaching a peak in Vietnam.

But impermanence—of residences, friends, sexual partners— is an unavoidable feature of an imperial army.

The welfare state reservations on which military families live are a tawdry endorsement of notions conservatives once advanced about the dignity of stable lives and secure private property. In the *American Journal of Orthopsychiatry* (1967), the mental health consultant Eli M. Bower asked of families on military bases— "ephemeral stopovers," he called them—"Why be overly concerned about the crumbling walls, the unfixed walks, the burned-out bulbs, petty vandalism, or lack of services in a home or community from which one might move next week, next month, or next year?"[107]

That Bower's description applied equally to U.S. military bases and eastern European public housing projects bothered not the conservatives, who in 1967 sternly disapproved of "bureaucrats" but went all weak in the knees at the sight of a man in a uniform. Besides, they were busy adopting the Vietnam War from its liberal parents.

"Mobility," wrote the psychiatrists Frank A. Pederson and Eugene J. Sullivan of Walter Reed General Hospital in their study of mentally disturbed military children, "is associated with psychiatric casualty rates among both adults and children."[108]

Or as Janice G. Rienerth wrote in "Separation and Female Centeredness in the Military Family," "The stressful effects of U.S. geographic mobility have been underestimated; moving often places inordinate demands on the individual to adapt and raises continued challenges to identity."[109] Mobility is the great sickness afflicting America, and militarism is among its most virulent carriers.

The military family is a parody of the traditional American family. "If Uncle Sam wanted you to have a wife, he would have issued one" went the gruff maxim of the old army. Military sociologists once spoke of "the loneliness of the long-distance wife," but today, mother the sergeant is lief as not e-mailing Katelynn and Dakota from a laptop six thousand miles away.

As Allan Carlson writes, "While the 1890 army of 24,700

officers and men could realistically remain a bachelor force, the same could not be true of a force numbering 1,000,000 or more."[110] So to strengthen the American family, we must shrink the armed services. Discharge fathers and mothers to their homier, infinitely more important duties. For the standing army is a ruthless manufactory of familial maladjustment.

"No other large group is exposed so uniformly to the pressures of father absence and geographical mobility," wrote a trio of military researchers.[111] The former can lead to "aggression, introversion . . . helplessness, defensiveness, and impulsivity" in children;[112] the costs of the latter may be tallied in every doleful admission that "I'm from nowhere." Or, even worse, the pathetic boast of one military brat essayist: "I am from nowhere, and I am from everywhere."[113]

In her study of *Military Brats* (1991), Mary Edwards Wertsch writes:

> There are two questions one can pose that reveal rootlessness as instantly as a litmus test.
>
> The first is *Where are you from?* Military brats do not relish the "where from?" question and go through life vainly trying to parry it. Some answer "Nowhere," others, "Everywhere" . . .
>
> The second litmus test is a question rarely posed in social situations, but one I posed to every interviewee: *Where do you want to be buried?* A person with roots always knows the answer . . . The response of a person without roots is quite different. "Wherever I am when I finish up," said one military brat. "I have no firm attachment to any geographic location." Another answered, "Buried? Never. I want to be cremated and my ashes scattered. I don't care where."[114]

These are profoundly depressing answers, but they drive home for us the emptiness of life as a servant of the empire. Conservatives—believers in what Russell Kirk called "the permanent things"—used to understand the need for roots. For a sense of permanence, of placefulness. But as Jeremy Beer, the coeditor of *American Conservatism: An Encyclopedia,* cogently observes, " 'Preserve,' 'save,' 'conserve,' 'sustain,' 'protect,' 'heritage,' 'tradition,' 'community,' 'place,' 'decentralized,' 'permanence,' 'beauty,' 'humane'—these former keywords of conservatism have largely migrated to other political quarters."[115]

In *Philosophy in a New Key* (1942), Susanne K. Langer writes, "Most people have no home that is a symbol of their childhood, not even a definite memory of one place to serve that purpose."[116]

This is true in spades of the military brat. Let's help the homeless: close the military bases and let these kids have a place worth calling home.

Manhattan-D.C. conservatives, eyes lit by the blazes of wars in far-off lands, cannot see (or will not concede) that militarism and empire are the most potently noxious enemies the American family has.

As first lady, Hillary Clinton played the wicked witch of bossy, man-suit-wearing feminism to the Republican Right, but as the carpetbagging senator from New York she has rendered herself acceptable to the Beltway–Manhattan–*Weekly Standard* Right with her support of the Iraq War, the Patriot Act, and the rattling of sabers at Israel's sworn foes. What hasn't changed is her approval of the military family. As first lady, she spoke gushingly of the armed forces, especially in their role as an agent of social change via babysitting.

Mrs. Clinton presided over an April 1997 White House Conference on Early Childhood Development and Learning at which the Pentagon was feted for its recognition, as a 1987 Army Family Action Plan put it, that "quality child development care" is "a crucial [military] program." What's that you say, hippie? War is not healthy for children and other living things? Au contraire: just listen to Hillary Clinton, mistress of war.

Allan Carlson had served as a Reagan appointee on the National Commission on Children and thus wrangled an invite to Hillary's conference. His report therefrom would have alarmed conservatives of the Nisbet and Kirk stripes, if any were left. Major General John G. Meyer, commanding general of the U.S. Army's Community and Family Support Center, "captivated an audience of institutional child-care enthusiasts with tales of military triumph in the nursery," relayed Carlson. The general declared, "Supporting the care and development of children is a responsibility the military readily assumes in exchange for the loyalty of their parents in uniform."

That is, care of the children of military men and women is socialized; myrmidon and dad pledge fealty to the state, and junior and sis will be raised in the state's nurseries. Over two hundred thousand American tykes are being raised in military day-care centers, which run twenty-four hours a day, seven days a week, 365 days a year, as the biggest day-care provider in the land of the semifree. The Pentagon calls this "the Total Army Family," and the whisper of dystopia may be heard over the tread of the tanks. "Contemporary military families are neither autonomous nor strong, the true measures of family health," wrote Carlson in lonely protest. "All are heavily dependent on special subsidy . . . The American armed forces are becoming agents of social change, instruments of social engineering committed in particular to eradicating belief in differences between the sexes, and building new family forms under complete control of the state."[117]

Newsweek's reporters summed up Hillary's White House conference by musing that "perhaps the Pentagon can fight a couple of land wars and simultaneously save the nation's children."[118] If you believe that, I'll preorder a copy of George W. Bush's memoirs for you.

I don't suppose Bush 43's ghostwriter will quote Stephen

Baskerville, president of the American Coalition for Fathers and Children, who has noted the "dramatic rise in military divorces" during Iraq War II. (Baskerville says of the Iraq War sunderings that "the divorces are almost all initiated by wives.")[119] Absence may make the heart grow fonder, but love requires presence. The Pentagon's own Defense Manpower Data Center acknowledges that the divorce rate for both officers and enlisted personnel almost doubled between 2001 and 2004. "We've seen nothing like this before," said the army chaplain Colonel Glen Bloomstrom, who added, "We've got some very loyal, dedicated military professionals stepping up to the plate, sometimes to the detriment of their kids."[120]

Ah, Chaplain, dear Sky Pilot, war may be a frequent metaphor but let us not metaphorize war. The soldiers are not "stepping up to the plate" in the Middle East. No one plays baseball there. The place to step up to the plate is in your backyard, or on the local diamond, with your daughter pitching and your son heckling you from shortstop. In which case the family is intact, the children are not suffering, and all is well with the world. The more manpower the Pentagon has on which to collect data, the worse off American families will be.

Contra Chaplain Bloomstrom, this is nothing new. The pernicious effect of militarism on the American family has long been known. Though intensified in wartime, the pressures of the armed services upon the family are present in peacetime as well. Even before the war, young military couples were "64 percent more likely to be divorced by age 24 than comparable civilian couples," according to Allan Carlson.[121] In March 2000, the *Telegraph* of London reported that "Armed Forces personnel are twice as likely to get divorced as civilian couples because of the strain Service life places on families."[122]

Never fear, however: in 2006 *Sesame Street* and Wal-Mart, the pus and canker of middle-class decay, announced "Talk, Listen,

Connect—Helping Families During Military Deployment," a program through which children deprived of fathers and mothers were consoled with DVDs of talking muppets. Big Brother meets Big Bird, brought to you by the Big Box.

George W. Bush, a putatively "pro-family" president, has in fact pursued military policies that are profoundly, heart-wrenchingly antifamily. This, really, ought to be a central indictment against Bush: he is, by policy, the most antifamily president in American history.

Behold the perversity as women reservists, young mothers of infants and small children, leave their families to go halfway 'round the world to act as cogs, expendable parts, in the machinery of empire. And hearken to the silence of the courtiers and grant grubbers of establishment conservatism, whose mingled amentia and cowardice testify to the gutlessness and wicked stupidity of what passes for the Right.

As a radical and a reactionary—a patriot of the old America—I am appalled by the violence done by the military-industrial complex at home as well as abroad. The images of families cleaved by the Iraqi War and occupation should outrage family-values conservatives—many of whom, especially at the grass roots, are sincere and decent, no matter how sleazy the Bennetts and Bauers are. Here is yet another issue on which good people of the greenish Left and anti-imperialist Right ought to unite: the first casualty of the militarized U.S. state is the family.

I once asked former secretary of defense Caspar Weinberger if the U.S. military wasn't "a government-subsidized uprooting of the population."[123] He replied, shall we say, in the negative; I may as well have asked Caspar the unfriendly ghost if he preferred the Clash or the Sex Pistols. But I was dead serious; the single greatest cause of rootlessness has been our standing army. (If it really were standing, it wouldn't be so bad; alas, it never stops moving.)

I could go on and on about the ways in which post–World War II militarism has eroded American family life. (I do go on and on elsewhere; see the chapter on the military vs. the family in my *With Good Intentions? Reflections on the Myth of Progress in America.*)[124] Divorce, dispersal, disruption of courtship patterns; ye shall know the warfare state by its rotten fruits. These include even the people-scattering Interstate Highway System, which was conceived during World War II by the top-down planner extraordinaire Rexford G. Tugwell and made concrete by a deracinated general named Dwight Eisenhower, who had admired Hitler's autobahn and got one of his own: the tellingly titled National System of Interstate and Defense Highways. Cohesive working-class neighborhoods in countless American cities were sacrificed to the Road Warriors.

By the late 1940s, sponsors of expensive, unconstitutional, or shockingly intrusive plans wised up to the fact that inserting *Defense* (the word *War* had been banished as insufficiently euphemistic) into the title of a bill enhanced greatly its chances of passage. Education, aviation, transportation—no field of human activity was so peaceable that it could not be sold as essential to "defense." Even children were now part of the arsenal.

Summer as Subversion

Conservatives used to regard education as a strictly local matter. Schools ought to be controlled at the grass roots, by parents and community leaders, and if Greenwich Village academies taught condom usage whilst those in Provo, Utah, cast aspersions upon Charles Darwin, well, that's the price—the glory, even—of letting a thousand flowers bloom. As late as 1996 the Republican Party platform called for abolishing the Department of Education, which had been a clumsy payoff from Jimmy Carter to the

National Education Association. But then along came the Bush men, and the GOP, rather enjoying the prospect of dictating policy to all those refractory school boards in flyover land, subjected the nation's schools and schoolchildren to unprecedented federal control. After all, we're fighting a war without end, a war against a shadowy and ill-defined enemy, and it behooves us all to be on the same page. Or in the same cage.

Militarism and empire long have been the allies of those who would centralize education. Take year-round schooling, that hobbyhorse of grim technocrats, of commissars of the god Efficiency, enemies of summer as we know it.

Proponents of putting schools on a schedule resembling that of a 7-Eleven store frequently have regarded children as the ductile means to some great national end, whether military or economic. Winning the Cold War, for instance. The United States "faces tough competition on both economic and military fronts," warned Grace and Fred M. Hechinger in the *New York Times* in 1960. "The Soviet pupil manages to spend about the same number of hours in school during his ten-year program as the American student does in twelve." (Those well-drilled pupils would go on to conquer Afghanistan and build the Mir.) "Is it sensible to leave this army of intellectual manpower unused for several months each year?" the Hechingers asked of the nation's teachers.[125] Note the martial imagery.

A Nation at Risk, the ballyhooed 1983 report of the National Commission on Excellence in Education, is also composed in the language of war. Education "undergirds American prosperity, security, and civility," we are told. "If an unfriendly foreign power had attempted to impose on America the mediocre educational performance that exists today, we might well have viewed it as an act of war." Indeed, we have "been committing an act of unthinking, unilateral educational disarmament."[126] And these preposterous tropes come from just the first two paragraphs!

The commission goes on to recommend longer school days (seven hours) and longer school years (220 days instead of the current 180). The former extension has been enacted widely in the years since, perhaps in recognition of the truth stated by the fire captain in Ray Bradbury's *Fahrenheit 451:* "Heredity and environment are funny things . . . The home environment can undo a lot you try to do at school. That's why we've lowered the kindergarten age year after year until now we're almost snatching them from the cradle."[127]

The school year in the average district remains closer to 180 days than 220, thanks to the blessed inertia and stubborn adherence to summer vacation of the typical American parent.

Sloth and camping trips: oh, how they vex the tyrant!

Empire centralizes and vulgarizes culture. It is the enemy not only of family but also of local life and art, for provincial arts and letters do not flourish in a centripetal age, as beaux esprits give way to Bill O'Reilly. In time of war, the mass media focus the attention of the public on the faraway—on Baghdad rather than one's backyard, and on the commercial products of New York and Los Angeles (which "bring us together") instead of on the particularistic culture of the town or neighborhood. The local is neglected or disparaged. A decentralized republic cultivates its Sarah Orne Jewetts; with empire, you get Madonna. Or as Sherwood Anderson said in 1939, "I suppose I am an isolationist . . . In a time of war any man working in the arts is sunk. His lamps are out. A new and strange ugliness comes into everyone about him. It is for him a time of death."[128]

The Cold War and our intermittent hot wars entailed mobility, the centralization of power, and the diminishing of the importance of the local. All must be subordinated to the struggle against the God That Failed the Neocon Ex-Communists or the God That Rewards Suicide Bombers. As I have written elsewhere

(*Dispatches from the Muckdog Gazette*, 2003), the real division in America is not left and right, or rich and poor, but mobile and immobile. The rulers of our political parties, the Fortune 500, the titans of the information/entertainment industry—all are displaced persons. The anchored are poorer, politically impotent, and under constant harassment by the mobile wielders of power. Our city neighborhoods were destroyed by urban renewal, highway construction, and busing; our small towns and rural areas are mocked by a vulgar popular culture, depopulated by war and its economic dislocations (just ask Kentucky). Our children are drafted, or they are eased into the military by a lack of local opportunities. There they fight the wars designed by the mobile. We are harassed by gun control and antismoking laws, and if parents in a rural township wish to have Genesis read in the classroom, they are ridiculed by the entertainment complex and pinned to the wall by the ukases of the courts. We are America's new niggers, and ain't no hate-speech laws gonna save us.

Those who direct U.S. foreign policy from Washington are, in a sense, homeless. Transient residents of mandarin suburbia, they lack any attachment to specific American places. "Defense," to them, is diffuse, overspilling the continental United States and taking in Australia, Israel, Japan, and other remote outposts of minimal interest to the vast majority of Americans.

The speechwriters for the savvier presidential candidates insert talismanic references to "community" into the teleprompter spiel, but all this loose talk ignores the precondition for community: stability, against which the culture of militarism militates. Frequent transfers; the stationing of servicemen and servicewomen far from the places they call home; subsidies lavished upon favored industries, bases, and military towns that lead to population drains and booms—community of anything but the most factitious and fugacious sort is impossible under such circumstances.

Empire stretches loyalties to a microscopic thinness. During the congressional debates over the admission of Alaska and Hawaii to the Union, Representative James Donovan of Manhattan's East Side begged his colleagues to "consider what happened to the pristine virtues of the Roman Republic when it started to take in the senator from Scythia, the senator from Mesopotamia, the senator from Egypt, the senator from Spain, the senators from Gaul; yes, even the senators from England. What happened to Roman culture? What happened to Roman unity?"[129] And what happens to American culture, American unity—or the glorious disunity that is a source of strength, too—when the American Empire cares more about Tehran and Tel Aviv than Oak Street and Washington Avenue?

Time Has Come Today

War obtrudes into our daily lives; it alters in the most fundamental ways the patterns of our days. It even corrupts the way we measure and the way we tell time. Take—please—daylight saving time.

Yes, spring ahead, fall back, that familiar ritual of mass timepiece rewinding ill-befitting freeborn Americans, is a war baby.

Today, we wonder who but the odd crank could object to the clock tinkering that brings us an extra hour of daylight on spring and summer nights. One such crank was the Canadian novelist Robertson Davies, whose grumpy alter ego Samuel Marchbanks wrote: "I object to being told that I am saving daylight when I am doing nothing of the kind. I even object to the implication that I am wasting something valuable if I stay in bed after the sun has risen. As an admirer of moonlight I resent the bossy insistence of those who want to reduce my time for enjoying it. At the back of the Daylight Saving scheme I detect the boney, blue-fingered hand of Puritanism, eager to push people into bed earlier, and get them up earlier, to make them healthy, wealthy, and wise in spite of themselves."[130]

Marchbanks was an acute detective. Benjamin Franklin, Mr. Healthy, Wealthy, and Wise himself, proposed a forerunner of daylight saving time in a whimsical 1784 essay,[131] though the notion's real father was the British architect and—crucially—golfer William Willett, who deplored "the waste of daylight" in a 1907 pamphlet. The British royal astronomer belittled Willett's plan, suggesting instead "that between the months of October and March the thermometer should be put up ten degrees."[132]

But it remained for the industrial and military complexes (in an age when the pair retained a modest degree of separation) to impose compulsory standardization on the nation's timekeepers.

Through most of American history, men and women lived and loved and died on local time, pegged to the transit of the sun. Towns and cities kept their own time, and if 12:15 in Rochester was 12:09 in Buffalo, so what? Isn't variety the spice of life?

Not to the iron horse. Idiosyncratic timekeeping was the bane of the railroaders, for whom decentralized chronometry was an evil worse than the Dalton Gang. Heaven forfend that states and cities might set their own times, wake to their own sunrises! So on November 18, 1883—"the day of two noons"—railroads and countless municipalities synchronized their collective watches all at once. The United States was divided into four zones. Standard time was born. Thus noon comes simultaneously to Detroit and Bangor, sun be damned.

Pockets of fierce resistance to standard time lined flinty New England and such time-zone outlying states as Ohio, Kentucky, and Michigan. In *Keeping Watch: A History of American Time*, Michael O'Malley found that the standard-time holdouts were not "silly, backward, and provincial." Rather, what "each found puzzling, saddening, or infuriating was the assumption that time was arbitrary, changeable, susceptible to the whims of the railroads or defined by mere commercial expediency. Surely the world ran by higher priorities than railroad scheduling."[133]

Surely it did not, editorialized *Railway Age*: "why should any other places, big or small, be allowed to retain the obsolete fashion? Local time must go."[134] It went. Commerce must be served. Ticktock. Ticktock. Time passed. And the battle was rejoined, on another front, as a direct result of Woodrow Wilson's war. The tribunes of Progress and Efficiency, two prominent noggins in the American godhead, imposed daylight saving time upon a bemused republic. The stated purpose was to conserve coal in wartime. (Similarly, the production of motion pictures was centralized in Southern California at this time as a consequence of the coal shortages brought on by the war.)

Farmers protested mightily against DST, but there was a war on, don't you know. Michael Downing, in his lively history *Spring Forward,* writes that "Daylight's proponents wrapped themselves in the flag, appropriated the war effort," and won.[135] They painted their foes—a "coalition of miners and farmers, Populists and Republicans, ministers and movie moguls"[136]—as, literally, the forces of darkness. These foes, or at least the first half of those enumerated, were also foes of the war, a contrary stance for which they were vilified as helpmeets of the hated Hun, home-front saboteurs sticking it to the valorous doughboys.

Evidence of energy savings was scant, but as Americans would learn soon enough, anything can be put over on the public if the sacred cause is munitions.

Congress repealed daylight saving time at war's end, overriding President Wilson's veto. (The farmer's "life and methods are more easily adjusted, I venture to think, than are those of the manufacturer and the merchant," lectured Wilson smugly.)[137] President Harding supported "voluntary" DST—that is, wake up earlier! Make the day's events conform to the sun's time; in spring and summer, begin work, school, and baseball games an hour later. But voluntarism attracts only a fraction of the partisans that compulsion does.

The 1919 repeal of DST marked the last victory for nature's (already standardized) time. An Illinois congressman called it "a contest between the golf stick and hoe,"[138] as daylight-craving recreationists were pitted against farmers, rustics, and other sundialing mossbacks. (President Wilson was crazy for golf, but he hid his putter under his hairshirt, emphasizing sacrifice rather than pleasure.) A Minnesota congressman called daylight saving time the "pet of the professional class, the semileisure class, the man of the golf club and the amateur gardener, the sojourner at the suburban summer resort." The golf club took on a sinister aspect to the time traditionalists, for as O'Malley writes, golf "symbolized the utter decadence that underlay the daylight saving movement."[139] (The decadence lobby can play it as it lies: movie interests later campaigned against DST.)

Mashies and niblicks failed to dislodge DST from the rough, but then came another war, and as always, all bets (and customs) were off. In 1942, FDR reimposed DST as a year-round measure. He called it "war time." Ah, yes. War time. Who ever objects to war time except enemy symps and fifth columnists? Wartime begat war time. Farmers, miners, populists, and Republicans were advised to keep their mouths shut and their clocks wound ahead.

Peace brought repeal. The choice of whether or not to spring ahead was left to states and localities. This produced diversity, which also goes under the name *confusion*—in one act of chronotyranny, Connecticut made it illegal to display the wrong time on a wristwatch—until the Uniform Time Act of 1966 whipped recalcitrants into line. (Arizona and Hawaii hold out still, with no apparent damage to the Republic.)

As Michael Downing has noted, by 2000 "the number of Americans living on farms was approximately equal to the number of Americans who were permanent residents of golf-course communities."[140] The bogeymen and the masters of war have trounced the dairymen and chased back the sun. Spring ahead, and fore!

No Litering

If the empire would forcibly alter our means of measuring time, would it not also compel Americans to change their way of reckoning distances and weights? You bet your liter it would.

And yet the metric system, so loathed by schoolboys of the baby-boom cohort, also suggests ways in which ordinary Americans resist empire—or at least those manifestations of empire that require conversion tables.

By now, only wrinkled crones and cowlick hillbillies were supposed to be reckoning in inches and quarts. The rest of America was to have been thoroughly metricized by the twenty-first century. "Early priority should be given to educating schoolchildren and the public at large to think in metric terms," commanded the Nixon administration's Department of Commerce.[141] Lord Ritchie-Calder, first chairman of the British Metrication Board, told a U.S. House of Representatives committee in 1973 that a metric America "is not only desirable but inevitable; those who do not come in will be out in the cold."[142]

Come now, Lord Ritchie-Calder; it's really not all that chilly out here. For upwards of thirty years Americans have warmed ourselves by bonfires made of meter-sticks. Mercurially, we have dumped Celsius thermometers like tea into Boston Harbor. The foot has not gotten the boot. For once—for now—NASA, the Department of Defense, and the Fortune 500 have been thwarted.

Lessons, anyone?

The inch, the primary unit of measurement in the customary

system, is based on the distance from the end of the middle finger to the first joint. The meter, the fundament of the metric system, is equal to one ten-millionth of the distance from the equator to the pole. Or so French scientists believed in 1795. They were wrong. One system is based on the human body—literally, a human scale—and the other is the mismeasurement of theoreticians, a "French fad" that has succeeded, as Frederick A. Halsey put it in *The Metric Fallacy* (1904), only "when backed by the policeman's club."[143]

John Quincy Adams, then secretary of state, prepared an 1821 report that bewrayed a certain sympathy for the metric system, but he realized that "the power of the legislator is limited over the will and actions of his subjects. His conflict with them is desperate, when he counteracts their settled habits, their established usages, their domestic and individual economy, their ignorance, their prejudices, and their wants: all which is unavoidable in the attempt to change . . . [the] system of weights and measures."[144]

Just as Adams understood that America goes not abroad in search of monsters to slay, so did he realize that if you give the metricists an inch they'll build a mile-long prison. The meter cannot be forced upon a people except by the rod.

In 1866, the United States legalized the use of metric measurements in contracts, but a committee of scientists reported to Congress in 1871 that Frenchmen, especially country people, had resisted the tyranny of meters, and predicted that "the conflict will be fierce in this country, where the people are freer and less habituated to blind obedience to imperial edicts."[145]

Liter lovers persisted in their efforts to standardize the world. *Voluntary* was not and is not a word in their lexicon. In 1902, Representative John F. Shafroth (R-CO), the prime congressional sponsor of a metric bill, observed of his pet system, "Germany adopted it by compulsory statute of the Reichstag, and I do not see how you can do it any other way."[146]

You can't. Metric, like empire, rests on force. Herbert Spencer, in *Against the Metric System* (1901), emphasized its antidemocratic qualities: "Ten thousand persons intend to make twenty million persons change their habits. The ten thousand are the men of science (by no means all), the Chambers of Commerce, and the leaders of some Trade-Unions—leaders only, for the question has never been put to the vote of the mass. The twenty million are the men and women of England, with those children who are old enough to be sent shopping."[147] The ten thousand carried the day, but then England was fast losing its habits of liberty in sacrifice to the Moloch of empire. The pint, it seems, was small beer indeed to those constructing an imperium upon which the poor sun would never be allowed to set.

The pound survived, unchallenged in America, until the Cold War, the single greatest impetus behind metrication. The Merlins of war demanded meters. Harold Urey, the Nobel Prize–winning chemist and Manhattan Project grandee, referred to the metric system as "a secret weapon of Communism."[148] Abandon the acre or risk losing Swaziland to the Reds! The Hungarian-born Dr. Strangelove, Edward Teller, warned Americans that we would be "overtaken by Russia" unless we rejected the rules of our fathers. The metric propagandist Frank Donovan declared in his peremptorily titled book *Prepare Now for a Metric Future* (1970), "Adherence to the inch-pound system is handicapping the United States in its conflict with Communism around the world."[149]

Donovan made explicit the link between military intervention and metrication: "Isolationism," he instructed, "which became a dirty word after World War II in most areas of American affairs, still prevails in the metric controversy."[150] But Donovan was sanguine, if also sanguinary. For reasons of "military strategy" and the "space program," nationwide conversion was inevitable. No two sectors of our increasingly militarized economy contained more enthusiastic metricists than the war and aerospace industries. The U.S. Army had gone metric in 1957; in 1970, NASA became the first (ostensibly) nondefense governmental department to convert from human-scale measurements to the cheerlessly linear French system. (Let us give one often deservedly maligned Frenchman his due. Napoleon said of metric, "It is a tormenting of the people for mere trifles."[151] He was half right; a torment it is, but the stakes could not be larger—or, more accurately, smaller.)

A series of carrots and sticks, of laws and executive orders were issued beginning in 1975 to destroy the customary system of weights and measures. The usual guff about competing in global marketplaces was coughed up, the ostrich took his accustomed metaphorical place in debate, and we were encouraged to panic over "the imminent isolation of the United States in an all-metric world."[152] Opponents were dismissed as labor union proles, dim-witted housewives, and crusty old-timers—that is, real people.

Smaller businesses on Main Street and in Middle America, the historic mercantile core of isolationism, fought metric through the National Federation of Independent Business. The NFIB declared: "Metric conversion benefits large, manufacturing industries and most of these are already undergoing conversion, but the metric system should not be forced down the throats of all businesses in America. The cost to small firms, in time lost and wasted materials, could never be recouped."[153]

Louis M. Sokol, president of the U.S. Metric Association, said in 1979 that "working people will be more efficient in using metric units on the job if they also use them in sports [and] hobbies."[154] Only "the Archie Bunkers in the country" opposed metric, sneered Sokol,[155] but the Archies' victory has been sugary sweet. Football fields are still one hundred yards long. The hoop is still ten feet from the floor. It's still a ninety-foot sprint from third base to home. Track, admittedly, has been lost. That inspiring blend of grace and endurance, the mile, is no more. Roger Bannister, Jim Ryun, Sebastian Coe . . . can anyone name a runner of the 1,500 meters?

The Galahad of the Holy Meter was Rhode Island senator Claiborne Pell, the daffy Democrat whose otherworldly interests—ESP, mentalism, parapsychology—made him an odd leader of the army of hyperrational scientists and apostles of drudgery who insist upon cutting off this nation's feet. But the movement has been bipartisan: the great metric strides—the creations of boards and mandates and studies—occurred under the Republican presidents Nixon, Ford, Reagan, and Bush 41. (Though Reagan, at the prodding of aide and western novelist Lyn Nofziger, did abolish the U.S. Metric Board.)

John Quincy Adams saw it coming: the metric lobby of big government, NASA, the military-industrial complex, and big science has been no match for the great spontaneous HELL NO! of the American people. The Maine artist Seaver Leslie, president of Americans for Customary Weight and Measure, called the French system "a language of technocracy and multinational trade,"[156] fit perhaps for science and some industries but not for everyday life. Leslie's side has carried the day—so far. The Federal Highway Administration has ceased defacing road signs with kilometric distances; and though a 1988 law declared metric to be Uncle Sam's "preferred system of measurement," his nieces and nephews beg to differ.

America's antimetrics have fulfilled the prophecy of one merry nineteenth-century song:

Then down with every "metric" scheme
Taught by the foreign school.
We'll worship still our Father's God!
And keep our Father's "rule"!
A perfect inch, a perfect pint,

The Anglo's honest pound,
Shall hold their place upon the earth,
Till Time's last trump shall sound![157]

Libya and Myanmar join our enisled land as metric holdouts, a queer pairing that the scolds of standardization never tire of throwing into our faces. With great forbearance do we resist pointing out the equally irrelevant fact that North Korea is metricized. Or perhaps that isn't so irrelevant . . .

Writing for the American Management Association in 1973, Alex Groner and George A. W. Boehm confidently described metrication as a way of clearing out the deadwood of tradition: "It should generate a spring cleaning that will make people look at existing practices and realize how many have accumulated just by habit and indifference, and how many can be effectively scrapped in the interest of efficiency."[158] That god of efficiency—he never is sated, is he?

The leading congressional defender of traditional measurements and critic of the imperialist metric system? Tennessee's Jimmy Duncan, the Taft Republican who has fought with guts and principle against G. W. Bush's crusade to remake the Middle East.[159]

In November 1989, as the cracks in the communist fissure revealed themselves, Allan Carlson called for a reassessment of defense policy on pro-family grounds, saying that "this may also be our last good opportunity to count up the price that has been paid for our recent crusade, morally and socially as well as financially. And this may be the time to chart alternative ways of reconciling national defense with the principles of republican government, to the benefit of both our liberties and our families."[160]

No one heard the call, though they would, eventually, heed the call-up.

Carlson understood that the love affair of "family-values" advocates with the Pentagon has been a disastrous shackup. No agency of the government has done as much to destroy the traditional American family as has the Department of Defense. A true family-values platform would not only end all federal involvement in day care and education, it would also demand radical reductions in the size and mission of the U.S. defense establishment. Please don't hold your breath waiting for some intrepid delegate to propose this linkage at the next GOP convention.

The leadership of the family-values Right is hopelessly compromised by its long-term adulterous affair with the Republican Party. But plenty of good folks who call themselves *conservatives* mean by that now-useless term that they believe in the integrity of families and small communities and detest the vulgar, home-wrecking, and even murderous intrusions of corporate capitalism and Big Government. As they watch this latest American diaspora, as young husbands and wives tearfully leave spouses and children and extended families to serve the empire, we should remind them that the only foreign policy compatible with healthy family life is one of peace and nonintervention.

CONCLUSION: COME HOME, AMERICA

"AS PROBLEMS OF every sort increase at home we realize that what happens to Israel or Ethiopia is not our first concern," wrote Felix Morley. "And this is not to be called a rebirth of 'isolationism,' but rather a recognition that federalism, even if we misname it democracy, is not adapted or adaptable to the path of empire."[1]

Hear, hear! One's crest falls, however, upon seeing that Morley incised that prophecy in 1959. The rebirth of federalism, or isolationism, never happened. Half a century on we are entangled ever more inextricably in Israeli affairs—and hold on, Ethiopia, we're a-comin'.

Hearing the wailing and gnashing of computer keys at *National Review* on August 10, 2006, the day after the sanctimonious pro-war liberal senator Joseph Lieberman was rejected in the Democratic primary by Connecticut voters, Daniel McCarthy of the *American Conservative* wrote:

> Not only is it not surprising that the war has been as polarizing as it has, but it also is not surprising that the polarization has broken down the way that it has. At least since Vietnam, and really going back some years earlier, most conservatives have been committed militarists and nationalists. Conservatives over the past five decades have frequently talked about government's incompetence and excessive spending—but virtually never have they applied these criticisms to the military, certainly not in a sustained and systematic fashion. It

would hardly be going too far to say that the military has been an object of veneration. Similarly, but to a slightly lesser degree, American military expansionism and interventionism have been supported by conservatives to a far greater degree than they have been supported by anyone else. Again, this is an old story. The one major exception to conservative foreign-policy bloodlust was the anomalous period in the mid-to-late '90s when Republicans weren't keen to get into Kosovo and bomb Serbia. Today, there's some hesitation on the Right about getting into Darfur and other African sinkholes, although some on the Christian Right—Sam Brownback in the Senate and Frank Wolf in the House come to mind—seem about as eager to do so as anyone on the Left.

There is no antiwar Right, at least not beyond the very limited number of contributors to and readers of magazines like *Chronicles* and *The American Conservative*. We could all fit into a college football stadium and still have plenty of seats to spare. There is, to be sure, a conservative intellectual tradition critical of war and militarism that outshines anything the belligerent Right or neoconservatives can offer. To one extent or another, Richard Weaver, Robert Nisbet, Michael Oakeshott, John Lukacs, and Russell Kirk are all in the antimilitarist camp. Up to a point, right-wing militarists can be brought around to the side of peace and nonintervention by showing them that the best conservative arguments are against war, especially total war, and a quasi-imperial foreign policy. But the number of conservatives who are smart enough to understand such arguments, or interested enough to listen, is very small indeed.

It gets steadily harder to deny that militarism is the *sine qua non* of "conservatism" as it is actually practiced in America.[2]

A sharp point, well-taken and impossible to blunt, which is why many of us who affirm values once associated with conservatism—decentralism, liberty, economy in government, religious faith, family-centeredness, parochialism, smallness—disdain the label *conservative*. It reeks of manslaughter and militarism. Yet that which the term once denoted is not dead, though it may be slumberous.

Look hard enough and there are sanguine signs and pleasing portents. Okay, there are rumors of revival, hints of hope. The antiwar voices in the U.S. Congress—which as yet are closer to an octet than a chorus—have included conservative Republicans (such as Tennessee representative Jimmy Duncan) and Democrats who cut reactionary cultural profiles (Senators Webb and Byrd and Representative Murtha). Across the land, local governments are rejecting the Patriot Act, and in a heartening number of cases these gallantly defiant cries of NO! are coming from the libertarian West, in allegedly "red" states such as Idaho and Montana. One cannot establish an empire on the ruins of the Republic without sparking one hell of a reaction: Vermont now boasts a lively and mediagenic secession movement that demands independence, for as its founder, Thomas Naylor, says, "Do you want to go down with the *Titanic*? No empire has survived the test of time."[3]

It may not be too late for the American Right—for Main Street America in all its conservative neighborliness, its homely yet life-giving blend of the communal and the libertarian—to rediscover the wisdom of its ancestors, who understood that empire is the enemy of the small and war is the enemy of the home.

In the first months of the second Iraq War, I spun the same 45 record every morning on our dusty old turntable: Freda Payne's "Bring the Boys Home," an isolationist anthem if ever there was one. Freda, best known for her bouncy drama of wedding-night impotence, "Band of Gold," recorded "Bring the Boys Home" in 1971 on the Invictus label. It never rose higher than number twelve on the charts. But it's a heartbreaker, one of the best antiwar pop songs because, like Jimmy Webb's "Galveston" or Eric Bogle's "And the Band Played Waltzing Matilda," it measures the cost of war on a human scale.

An affecting mixture of Motown and dirge, the song begins with Freda's lament:

Fathers are pleading
Lovers are all alone
Mothers are praying
Send our sons back home

Freda and her backup singers beseech, implore, demand that the boys be brought home from "a senseless war." She imagines "all the soldiers that are dying . . . just trying to get home," and she ends with a beautifully furious question:

What they doin' over there?
When we need 'em over here?

Thirty-five-plus years later, as brave American boys once again die for nothing halfway around the globe, our rulers still haven't answered that question. But until the Department of Homeland Security confiscates seditious pop records, Freda Payne will keep asking the same question Felix Morley asked, albeit more euphoniously.

From the turbid murk of the Cold War, Morley's hopeful words still pierce the darkness: "In recent years Americans have been abroad, in more than the literal sense. We can stay abroad, or we can come home. We shall never make the world safe for democracy. But we can keep and continuously strengthen the power in the people, here at home. Only thus will the light of this Republic continue to shine before mankind, as a beacon unique in history."[4]

We will come home only if there is something to come home to. Robert Nisbet wrote in 1975 that "the greatest need in our age is that of somehow redressing the balance between political-military power on the one hand and the structure of authority that lies in human groups such as neighborhood, family, labor union, profession, and voluntary association."[5] In reviving the local, the particular, the human scale, we chip away—like gleeful Berliners at that horrid wall—at the colossus of the military-industrial complex. Flowers push up between the cracks. Will we nurture them or sit by as the agents of the monster spray baneful pesticides?

I thought on these things of a recent April week, which I began by basking in applause and ended by wallowing in garbage, or at least the contemplation thereof.

The community college in my hometown of Batavia, New York, hosted its annual celebration of the writings of native son John Gardner, the late novelist best known for *Grendel* and his massive *The Sunlight Dialogues,* which is really more of a windy monologue, if I may say. Gardner once called our fair burg "a good symbol" of "the decline of Western civilization,"[6] which is a tough line for our tourism bureau to exploit. But he was, at heart, a plowboy, and indissolubly ours, the product of eccentric parents locally famous for reciting Poe and Shakespeare to the cows as they milked.

My keynote address to the gathered Gardnerians was irreverently respectful, though I subtly advanced my own claim to be Batavia's Great Writer. Practice paid dividends, as carefully scripted lines came off as witty ad-libs. I was even forgiven an atrocious joke: that the favorite play of the Gardner kine was *Othello,* the Moo-er of Venice. You may groan.

My wife, daughter Gretel, and I are also inveterate read-alouders, to each other if not to bovines, and we saw the month out by declaiming "I love to hunt for violets in April-time" by the early-nineteenth-century New England poet N. P. Willis.[7] Gretel and I tossed the softball back and forth in our yard, which seemingly overnight was awash in daffodils and violets. The flowers provided a beautiful purple-and-yellow coda to a cold and snowy late winter. The brutal storms were an inclement complement to this extended winter of our dissolution, when the vestiges of our beloved American Republic have been finally swept away by the deeply anti-American Empire whose repellent avatar is Dick Cheney, for whom the only good daffodil is a dead daffodil.

The empire despises spring, flowers, baseball. The docile subject of globalism is expected to eat the same chain fare, wear the same sweatshop-stitched togs, watch the same moronic and degenerate TV shows, and kick the same damnable soccer ball as collaborators and would-be Esperanto speakers throughout the world.

Well, not in our yard, Jack.

Baseball, the American game, and softball, its variant for girls, have not traveled well. The empire exports software and soft porn but never softball, God bless the sport's incomprehensible soul. You will forgive me if I boast that Gretel's fastball is gaining velocity by the day.

Rain had washed out our daily game of catch by week's end, when, with John Gardner's rapturous descriptions of our countryside in mind, I drove fifteen miles (I'll be damned if I ever measure in kilometers) to Albion. Nothing perfidious about this Albion, a village of lovely brick storefronts and modest but dignified homes along the Erie Canal.

But Albion finds itself threatened by the unholy marriage of state and commerce, as a waste company with friends in high places seeks to site a 190-foot-high garbage dump on the bluebird-stippled banks of the Erie Canal. The garbage would be trucked in from distant megalopolitan centers. Saith Urban Man to his country cousins: Eat shit.

The town board was to vote this night to fight the garbage dumpers to the bitter—or perhaps sweet—end. A thousand Davids had aimed their slingshots at Goliath. This was to be democracy in action, as foreign to Bush and McCain and the People in Gray as baseball is to the Husseins.

Our satisfaction was deferred when my boat-rocking pal Marty Stucko and I arrived to find that the meeting had been canceled.

Goliath, anticipating the ambuscade of stones, had requested and been granted a month's delay. But don't worry; the slingshots stayed loaded. Vigilance, desperation, love, laughter—we have weapons yet. Ours is the America not of the home run but of the sacrifice bunt. We haven't forgotten how to lay it down.

The decline of Western civilization? I see it writ across George W. Bush's petulantly vacant mug. As for John Gardner, daffodils, baseball, bluebirds, my daughter, and the Davids of Albion—hell, they're the only hope our little corner of American civilization has left.

Come home, America. Reject the empire.

Please.

NOTES

Introduction: I'll Just Stay Here, Thanks

1. Gore Vidal, "Foreword," in Bill Kauffman, *America First! Its History, Culture, and Politics* (Amherst, N.Y.: Prometheus, 1995), p. 10.
2. Garet Garrett, *The People's Pottage* (Caldwell, Idaho: Caxton, 1953), pp. 127–58.
3. Ibid., p. 167.
4. Quoted in *Congressional Record*, 86th Congress, 1st session, March 11, 1959, p. 3887.
5. *Congressional Record*, 83rd Congress, 1st session, March 10, 1953, p. 1801.
6. John Greenleaf Whittier, "The Haschish," in *The Complete Poetical Works of Whittier* (Boston: Houghton Mifflin, 1894), p. 317.
7. Robert Nisbet, *Conservatism: Dream and Reality* (Minneapolis: University of Minnesota Press, 1986), p. 104.
8. Quoted in Shailagh Murray and Dan Balz, "GOP Jabs as Dems Back Lamont," *Rochester Democrat and Chronicle,* August 10, 2006.
9. Felix Morley, *Freedom and Federalism* (Indianapolis: Liberty Press, 1981 [1959]), p. 121.
10. Senator Robert A. Taft, *Congressional Record,* 82nd Congress, 1st session, January 5, 1951, p. 55.
11. Edgar Lee Masters, *Lincoln: The Man* (New York: Dodd, Mead, 1931), p. 85.
12. George W. Bush, "State of the Union Address by the President," January 31, 2006, www.whitehouse.gov/stateoftheunion/2006.

13. "Bush's Concern over Isolationism Reflects More Than Just Rhetoric," press release, Pew Research for the People and the Press, February 3, 2006.
14. Quoted in Llewellyn H. Rockwell Jr., "Patriot Games," *Free Market* (June 1997), p. 4.

Chapter 1. "The Greatest Curse That Ever Befell Us":
An Empire Is Born

1. *The Debates in the Several State Conventions on the Adoption of the Federal Constitution,* vol. 3, selected and revised by Jonathan Elliott (Philadelphia: Lippincott, 1836), p. 379.
2. Ibid., Madison, p. 381.
3. For the genesis of the address, see Felix Gilbert, *To the Farewell Address: Ideas of Early American Foreign Policy* (Princeton, N.J.: Princeton University Press, 1961).
4. Ibid., pp. 144–47.
5. Thomas Jefferson to Elbridge Gerry, January 26, 1799, *The Papers of Thomas Jefferson,* vol. 30, edited by Barbara B. Oberg (Princeton: Princeton University Press, 2003), p. 646.
6. Merrill Jensen, *The Articles of Confederation: An Interpretation of the Social-Constitutional History of the American Revolution, 1774–1781* (Madison: University of Wisconsin Press, 1966 [1940]), p. 194.
7. *The Records of the Federal Convention of 1787,* vol. 2, edited by Max Farrand (New Haven: Yale University Press, 1911), p. 617.
8. Quoted in Jon Kukla, *A Wilderness So Immense: The Louisiana Purchase and the Destiny of America* (New York: Knopf, 2003), p. 65.
9. *The Debates in the Several State Conventions on the Adoption of the Federal Constitution,* vol. 3, p. 608.
10. Quoted in Kukla, *A Wilderness So Immense,* p. 292.
11. Quoted in Thomas Fleming, *The Louisiana Purchase* (Hoboken, N.J.: Wiley, 2003), p. 135.
12. Quoted in Kukla, *A Wilderness So Immense,* p. 293.
13. Quoted in Charles A. Cerami, *Jefferson's Great Gamble: The Remarkable Story of Jefferson, Napoleon, and the Men Behind the Louisiana Purchase* (Naperville, Ill.: Sourcebooks, 2003), p. 255. See also Roger Griswold to Oliver Wolcott, March 11, 1804, in *Documents Relating to New England Federalism, 1800–1815,* edited by Henry Adams (Boston: Little Brown, 1905), pp. 354–58.
14. Quoted in Kukla, *A Wilderness So Immense,* p. 295.
15. Timothy Pickering to Richard Peters, December 24, 1803, in *Documents Relating to New England Federalism, 1800–1815,* p. 338. See also

Kevin M. Gannon, "Escaping 'Mr. Jefferson's Plan of Destruction': New England Federalists and the Idea of a Northern Confederacy, 1803–1804, *Journal of the Early Republic* 21 (Fall 2001): 413–43.

16. Kukla, *A Wilderness So Immense,* p. 307.

17. Quoted in ibid., p. 301.

18. Thomas Jefferson, *Notes on the State of Virginia,* in *Writings* (New York: Library of America, 1984 [1787]), pp. 290–91.

19. Quoted in Russell Kirk, *John Randolph of Roanoke: A Study in American Politics* (Indianapolis: Liberty Press, 1978 [1951]), pp. 204–5. See also Henry Adams, *John Randolph* (Boston: Houghton Mifflin, 1882), pp. 88–95.

20. Henry Adams, *History of the United States of America During the First Administration of Thomas Jefferson,* vol. 2 (New York: Scribner's, 1909), p. 90.

21. Quoted in Margaret L. Coit, *John C. Calhoun: American Portrait* (Boston: Houghton Mifflin, 1961 [1950]), p. 116.

22. William Cullen Bryant, "Autumn Woods," in *The Poetical Works of William Cullen Bryant* (New York: AMS Press, 1972 [1903]) p. 68.

23. William Cullen Bryant, *The Embargo,* with notes by Thomas O. Mabbott (Gainesville, Fla.: Scholars' Facsimiles and Reprints, 1955 [1808]), pp. 35–48. I have quoted from Bryant's 1809 revision of the poem.

24. Ibid., p. 13.

25. John Bigelow, *William Cullen Bryant* (Boston: Houghton Mifflin, 1890), p. 69.

26. Parke Godwin, *The Life and Works of William Cullen Bryant,* vol. 1 (New York: Appleton, 1883), p. 75.

27. Quoted in Edgar Lee Masters, *Whitman* (New York: Scribner's, 1937), p. 269.

28. William Cullen Bryant, "Freedom of Exchange," in *Prose Writings of William Cullen Bryant,* vol. 2, edited by Parke Godwin (New York: Appleton, 1884), p. 250.

29. I borrow the fittingly nigrescent sobriquet for Randolph from that wonderful historian of old Virginia, Alan Crawford.

30. Lemuel Sawyer, *A Biography of John Randolph, with a Selection from His Speeches* (New York: William Robinson, 1844), p. 9.

31. Alan Pell Crawford, *Unwise Passions: A True Story of a Remarkable Woman—and the First Great Scandal of Eighteenth-Century America* (New York: Simon and Schuster, 2000), p. 271.

32. Ibid., p. 188.

33. Quoted in ibid., p. 178.

34. Kirk, *John Randolph of Roanoke,* p. 138.

35. Quoted in ibid., p. 205.
36. Quoted in ibid., p. 206.
37. Ibid., p. 139.
38. *The Debates in the Several State Conventions on the Adoption of the Federal Constitution,* vol. 4, selected and revised by Jonathan Elliott, p. 441.
39. Quoted in Robert V. Remini, *Henry Clay: Statesman for the Union* (New York: Norton, 1991), p. 778.
40. Quoted in Coit, *John C. Calhoun,* p. 76.
41. Quoted in Harry L. Coles, *The War of 1812* (Chicago: University of Chicago Press, 1965), p. 27.
42. Quoted in Julius W. Pratt, *Expansionists of 1812* (Gloucester, Mass.: Peter Smith, 1957 [1925]), p. 40.
43. Quoted in ibid., p. 52.
44. Quoted in ibid., p. 125.
45. Ibid., p. 9.
46. Thomas Jefferson to General Thaddeus Kosciusko, June 28, 1812, in *The Writings of Thomas Jefferson,* edited by Paul Leicester Ford (New York: Putnam's, 1898), pp. 360–64.
47. Henry Adams, *History of the United States During the Second Administration of James Madison* (New York: Scribner's, 1891), p. 229.
48. Samuel Eliot Morison, "Dissent in the War of 1812," in *Dissent in Three American Wars,* by Morison, Frederick Merk, and Frank Freidel (Cambridge: Harvard University Press, 1970), p. 3.
49. Daniel Webster, speech of December 9, 1814, reprinted in *New Individualist Review* 4, no. 4 (Spring 1967): 876–77.
50. John Randolph, speech of December 10, 1811, reprinted in Kirk, *John Randolph of Roanoke,* pp. 355–79.
51. Quoted in Robert Dawidoff, *The Education of John Randolph* (New York: Norton, 1979), p. 198.
52. Quoted in Julian Hawthorne, *Nathaniel Hawthorne and His Wife: A Biography,* vol. 2 (Boston: James R. Osgood, 1885), p. 277.
53. John Greenleaf Whittier, "Randolph of Roanoke," in *The Complete Poetical Works of Whittier* (Boston: Houghton Mifflin, 1894), p. 303.
54. Kirk, *John Randolph of Roanoke,* p. 208.
55. A Massachusetts Farmer (John Lowell), "Thoughts in a Series of Letters, in Answers to a Question Respecting the Division of the States," 1813. I write about Lowell's proposal to sever the original thirteen from the new states in my forthcoming book on secession from Chelsea Green.

56. Quoted in Gay Wilson Allen, *Waldo Emerson: A Biography* (New York: Viking, 1981), p. 446. See also John C. Calhoun, "Speech on the War Appropriation Bill," February 9, 1847, in *The Essential Calhoun: Selections from Writings, Speeches, and Letters,* edited by Clyde N. Wilson (New Brunswick, N.J.: Transaction, 2000 [1992]), p. 132.

57. Quoted in Frederick Merk, "Dissent in the Mexican War," in *Dissent in Three American Wars,* p. 40.

58. Ibid., pp. 43–44.

59. Quoted in Rudolph Van Abele, *Alexander H. Stephens: A Biography* (New York: Knopf, 1946), p. 97.

60. Bill Kauffman, "A Mighty Long Fall: An Interview with Eugene McCarthy," *Chronicles,* July 1996, p. 16.

61. Quoted in K. Jack Bauer, *The Mexican War, 1846–1848* (New York: Macmillan, 1974), p. 369.

62. Quoted in Frederick Merk, *Manifest Destiny and Mission in American History: A Reinterpretation* (New York: Knopf, 1963), p. 46.

63. Herbert Agar, *The People's Choice* (Boston: Houghton Mifflin, 1933), p. 149.

64. Thomas Corwin, speech of February 11, 1847, in *Life and Speeches of Thomas Corwin,* edited by Josiah Morrow (Cincinnati: W. H. Anderson, 1896), p. 305. See also Michael F. Holt, *The Rise and Fall of the American Whig Party: Jacksonian Politics and the Onset of the Civil War* (New York: Oxford University Press, 1999), pp. 248–50.

65. Corwin, *Life and Speeches,* pp. 280–84.

66. Ibid., p. 303.

67. Quoted in ibid., p. 88.

68. Ibid., p. 90.

69. Quoted in Charles J. DeWitt, "Crusading for Peace in Syracuse During the War with Mexico," *New York History* 31 (1933): 104.

70. Ibid., 109.

71. Quoted in Robert Remini, *Daniel Webster: The Man and His Time* (New York: Norton, 1997), p. 647.

72. Quoted in David Lowenthal, *George Perkins Marsh: Versatile Vermonter* (New York: Columbia University Press, 1958), pp. 103, 106.

73. "Biographical Memoir of George Perkins Marsh," in *National Academy of Sciences Biographical Memoirs,* vol. 6 (Washington, D.C., 1909), p. 73.

74. Whittier, "The Crisis," in *The Complete Poetical Works of Whittier,* p. 309.

75. Quoted in William M. Armstrong, *E. L. Godkin and American Foreign Policy, 1865–1900* (New York: Bookman Assoc., 1957), p. 103.

76. Quoted in Joseph Frazier Wall, *Andrew Carnegie* (New York: Oxford University Press, 1970), p. 694.

77. Quoted in Allan Nevins, *Grover Cleveland: A Study in Courage* (New York: Dodd, Mead, 1932), p. 553.

78. Henry F. Graff, *Grover Cleveland* (New York: Times Books, 2002), p. 35.

79. Grover Cleveland, "Inaugural Address of March 4, 1885," in *Inaugural Addresses of the Presidents of the United States* (Washington, D.C.: U.S. Government Printing Office, 1961), p. 151.

80. Graff, *Grover Cleveland*, p. 77.

81. Nevins, *Grover Cleveland: A Study in Courage*, p. 549.

82. Ibid., p. 560.

83. Grover Cleveland, statement to the Associated Press, January 24, 1898, in *Letters of Grover Cleveland, 1850–1908*, edited by Allan Nevins (Boston: Houghton Mifflin, 1933), p. 491.

84. Ibid., p. 492.

85. Grover Cleveland to Richard Olney, July 8, 1898, ibid., p. 502.

86. William Graham Sumner, "The Fallacy of Territorial Extension," in *On Liberty, Society, and Politics: The Essential Essays of William Graham Sumner,* edited by Robert C. Bannister (Indianapolis: Liberty Fund, 1992), p. 268.

87. John Lukacs, "The Meaning of '98," *American Heritage* (May–June 1998), p. 78.

88. Quoted in John V. Denson, "Introduction," *Reassessing the Presidency: The Rise of the Executive State and the Decline of Freedom* (Auburn, Ala.: Mises Institute, 2001), p. xx.

89. Quoted in Thomas Beer, *Hanna* (New York: Knopf, 1929), p. 236.

90. Quoted in William M. Gibson, "Mark Twain and Howells: Anti-Imperialists," *New England Quarterly* 20 (1947): 437.

91. Quoted in Margaret Leech, *In the Days of William McKinley* (New York: Harper and Brothers, 1959), p. 345.

92. Robert L. Beisner, *Twelve Against Empire: The Anti-Imperialists* (New York: McGraw-Hill, 1968), p. x.

93. Morley, *Freedom and Federalism*, p. 118.

94. Beisner, *Twelve Against Empire*, p. 238.

95. Quoted in Patricia O'Toole, *When Trumpets Call: Theodore Roosevelt After the White House* (New York: Simon and Schuster, 2005), p. 363.

96. Fred H. Harrington, "The Anti-Imperialist Movement in the United States, 1898–1900," *Mississippi Valley Historical Review* 22, no. 2 (September 1935): 211.

97. Harold Francis Williamson, *Edward Atkinson: The Biography of an American Liberal, 1827–1905* (Boston: Old Corner Book Store, 1934), p. v.
98. Ibid., p. 236.
99. Beisner, *Twelve Against Empire*, pp. 88, 90.
100. Williamson, *Edward Atkinson*, p. 228.
101. Robert L. Beisner, "1898 and 1968: The Anti-Imperialists and the Doves," *Political Science Quarterly* 85, no. 2 (June 1970): 194.
102. Quoted in Beisner, *Twelve Against Empire*, pp. 205, 209.
103. William Belmont Parker, *The Life and Public Services of Justin Smith Morrill* (Boston: Houghton Mifflin, 1924), p. 346.
104. George S. Boutwell, *Reminiscences of Sixty Years in Public Affairs*, vol. 2 (New York: McClure, Phillips, 1902), p. 324. Far into his dotage, Boutwell finally redeemed the promise that no less than Bronson Alcott had seen in him: "And one of the most hopeful aspects of our national affairs," wrote the transcendentalist preceptor of Concord in 1872, "is the coming into importance and power of plain, sensible men, like Grant and Boutwell,—men owing their places to their honesty and useful services." Er, ahem, yes. A. Bronson Alcott, *Concord Days* (Boston: Roberts Brothers, 1872), p. 168.
105. Boutwell, *Reminiscences*, pp. 334–35.
106. Quoted in E. Berkeley Tompkins, "Scylla and Charybdis: The Anti-Imperialist Dilemma in the Election of 1900," *Pacific Historical Review* 36, no. 2 (May 1967): 150.
107. Ibid., p. 147. During the Vietnam War, the Tory Confederate Arkansas Democratic senator J. William Fulbright, a wise critic of empire, found in Hoar a brother dissenter. See Bill Kauffman, "Fulbright: The First Arkansas Bill," in *America First!: Its History, Culture and Politics* (Amherst, N.Y.: Prometheus, 1995), pp. 143–54.
108. Quoted in ibid., p. 152.
109. *Congressional Record,* 55th Congress, 3rd session, January 9, 1899, pp. 493–502.
110. Ibid., February 2, 1899, p. 1384.
111. Quoted in James McGurrin, *Bourke Cockran: A Free Lance in American Politics* (New York: Scribner's, 1948), p. 193.
112. Frances Bartlett, "Triumph: Hoar of Massachusetts," in *Liberty Poems: Inspired by the Crisis of 1898–1900* (Boston: James H. West, 1900), p. 66.
113. Quoted in Armstrong, *E. L. Godkin and American Foreign Policy*, p. 192.
114. Quoted in Beisner, *Twelve Against Empire*, p. 79.
115. Armstrong, *E. L. Godkin and American Foreign Policy*, p. 199.

116. Quoted in McGurrin, *Bourke Cockran*, p. 232.

117. Ibid., pp. 331–32.

118. Quoted in ibid., p. xiv.

119. Quoted in ibid., pp. 322, 325.

120. Quoted in Graff, *Grover Cleveland*, p. 51.

121. Quoted in McGurrin, *Bourke Cockran*, p. 196.

122. Quoted in ibid., p. 332.

123. "Democratic Platform of 1900," in *National Party Platforms, 1840–1972,* compiled by Donald Bruce Johnson and Kirk H. Porter (Urbana: University of Illinois Press, 1973), p. 112.

124. Quoted in E. Berkeley Tompkins, "Scylla and Charybdis: The Anti-Imperialist Dilemma in the Election of 1900," p. 146.

125. Ernest Crosby, "Rebels," in *Liberty Poems,* p. 48.

126. Grover Cleveland to Richard Olney, April 12, 1899, in *Letters of Grover Cleveland,* pp. 513–14.

127. Beisner, *Twelve Against Empire,* p. 222.

128. Quoted in ibid., p. 162.

129. James T. DuBois, "Expansion," in *Liberty Poems,* pp. 82–83.

130. Quoted in Beisner, "1898 and 1968," p. 202.

131. Quoted in Armstrong, *E. L. Godkin and American Foreign Policy,* p. 177.

132. Quoted in H. Wayne Morgan, *America's Road to Empire: The War with Spain and Overseas Expansion* (New York: Wiley, 1965), p. 107.

133. Quoted in Fred Harvey Harrington, "Literary Aspects of American Anti-Imperialism, 1898–1902," *New England Quarterly* (December 1937): 667.

134. Quoted in Richard E. Welch Jr., *Response to Imperialism: The United States and the Philippine-American War, 1899–1902* (Chapel Hill: University of North Carolina Press, 1979), p. 62.

135. Quoted in William B. Hixson Jr., *Moorfield Storey and the Abolitionist Tradition* (New York: Oxford University Press, 1972), p. 38.

136. August Derleth, "American Portrait," in *Selected Poems* (Prairie City, Ill.: James A. Decker, 1944), p. 162.

137. Quoted in Hixson, *Moorfield Storey and the Abolitionist Tradition,* p. 66.

138. Thomas Bailey Aldrich, "Unguarded Gates," in *The Poems of Thomas Bailey Aldrich* (Boston: Houghton Mifflin, 1907), pp. 275–76.

139. Quoted in Harrington, "Literary Aspects of American Anti-Imperialism," p. 666.

140. Corporal John Mulcahy, "In the Trenches," in *Liberty Poems,* pp. 8–9. There is some confusion over the correct spelling of the poet's name. On the assumption that this is the itinerant poet John Mulcahy, I have gone with the *e*-less spelling.

141. Howard Hickson, "Poem of Murder," August 27, 2001, http: outbacknevada.us/howh/Poet.htlml, from *Northeastern Nevada Historical Society Quarterly* (Winter 1987). Also letter to the author from Howard Hickson, April 7, 2006.
142. Maurice F. Brown, *Estranging Dawn: The Life and Works of William Vaughn Moody* (Carbondale: Southern Illinois University Press, 1973), p. 171.
143. Ibid., p. 112.
144. William Vaughn Moody, "An Ode in the Time of Hesitation," in *Poems* (Boston: Houghton Mifflin, 1901), p. 18.
145. Ibid., p. 16.
146. William Vaughn Moody, "On a Soldier Fallen in the Philippines," in *Poems*, pp. 24–25.
147. Quoted in Brown, *Estranging Dawn*, p. 171.
148. Quoted in Armstrong, *E. L. Godkin and American Foreign Policy*, p. 194.

Chapter 2. "It's Not Our Fight": Saying No to World Wars

1. Agar, *The People's Choice*, p. 301.
2. Frederick E. Drinker, *Our War for Human Rights* (Washington, D.C.: National Publishing, 1917), p. vi.
3. Ibid., p. vii.
4. Quoted in Beisner, *Twelve Against Empire*, p. 168.
5. Walter Millis, *Road to War: America, 1914–1917* (Boston: Houghton Mifflin, 1935), p. 243.
6. Quoted in ibid., p. 303.
7. Quoted in ibid., pp. 454–55.
8. Alex Mathews Arnett, *Claude Kitchin and the Wilson War Policies* (Boston: Little, Brown, 1937), p. 42.
9. Quoted in ibid., p. 214.
10. Quoted in ibid., p. 237.
11. Quoted in ibid., p. 275.
12. Quoted in ibid., p. 227.
13. Quoted in Millis, *Road to War*, p. 454.
14. Quoted in David M. Kennedy, *Over Here: The First World War and American Society* (New York: Oxford University Press, 1980), p. 23.
15. Quoted in Richard M. Gamble, *The War for Righteousness: Progressive Christianity, the Great War, and the Rise of the Messianic Nation* (Wilmington, Del.: ISI Books, 2003), p. 152.
16. Quoted in Warren I. Cohen, ed., *Intervention, 1917: Why America Fought* (Boston: Heath, 1966), p. 17.

17. Woodrow Wilson, "For Declaration of War Against Germany," April 2, 1917, in *War and Peace: The Public Papers of Woodrow Wilson,* vol. 1, edited by Ray Stannard Baker and William E. Dodd (New York: Harper and Bros., 1927), p. 16.

18. William Alexander Percy, *Lanterns on the Levee: Recollections of a Planter's Son* (New York: Knopf, 1941), p. 143.

19. Quoted in William F. Holmes, *The White Chief: James Kimble Vardaman* (Baton Rouge: Louisiana State University Press, 1970), p. 292.

20. Quoted in ibid., p. 369.

21. Quoted in ibid., p. 374.

22. Joseph E. Fortenberry, "James Kimble Vardaman and American Foreign Policy, 1913–1919," *Journal of Mississippi History* 35, no. 2 (May 1973): 132.

23. Ibid., p. 139.

24. Quoted in ibid., p. 131.

25. Quoted in Holmes, *The White Chief,* p. 317.

26. Quoted in Fortenberry, "James Kimble Vardaman and American Foreign Policy, 1913–1919," p. 135.

27. Quoted in ibid., p. 136.

28. Quoted in Millis, *Road to War,* p. 448.

29. Quoted in Gilbert C. Fite and H. C. Peterson, *Opponents of War, 1917–1918* (Madison: University of Wisconsin Press, 1957), p. 6.

30. Holmes, *The White Chief,* p. xii.

31. Quoted in Fite and Peterson, *Opponents of War,* p. 155.

32. Quoted in ibid., pp. 5–6.

33. Quoted in ibid., pp. 36–37.

34. Robert Nisbet, *Twilight of Authority* (New York: Oxford University Press, 1975), p. 179.

35. Quoted in Robert Nisbet, *The Present Age* (New York: Harper and Row, 1988), p. 43.

36. Nisbet, *Twilight of Authority,* p. 180.

37. Quoted in Fite and Peterson, *Opponents of War,* p. 209.

38. Ruth Suckow, *Country People* (New York: Knopf, 1924), p. 100.

39. Ibid., p. 103.

40. Quoted in Kennedy, *Over Here,* p. 18.

41. Edward Bellamy, *Looking Backward, 2000–1887* (New York: Modern Library, 1951 ([1887]), p. 46.

42. Quoted in E. James Lieberman, "American Families and the Vietnam War," *Journal of Marriage and the Family* 33, no. 4 (November 1971): 717–18.

43. William K. Shearer, "Rep. George Holden Tinkham of Massachusetts," *California Statesman,* January–February 1997, p. 1.
44. Will Lang, "Tinkham the Mighty Hunter," *Life,* December 16, 1940, p. 69.
45. Quoted in Shearer, "Rep. George Holden Tinkham of Massachusetts," p. 6.
46. Quoted in Lang, "Tinkham the Mighty Hunter," p. 72.
47. Richard D. Challener, "Veterans of Future Wars," from Alexander Leitch, *A Princeton Companion* (Princeton: Princeton University Press, 1978), http://etcweb1.princeton.edu/CampusWWW/Companion.
48. "Future Veterans," *Time,* March 30, 1936, p. 38.
49. "The Veterans of Future Wars," www.museumofhoaxes.com/pranks/veterans.html.
50. "Future Veterans," *Time.*
51. Robert McG. Thomas Jr., "Lewis J. Gorin, Jr., Instigator of a 1930's Craze, Dies at 84," *New York Times,* January 31, 1999.
52. "The Veterans of Future Wars."
53. See Ernest C. Bolt Jr., *Ballots Before Bullets: The War Referendum Approach to Peace in America, 1914–1941* (Charlottesville: University Press of Virginia, 1977) and Kauffman, *America First!,* pp. 225–27.
54. Justus D. Doenecke, *In Danger Undaunted: The Anti-Interventionist Movement of 1940–1941 as Revealed in the Papers of the America First Committee* (Stanford, Calif.: Hoover Institution Press, 1990), p. 9.
55. Quoted in Ruth Sarles, *A Story of America First: The Men and Women Who Opposed U.S. Intervention in World War II* (Westport, Conn.: Praeger, 2003), p. lv–lvi.
56. Ibid., p. 88.
57. Irwin H. Palmer, "Just Stay This Side of the Pond," Aberdeen, South Dakota, 1938.
58. Anne Morrow Lindbergh, *War Within and Without: Diaries and Letters of Anne Morrow Lindbergh, 1939–1944* (New York: Harcourt Brace Jovanovich, 1980), pp. 119–20.
59. Quoted in William Manchester, *Disturber of the Peace: The Life of H. L. Mencken* (Amherst: University of Massachusetts Press, 1986 [1951]), p. 290. Mencken believed the Second World War sapped the libertarian American spirit. In February 1945 he wrote the African American journalist-novelist George S. Schuyler: "The American people have lost altogether their old impatience of regimentation. They now fall into the goose-step with the utmost docility. In brief, slavery has staged a revival, and I am thinking seriously of proposing

formally that the Emancipation Proclamation be repealed. I don't propose, of course, that the dark brethren alone be enslaved; the ofays deserve a massive dose out of the same bottle." Mencken to Schuyler, February 5, 1945, in *The New Mencken Letters,* edited by Carl Bode (New York: Dial Press, 1977), p. 550.

60. Quoted in Barbara Branden, *The Passion of Ayn Rand* (Garden City, N.Y.: Doubleday, 1986), p. 160.

61. Quoted in Howard Teichman, *Alice: The Life and Times of Alice Roosevelt Longworth* (Englewood Cliffs, N.J.: Prentice-Hall, 1979), p. 180.

62. Morley, *Freedom and Federalism,* pp. xiv–xv.

63. Quoted in Donald Bruce Johnson, *The Republican Party and Wendell Willkie* (Urbana: University of Illinois Press, 1960), p. 60.

64. Quoted in ibid., p. 76.

65. Quoted in Teichman, *Alice,* p. 181.

66. Quoted in James T. Patterson, *Mr. Republican: A Biography of Robert A. Taft* (Boston: Houghton Mifflin, 1972), p. 221.

67. Quoted in "The Road Back," *Time,* October 7, 1940, pp. 14–16.

68. Quoted in Johnson, *The Republican Party and Wendell Willkie,* p. 124.

69. Quoted in ibid.

70. Quoted in Virginia Spencer Carr, *Dos Passos: A Life* (Garden City, N.Y.: Doubleday, 1984), p. 410.

71. Wendell L. Willkie, *An American Program* (New York: Simon and Schuster, 1944), p. 4. Here is the obtuse Willkie offering an alternative explanation of the Soviet purges: "It would be my guess . . . that Stalin likes a pretty heavy turnover of young people in his immediate entourage in the Kremlin. It is his way, I think, of keeping his ear to the ground." Coming soon from Freedom House: Leadership Secrets of Joseph Stalin! You will not find a single remark about Hitler by an America First leader that is anywhere close to exhibiting such blindness (and blitheness) toward evil. Wendell L. Willkie, *One World* (New York: Simon and Schuster, 1943), p. 84.

72. "Through the Mill," *Time,* November 20, 1944, p. 23.

73. Quoted in Wayne S. Cole, *America First: The Battle Against Intervention, 1940–41* (Madison: University of Wisconsin Press, 1953), p. 136.

74. Quoted in Sarles, *A Story of America First,* p. 226. The standard works on the committee are Wayne S. Cole, *America First: The Battle Against Intervention, 1940–1941,* and two books by Justus D. Doenecke: *Storm on the Horizon: The Challenge to American Intervention, 1939–1941* (Lanham, Md.: Rowman and Littlefield, 2000), and *In Danger Undaunted,* which he edited. Cole and Doenecke, though

sometimes critical of the committee's strategy, find no evidence of an anti-Semitic coloration to the AFC. See also Cole's *Charles A. Lindbergh and the Battle Against American Intervention in World War II* (New York: Harcourt Brace Jovanovich, 1974) and his masterwork, *Roosevelt and the Isolationists, 1932–1945* (Lincoln: University of Nebraska Press, 1983).

75. Quoted in ibid., p. 109.
76. Quoted in ibid., p. 110.
77. Quoted in ibid., p. 121.
78. Quoted in ibid., pp. 54–55. Lindbergh had a reputation for sternly discouraging ethnic jokes and remarks. He raised his "children never to say, never to think, such things," recalled his daughter, Reeve. Reeve Lindbergh, *Under a Wing: A Memoir* (New York: Simon and Schuster, 1998), p. 201.
79. Gerald Nye, "War Propaganda," *Vital Speeches,* September 15, 1941, p. 721.
80. Quoted in Frederick R. Barkley, "Flynn Says Films Bar Peace Side," *New York Times,* September 12, 1941.
81. Norman Thomas to General R. E. Wood, September 17, 1941, America First Collection, box 291, Hoover Institution.
82. Kurt Vonnegut, "We Chase a Lone Eagle and End Up on the Wrong Side of the Fence," *Cornell Daily Sun,* October 13, 1941, editorial page. Four years later, the infantryman Vonnegut, a POW held by the Germans, would witness the destruction of Dresden, which he memorialized in *Slaughterhouse-Five* (1969).
83. Lincoln Colcord to General Robert E. Wood, January 6, 1941, in *In Danger Undaunted,* p. 221.
84. Quoted in Christopher Lasch, "Lincoln Colcord and Colonel House: *Dreams of Terror and Utopia,*" in *The New Radicalism in America, 1889–1963* (New York: Knopf, 1965), p. 221.
85. Wayne S. Cole, *Determinism and American Foreign Relations During the Franklin D. Roosevelt Era* (Lanham, Md.: University Press of America, 1995), p. 42.
86. For a roundhouse right thrown by the avenging ghost of Burton K. Wheeler, see Bill Kauffman, "Heil to the Chief," *American Conservative,* September 27, 2004, pp. 28–31.
87. Milton Mayer, *Robert Maynard Hutchins: A Memoir,* edited by John H. Hicks (Berkeley: University of California Press, 1993), pp. 216–17.
88. Cole, *Determinism and American Foreign Relations During the Franklin D. Roosevelt Era,* p. 46.

89. Quoted in Kai Bird, *The Chairman: John J. McCloy, the Making of the American Establishment* (New York: Simon and Schuster, 1992), p. 147.

Chapter 3. "Ill-Fated, Unnecessary, and Un-American": Following a Cold War into Asia

1. Felix Morley, *The Power in the People* (Los Angeles: Nash, 1972 [1949]), p. 231.
2. Felix Morley, "In the Course of Human Events," *Reason*, February 1978, p. 35.
3. Ibid., p. 34.
4. Justus D. Doenecke, *Not to the Swift: The Old Isolationists in the Cold War* (Lewisburg, Pa.: Bucknell University Press), p. 40.
5. Quoted in Jefferson Morley, "Irreconcilable Conflicts," *Washington Post*, August 12, 1995, letters page.
6. The Manhattan Project, which birthed that bomb which in addition to laying waste two Japanese cities had the unfortunate domestic effect of focusing antiwar energies on weaponry rather than foreign policy, and thus privileging in debate those who had mastered the jargon of technology, horrified Robert Nisbet as a study in cog-hood. Nisbet marveled at "the spectacle of tens of thousands of workers and scientists working for a period of years on a product the nature of which few of them knew or were permitted to discover. Life was almost wholly circumscribed by security regulations, formal organizational patterns, technical instructions, and complicated machines, all pointing toward a goal that was undiscoverable by the individual worker or lesser scientist. Even to look too closely into the identity of fellow workers was not encouraged." Robert Nisbet, *The Quest for Community: A Study in the Ethics of Order and Freedom* (San Francisco: Institute for Contemporary Studies, 1990 [1953]), pp. 33–34.

   The "secrecy and depersonalization" of wartime enterprises carried over into the postwar world, though the term *postwar* is something of a misnomer. For when since 1941 has the United States *not* been at war? As the "indispensable nation"—in the repellent phrase of Clinton's secretary of state Madeleine Albright—our government has become godlike in its unwillingness to let a single sparrow or regime fall unattended.
7. Morley, *The Power in the People*, p. 231.
8. Quoted in Joseph R. Stromberg, "Felix Morley: An Old Fashioned Republican Critic of Statism and Interventionism," *Journal of Libertarian Studies* 2, no. 3 (Fall 1978): 271.

9. Felix Morley, *Freedom and Federalism* (Indianapolis: Liberty Press, 1981 [1959]), p. 114.

10. Stromberg, "Felix Morley," p. 275.

11. Morley, *The Power in the People,* pp. 265–66.

12. Quoted in Stromberg, "Felix Morley," p. 271.

13. Morley, *The Power in the People,* p. 266.

14. Morley, "In the Course of Human Events," pp. 35–36.

15. "The North Atlantic Treaty Organization," in *Two Centuries of U.S. Foreign Policy: The Documentary Record,* edited by Stephen J. Valone (Westport, Conn.: Praeger, 1995), p. 120.

16. Quoted in Ted Galen Carpenter, "The Dissenters: American Isolationists and Foreign Policy, 1945–1954," Ph.D. dissertation, University of Texas, 1980, p. 152.

17. Quoted in Robert Griffith, "Old Progressives and the Cold War," *Journal of American History* 66, no. 2 (September 1979): 338.

18. Quoted in ibid., p. 342.

19. Quoted in Carpenter, "The Dissenters," p. 240.

20. John T. Flynn, *The Road Ahead: America's Creeping Revolution* (New York: Devin-Adair, 1949), p. 156.

21. Quoted in "National Security," in *Congress and the Nation: A Review of Government and Politics, 1945–1964* (Washington, D.C.: Congressional Quarterly, 1965), p. 263.

22. Joseph P. Kennedy, "Present Policy Is Politically and Morally Bankrupt," *Vital Speeches,* January 1, 1951, p. 173.

23. Herbert Hoover, "Our National Policies in This Crisis," in *Addresses upon the American Road, 1950–1955* (Stanford, Calif.: Stanford University Press, 1955), pp. 3–10.

24. "Hoover's Folly," *The Nation,* December 30, 1950, p. 688.

25. "Can We Save World Peace?" *The New Republic,* January 1, 1951, pp. 5–6. For the story of how a Soviet spy came to back Truman, see Michael Straight, *After Long Silence* (New York: Norton, 1983).

26. Senator Robert Taft, *Congressional Record,* January 5, 1951, pp. 54–61.

27. Quoted in Coit, *John C. Calhoun,* p. 441.

28. *Congressional Record,* January 5, 1951, p. 58.

29. Ibid., p. 55.

30. "Washington Wire," *New Republic,* January 15, 1951, p. 3.

31. Quoted in *Congress and the Nation,* p. 265.

32. Quoted in *Congressional Record,* January 5, 1951, p. 59. My favorite sally from the last ditch, a poignant attempt to preserve boyhood, was an amendment by Senator Francis Case, a South Dakota Republican,

to set a minimum age of twenty for troops sent to Europe. It failed 62–27, with a majority of Republicans—25–18—in support but virtually all Democrats—44–2—opposed. Damned ephebe stealers!

33. Thomas E. Mahl, *Desperate Deception: British Covert Operations in the United States, 1939–44* (Dulles, Va.: Brassey's, 1998), p. 140.

34. Harry S. Truman, "Sixth Annual Message," January 8, 1951, in *The State of the Union Messages of the Presidents,* vol. 3 (New York: Chelsea House, 1967), pp. 2976–83.

35. Quoted in Griffith, "Old Progressives and the Cold War," p. 343.

36. Quoted in Roger Lowenstein, *Buffett: The Making of an American Capitalist* (New York: Random House, 1995), pp. 5, 11.

37. Quoted in ibid., p. 18.

38. Ibid., p. 27.

39. Quoted in Murray N. Rothbard, "The Foreign Policy of the Old Right," *Journal of Libertarian Studies* 2, no. 1(Winter 1978): 91.

40. Quoted in Lowenstein, *Buffett,* p. 27.

41. Quoted in Murray N. Rothbard, "The Transformation of the American Right," *Continuum* (Summer 1964): 222.

42. Quoted in Carpenter, "The Dissenters," p. 138.

43. Quoted in Richard Harris, *Decision* (New York: Dutton, 1971), p. 110.

44. Quoted in Murray N. Rothbard, "Confessions of a Right-Wing Liberal," *Ramparts,* June 15, 1968, p. 48.

45. Carl Oglesby, "Vietnamese Crucible: An Essay on the Meanings of the Cold War," in *Containment and Change* (New York: Macmillan, 1971 [1967]), pp. 166–67.

46. Howard Buffett, "An Opportunity for the Republican Party," *New Individualist Review* 2, no. 2 (Summer 1962): 251.

47. Milton and Rose Friedman, *Two Lucky People* (Chicago: University of Chicago Press, 1998), p. 380. See also David R. Henderson, "The Role of Economists in Ending the Draft," *Econ Journal Watch* 2, no. 2 (August 2005): 362–76.

48. Then again, I was an associate editor at AEI's flagship, the *American Enterprise,* from 1994 to 2006, an admittedly bizarre mésalliance due solely to my friendship with *TAE*'s editor, Karl Zinsmeister, a dear chum since our Moynihan daze. Friendship must always—always—trump politics.

49. Nisbet, *The Quest for Community,* pp. 8–9.

50. Nisbet, his biographer Brad Lowell Stone notes, spent two years of his boyhood in Macon, Georgia, and had a "very strong feeling" that he was a southerner. Brad Lowell Stone, *Robert Nisbet: Communitarian Traditionalist* (Wilmington, Del.: ISI Books, 2000), p. 2.

51. Robert Nisbet, "Uneasy Cousins," in *Freedom and Virtue: The Conservative/Libertarian Debate,* edited by George W. Carey (Lanham, Md.: University Press of America, 1984), p. 19.

52. Nisbet, *Twilight of Authority,* p. 78.

53. Nisbet, "Uneasy Cousins," p. 17.

54. Nisbet, *Twilight of Authority,* pp. 191–92.

55. William A. Schambra, "Foreword," *The Quest for Community,* p. xv.

56. Nisbet, *Conservatism: Dream and Reality,* p. 105.

57. Nisbet, *The Quest for Community,* p. 107.

58. Robert Nisbet, "The Present Age and the State of Community," *Chronicles,* June 1988, p. 11.

59. Nisbet, *Twilight of Authority,* p. 183.

60. Ibid., p. 66.

61. Nisbet, *Conservatism: Dream and Reality,* p. 105.

62. Nisbet, *The Quest for Community,* p. 35.

63. Nisbet, *Twilight of Authority,* p. 220.

64. Thomas E. Woods Jr., "Twilight of Conservatism," *American Conservative,* www.amconmag.com/2005/2005_12_05, December 5, 2005.

65. Quoted in Russell Kirk, *The Politics of Prudence* (Wilmington, Del.: ISI Books, 1993), p. 176.

66. Nisbet, *The Quest for Community,* p. 33.

67. Quoted in Coit, *John C. Calhoun,* p. 101.

68. Nisbet, *Twilight of Authority,* pp. 187–88.

69. Quoted in Leonard P. Liggio, "Vietnam and the Republicans," *Left and Right* 3, no. 2 (Spring–Summer 1967): 50.

70. "I'm Not Going to Take the Easy Way," *Life,* June 21, 1954, p. 128.

71. Quoted in "Harold Royce Gross," *Current Biography, 1964* (New York: H. W. Wilson), p. 172.

72. Representative H. R. Gross, *Congressional Record,* 88th Congress, 1st session, December 2, 1963, p. 22979.

73. Bart Barnes, "Former Iowa Rep. H. R. Gross Dies at 88," *Washington Post,* September 24, 1987.

74. Vernon Louviere, "The House Is Losing Its 'Conscience,' " *Nation's Business,* June 1974, p. 26.

75. Quoted in "The Useful Pest," *Time,* June 15, 1962, p. 21.

76. *Current Biography, 1964,* p. 173.

77. Quoted in "Former Iowa Rep. H. R. Gross Dies at 88."

78. " 'Gyrating' Dances, 'Peekaboo' Dresses," *U.S. News and World Report,* May 23, 1966, p. 10.

79. Quoted in "The House Is Losing Its 'Conscience,' " p. 29.

80. *Current Biography, 1964,* p. 173.

81. "The House Is Losing Its 'Conscience,' " p. 26.
82. Quoted in ibid., p. 29.
83. David T. and Linda Royster Beito, "The Christian Conservative Who Opposed the Vietnam War," antiwar.com, August 22, 2006.
84. Quoted in Andrew L. Johns, "Doves Among Hawks: Republican Opposition to the Vietnam War, 1964–1968," *Peace and Change* 31, no. 4 (October 2006): 589.
85. Leonard Liggio, letter to the author, September 6, 2006.
86. Johns, "Doves Among Hawks," p. 597.
87. Quoted in ibid., p. 598.
88. Ibid., p. 585.
89. Thruston B. Morton, "Only the G.O.P. Can Get Us Out of Vietnam," *Saturday Evening Post,* April 6, 1968, pp. 10–11.
90. Quoted in John Perham, "Business and Vietnam," *Dun's Review,* April 1966, p. 94.
91. John H. Bunzel, *The American Small Businessman* (New York: Knopf, 1962 [1956]), p. 227.
92. Ron Paul, interview with the author, Summer 1986.
93. Kenneth Crawford, "Peacenik Wall Street," *Newsweek,* March 18, 1968, p. 56.
94. Steve Weissman, "Businessmen Against the War (Sic)," *Ramparts,* December 1970, p. 32.
95. James Clotfelter, "Millions for Defense, But . . . ," *Nation,* January 25, 1971, p. 110.
96. Quoted in Stromberg, "Felix Morley," p. 272.
97. Rothbard, "Confessions of a Right-Wing Liberal," p. 48.
98. Rothbard, "The Foreign Policy of the Old Right," pp. 94–95.
99. Quoted in Stephen E. Ambrose, *The Wild Blue: The Men and Boys Who Flew the B-24s over Germany* (New York: Simon and Schuster, 2001), large print edition, p. 38.
100. George McGovern, *Grassroots: The Autobiography of George McGovern* (New York: Random House, 1977), p. 10.
101. Ibid., p. 14.
102. Quoted in Robert Sam Anson, *McGovern: A Biography* (New York: Holt, Rinehart and Winston, 1972), p. 16.
103. All quotes by George McGovern in this paragraph and the next two paragraphs are from an interview with the author, November 3, 2005.
104. Quoted in George McGovern, *The Essential America: Our Founders and the Liberal Tradition* (New York: Simon and Schuster, 2004), p. 69.

105. McGovern, interview with the author.

106. McGovern, *Grassroots,* p. 164.

107. Ibid., p. 167.

108. Anson, *McGovern: A Biography,* p. 287.

109. McGovern, interview with the author.

110. McGovern, *Grassroots,* p. 8.

111. Gary Aguiar, "Congressional Experiences, Congressional Legacies," in *George McGovern: A Political Life, a Political Legacy,* edited by Robert P. Watson (Pierre: South Dakota State Historical Society Press, 2004), p. 55.

112. *McGovern: The Man and His Beliefs,* edited by Shirley MacLaine (New York: Artists and Writers for McGovern, 1972), p. 33.

113. Ambrose, *The Wild Blue,* p. 21.

114. McGovern, interview with the author.

115. McGovern, *Grassroots,* p. 228.

116. Ibid., p. 13.

117. McGovern, interview with the author.

118. McGovern, *Grassroots,* p. 160.

119. McGovern, interview with the author.

120. George McGovern, *An American Journey: The Presidential Campaign Speeches of George McGovern* (New York: Random House, 1974), pp. 219–20.

121. The best discussion of the Eagleton fiasco is in Hunter S. Thompson, *Fear and Loathing on the Campaign Trail '72* (New York: Popular Library, 1973).

122. McGovern, *Grassroots,* p. 182.

123. McGovern, interview with the author.

124. McGovern, *An American Journey,* pp. 179–81.

125. Karl Hess, "An Open Letter to Barry Goldwater," *Ramparts,* August 1969, pp. 28–29.

126. McGovern, *An American Journey,* p. 192.

127. Ibid., p. 21.

128. McGovern, *Grassroots,* p. 169.

129. McGovern, interview with the author.

130. Quoted in George McGovern, *The Third Freedom: Ending Hunger in Our Time* (New York: Simon and Schuster, 2001), p. 16.

131. McGovern, *The Essential America,* pp. 142–44.

132. McGovern, interview with the author.

133. McGovern, *The Essential America,* p. 147.

134. Oglesby, "Vietnamese Crucible," p. 166.

135. Ibid., p. 165.
136. Paul M. Buhle and Edward Rice-Maximin, *William Appleman Williams: The Tragedy of Empire* (New York: Routledge, 1995), p. 13.
137. Ibid., p. 162.
138. Ibid., p. xiv.
139. Ibid., p. 1.
140. Quoted in ibid., p. 9.
141. Ibid., p. 21.
142. Ibid., p. 42.
143. Quoted in "Old Right/New Left," *Left and Right* 2, no. 1 (Winter 1966): 5.
144. Quoted in Buhle and Rice-Maximin, *William Appleman Williams*, p. 110.
145. William Appleman Williams, *The Contours of American History* (Chicago: Quadrangle, 1966 [1961]), p. 429.
146. Quoted in Buhle and Rice-Maximin, *William Appleman Williams*, p. 82.
147. Quoted in ibid., pp. 114–15.
148. Ibid., p. 150.
149. Ibid., p. 161.
150. William Appleman Williams, *Empire as a Way of Life: An Essay on the Causes and Character of America's Present Predicament Along with a Few Thoughts About an Alternative* (New York: Oxford University Press, 1980), p. 226.
151. Bob Dylan, *Chronicles* (New York: Simon and Schuster, 2004), p. 292.
152. Tor Egil Forland, "Bringing It All Back Home *or* Another Side of Bob Dylan: Midwestern Isolationist," *Journal of American Studies* 26, no. 3 (1992): 337.
153. Jimmy McDonough, *Shakey: Neil Young's Biography* (New York: Random House, 2002), p. 588.

Chapter 4. "Meddlers in the Affairs of Distant Nations"; or, Since When Did Iraq Define Conservatism?

1. Felix Morley, "American Republic or American Empire?" *Modern Age* 1, no. 1 (Summer 1957): 20.
2. Mark O. Hatfield, "For Me, Choice for President Is Clear: Bush," *Oregonian,* September 23, 2004, editorial page.
3. Patrick J. Buchanan, *A Republic, Not an Empire: Reclaiming America's Destiny* (Washington, D.C.: Regnery, 1999), p. 5.
4. Russell Kirk, "Conscription Ad Infinitum," *South Atlantic Quarterly* 45, no. 3 (July 1946): 313–19.

5. Jeffrey Hart, *The Making of the American Conservative Mind:* National Review *and Its Times* (Wilmington, Del.: ISI Books, 2005), p. 48.

6. Washington Irving, "The Legend of Sleepy Hollow," in *The Sketch Book* (New York: Dodd, Mead, 1954 [1819]), p. 373.

7. Hart, *The Making of the American Conservative Mind,* p. 48.

8. Russell Kirk, *The Sword of Imagination: Memoirs of a Half-Century of Literary Conflict* (Grand Rapids, Mich.: Eerdmans, 1995), pp. 331–32.

9. "Nixon Reacts to Eastertide," in "The Cold War Files: Interpreting History Through Documents," www.coldwarfiles.org, April 4, 1972.

10. Kirk, *The Sword of Imagination,* p. 334.

11. Russell Kirk, *The Politics of Prudence* (Wilmington, Del.: ISI Books, 2004 [1993]), p. 70.

12. Ibid., p. 157.

13. Ibid., p. 217.

14. See Kirk's "Libertarians: The Chirping Sectaries," *Modern Age* 25, no. 4 (Fall 1981): 343–51.

15. Kirk, *The Politics of Prudence,* p. 158.

16. Ibid., p. 180.

17. Ibid., p. 221.

18. Ibid., p. 212.

19. Ibid., pp. 221–22.

20. Llewellyn H. Rockwell Jr., "Libertarians and the Old Right," interview by Brian Doherty, lewrockwell.com, February 1999. Rockwell confirmed Kirk's remarks in a letter to the author.

21. Jeremy Beer, "What Is Left? What Is Right? Does It Matter?" *American Conservative,* August 28, 2006, pp. 5–6.

22. Unless otherwise indicated, all quotations by John J. Duncan Jr., are from his interview with the author, June 30, 2005.

23. Janet Ayer Fairbank, *The Lions' Den* (Indianapolis: Bobbs-Merrill, 1930), p. 357.

24. Hearing of the House Government Reform Committee, June 20, 2002.

25. Congressman John J. Duncan Jr., *Washington Report,* April 2004, p. 6.

26. Ibid., August 2003, p. 2.

27. Ibid., p. 3.

28. John J. Duncan Jr., "The Independent Way," *Knoxville Metro Pulse,* July 1, 2004, p. 13.

29. Congressman John J. Duncan Jr., *Washington Report,* February 2005, p. 4.

30. Morley, *Freedom and Federalism,* p. 125.

31. Quoted in Ted Galen Carpenter, "Reject False Prophets," *Chronicles,* March 2007, p. 24.

32. Bill Berkowitz, "Evangelicals Rally Their Flocks Behind Israel," April 6, 2006, antiwar.com.

33. Quoted in John Edward Weems, *To Conquer a Peace: The War Between the United States and Mexico* (College Station, Tex.: Texas A&M University Press, 1988 [1974]), p. 346.

34. William G. Eggleston, "Our New National Hymn," in *Liberty Poems,* p. 27.

35. Patrick J. Buchanan, "No, This Is Not 'Our War,' " antiwar.com, July 21, 2006.

36. Gore Vidal, "The Empire Lovers Strike Back," *The Nation,* March 22, 1986, p. 353.

37. Quoted in Jeff Zeleny, "12 Republicans Break Ranks on Iraq Resolution," *New York Times,* February 15, 2007.

38. Kimberly Hefling, "War Losses Mount for Nation's Small Towns," Associated Press, *Batavia Daily News,* February 24, 2007.

39. Cal Thomas, "Too Many Cooks in Foreign Policy," *Batavia Daily News,* December 24, 1986, editorial page.

40. Cal Thomas, "Taliban Democrats," August 10, 2006, www.townhall .com/columnists/CalThomas.

41. *Life and Speeches of Thomas Corwin,* p. 288.

42. Patrick J. Buchanan, "Why Neo-Conservatives Love Lieberman," Human Events Online, August 10, 2006.

43. Quoted in William B. Hixson Jr., *Moorfield Storey and the Abolitionist Tradition,* pp. 60–61.

Chapter 5. Blood, Treasure, Time, Family:
The Costs of American Empire

1. Quoted in Gordon S. Wood, *Revolutionary Characters: What Made the Founders Different* (New York: Penguin, 2006), pp. 166–67.

2. Quoted in Justin Raimondo, *Reclaiming the American Right: The Lost Legacy of the Conservative Movement* (Burlingame, Calif.: Center for Libertarian Studies, 1993), p. 177.

3. G. K. Chesterton, *The Napoleon of Notting Hill* (London: John Lane, 1928 [1904]), p. 134.

4. J. William Fulbright, "The Price of Empire," August 8, 1967, in Haynes Johnson and Bernard M. Gwertzman, *Fulbright: The Dissenter* (Garden City, N.Y.: Doubleday, 1968), p. 311.

5. Alexis de Tocqueville, *Democracy in America* (New York: New American Library, 1956 [1835]), p. 278.

6. Quoted in Kirk, *John Randolph of Roanoke,* p. 143.

7. Quoted in Riley Yates, "Gingrich Raises Alarm at Event Honoring Those Who Stand Up for Freedom of Speech," *Manchester Union-Leader,* November 28, 2006.

8. Quoted in Justus D. Doenecke, "American Dissidents," *Reason,* December 1979, p. 47.

9. Garrett, *The People's Pottage,* p. 16. See also Carl Ryan, *Profit's Prophet: Garet Garrett (1878–1954)* (Selinsgrove, Pa.: Susquehanna University Press, 1989).

10. Ibid., p. 25.

11. Ibid., p. 92.

12. Ibid., p. 117.

13. Robert Higgs, "America Won, Americans Lost," *Liberty,* April 2006, p. 17.

14. Ibid., p. 19.

15. Edmund Wilson, *Patriotic Gore: Studies in the Literature of the American Civil War* (New York: Oxford University Press, 1962), p. xxiii.

16. Edmund Wilson, *The Cold War and the Income Tax: A Protest* (New York: New American Library 1964 [1963]), p. 9.

17. Ibid., p. 33.

18. Wilson, *Patriotic Gore,* p. xxxii.

19. Wilson, *The Cold War and the Income Tax,* p. 101.

20. Ibid., p. 103.

21. Ibid., p. 128.

22. Ibid., p. 117.

23. Wilson, *Patriotic Gore,* p. xxviii.

24. Brian Doherty, "Best of Both Worlds," *Reason,* June 1995.

25. Quoted in "Grips and Taxes—II," *The New Yorker,* February 10, 1951, p. 40.

26. Quoted in Joseph M. Weresch, "A Girl with a Grip of Steel," *Nation's Business,* August 1941, pp. 46, 56.

27. Vivien Kellems, "Taxes," *Vital Speeches,* August 15, 1948, p. 651.

28. Vivien Kellems, *Toil, Taxes, and Trouble* (New York: Dutton, 1952), p. 77.

29. Kellems, "Taxes," p. 652.

30. Ibid., p. 651.

31. "Grips and Taxes—II," p. 39. See also *Current Biography, 1948* (New York: H. W. Wilson), pp. 340–42.

32. Quoted in ibid., p. 43.

33. Kellems, *Toil, Taxes, and Trouble,* p. 103.

34. Ibid., p. 89.

35. Ibid., p. 86.
36. William Kristol and David Brooks, "What Ails Conservatism?" *Wall Street Journal,* September 15, 1997.
37. *T. Coleman Andrews: A Collection of His Writings,* edited by Edward N. Coffman and Daniel L. Jensen (Columbus: Ohio State University/ Accounting Hall of Fame, 1996), p. xvi.
38. Ibid., p. xxi.
39. Henry David Thoreau, "On the Duty of Civil Disobedience," in *Walden, or Life in the Woods, and On the Duty of Civil Disobedience* (New York: New American Library, 1960 [1849]), p. 260.
40. "Interview with T. Coleman Andrews," *U.S. News and World Report,* May 25, 1956, p. 62.
41. *T. Coleman Andrews: A Collection of His Writings,* p. 420.
42. Ibid., pp. 436–37.
43. Ibid., p. 443.
44. Ibid., p. 487.
45. Quoted in Charles E. Egan, "States Rights Party Nominates Andrews," *New York Times,* October 16, 1956.
46. John T. Flynn, "Fifty Million Americans in Search of a Party," *American Mercury,* February 1955, pp. 5–10.
47. Doenecke, *Not to the Swift,* pp. 234–35.
48. "Off the Hot Seat," *Newsweek,* October 24, 1955, p. 28.
49. Quoted in Dennis L. Lythgoe, *Let 'Em Holler: A Political Biography of J. Bracken Lee* (Salt Lake City: Utah State Historical Society, 1982), pp. 117–32.
50. Quoted in ibid., p. 245.
51. Quoted in ibid., pp. 300–301.
52. Quoted in ibid., p. 322. The Mormon founder Joseph Smith favored pardoning "every convict" in the state penitentiaries and "blessing them as they go, and saying to them in the name of the Lord, *go thy way and sin no more.*" See the section "Joseph Smith's Presidential Platform," in *Dialogue: A Journal of Mormon Thought* 3, no. 3 (Autumn 1968): 17–36. See also Bill Kauffman, "The Prophet Who Ran for President," *American Enterprise,* September 2004, p. 47.
53. Wilson, *The Cold War and the Income Tax,* pp. 58–59.
54. Oliver Wendell Holmes, "Wind-Clouds and Star-Drifts," in *The Complete Poetical Works of Oliver Wendell Holmes* (Boston: Houghton Mifflin, 1895), p. 174.
55. Quoted in Brian W. Aldiss, *Billion Year Spree: The True History of Science Fiction* (New York: Doubleday, 1973), p. 286.

56. Percival Lowell, *Mars and Its Canals* (New York: Macmillan, 1906), p. 376.
57. Quoted in A. Lawrence Lowell, *Biography of Percival Lowell* (New York: Macmillan, 1935), p. 9.
58. Percival Lowell, *Mars* (Boston: Houghton Mifflin, 1895), p. 158.
59. Ibid., p. 128.
60. Lowell, *Mars and Its Canals*, p. 175.
61. Ibid., pp. 376–78.
62. Ibid., p. 377.
63. Lowell, *Mars*, p. 210.
64. Clyde W. Tombaugh and Patrick Moore, *Out of the Darkness: The Planet Pluto* (New York: New American Library, 1980), p. 20.
65. Arthur C. Clarke, *The Exploration of Space,* revised edition (New York: Harper and Row, 1959), p. 182.
66. Edward Abbey, *Good News* (New York: Dutton, 1980), p. 187.
67. Howard E. McCurdy, *Space and the American Imagination* (Washington, D.C.: Smithsonian Institution Press, 1997), p. 18.
68. Quoted in ibid., p. 53.
69. Quoted in ibid., p. 64.
70. Ibid., p. 68.
71. Quoted in Henry C. Dethloff, *Suddenly Tomorrow Came . . . A History of the Johnson Space Center* (Washington, D.C.: NASA, 1993), p. 28.
72. Quoted in McCurdy, *Space and the American Imagination,* p. 62.
73. Quoted in Phillip Longman, *The Empty Cradle: How Falling Birthrates Threaten World Prosperity and What to Do About It* (New York: Perseus, 2004), p. 57.
74. Dwight D. Eisenhower, "Eisenhower's Farewell Address," January 17, 1961, in *Documents of American History,* edited by Henry Steele Commager (New York: Appleton-Century-Crofts, 1963), pp. 686–87.
75. Quoted in Walter A. McDougall, *The Heavens and the Earth: A Political History of the Space Age* (New York: Basic Books, 1985), p. 303.
76. Quoted in James Lee Kauffman, *Selling Outer Space: Kennedy, the Media, and Funding for Project Apollo, 1961–1963* (Tuscaloosa: University of Alabama Press, 1994), p. 118.
77. Quoted in McDougall, *The Heavens and the Earth,* p. 393.
78. Quoted in Kauffman, *Selling Outer Space,* p. 120.
79. Lewis Mumford, *The Myth of the Machine,* vol. 2: *The Pentagon of Power* (New York: Harcourt Brace Jovanovich, 1970), p. 305.
80. Ibid., p. 310.

81. Russell Kirk, "Fairy Castles of the Moon," *Confessions of a Bohemian Tory* (New York: Fleet, 1963), pp. 275–76.
82. Robert Frost, "Some Science Fiction," in *In the Clearing* (New York: Holt, Rinehart, and Winston, 1962), pp. 89–90.
83. Quoted in John M. Logsdon, *The Decision to Go to the Moon* (Cambridge, Mass.: MIT Press, 1970), p. 3.
84. Bob Dylan, "License to Kill," *Infidels* (1983). A less-talented versifier, the military brat Jim Morrison of the Doors, mocked the moondoggle in "Ship of Fools." The dead Door was an especial admirer of the left-conservative Norman Mailer, whose proposal to make New York City the fifty-first state captured Morrison's imagination. Mailer, in turn, was one of the few writers on the "left" to appreciate the populist-isolationist candidacies of Pat Buchanan.
85. Carl Sagan, *Pale Blue Dot: A Vision of the Human Future in Space* (New York: Random House, 1994), p. xii.
86. Leslie C. Peltier, *Starlight Nights: The Adventures of a Star-Gazer* (Cambridge, Mass.: Sky Publishing, 1965), p. 235.
87. Arthur A. Ekrich Jr., *The Civilian and the Military* (New York: Oxford University Press, 1956), p. 43.
88. Daniel Webster, speech of December 9, 1814, *New Individualist Review*, p. 879.
89. Josephine D. Abbott, "What of Youth in Wartime?" *Survey Midmonthly* 79 (October 1943): 265.
90. Quoted in C. Calvin Smith, *War and Wartime Changes: The Transformation of Arkansas, 1940–1945* (Fayetteville: University of Arkansas Press, 1986), p. 48.
91. "One Thing Leads to Another: Juvenile Delinquency Rises," *Life on the Home Front: Oregon Responds to World War II,* Oregon State Archives, http://arcweb.sos.state.or.us/exhibits/ww2, February 21, 2007.
92. Quoted in William M. Tuttle Jr., *"Daddy's Gone to War": The Second World War in the Lives of America's Children* (New York: Oxford University Press, 1993), p. 74.
93. Ellen Reese, "Maternalism and Political Mobilization: How California's Postwar Child Care Campaign Was Won," *Gender and Society* 10, no. 5 (October 1996): 574.
94. Richard Polenberg, *War and Society: The United States, 1941–1945* (Philadelphia: Lippincott, 1972), p. 149.
95. *The Charter of the United Nations, Hearings Before the Committee on Foreign Relations,* United States Senate, 79th Congress, 1st session, 1945, p. 356.

96. John W. Jeffries, *Wartime America: The World War II Home Front* (Chicago: Ivan R. Dee, 1996), p. 70.

97. James H. S. Bossard, "Family Backgrounds of Wartime Adolescents," *Annals of the American Academy of Political and Social Science* 236 (November 1944): 40.

98. Ibid., p. 41.

99. George E. Gardner and Harvey Spencer, "Reactions of Children with Fathers and Brothers in the Armed Forces," *American Journal of Orthopsychiatry* 14 (1944): 38.

100. Quoted in Tuttle, *"Daddy's Gone to War,"* p. 30.

101. E. James Lieberman, "American Families and the Vietnam War," *Journal of Marriage and the Family* 33, no. 4 (November 1971): 715.

102. Quoted in Herbert J. Storing, *What the Anti-Federalists Were For* (Chicago: University of Chicago Press, 1981), p. 20.

103. Beisner, *Twelve Against Empire,* p. 97.

104. Quoted in ibid., p. 101.

105. Edgar Lee Masters, *Spoon River Anthology* (New York: Macmillan, 1916), pp. 185–86.

106. Quoted in Welch, *Response to Imperialism,* p. 47.

107. Eli M. Bower, "American Children and Families in Overseas Communities," *American Journal of Orthopsychiatry* 37, no. 4 (1967): 791.

108. Frank A. Pederson and Eugene J. Sullivan, "Relationships Among Geographical Mobility, Parental Attitudes and Emotional Disturbances in Children," *American Journal of Orthopsychiatry* 34 (1964): 575.

109. Janice G. Rienerth, "Separation and Female Centeredness in the Military Family," in *Military Families: Adaptation to Change,* edited by Edna J. Hunter and Stephen Nice (New York: Praeger, 1978), pp. 172–73.

110. Allan Carlson, " 'You're in the Army Now': The Troubled State of the Military Family," *Family in America,* November 1989, p. 2.

111. Hamilton I. McCubbin, Barbara B. Dahl, and Edna J. Hunter, "Research on the Military Family: A Review," in *Families in the Military System,* edited by McCubbin, Dahl, and Hunter (Beverly Hills: Sage, 1976), p. 293.

112. Edna J. Hunter, *Families Under the Flag* (New York: Praeger, 1982), p. 44.

113. Jennifer J. Crispin, "No Place Like Home," *Newsweek,* May 26, 1997, p. 16.

114. Mary Edwards Wertsch, *Military Brats: Legacies of Childhood Inside the Fortress* (New York: Harmony, 1991), pp. 249–50.

115. Beer, "What Is Left? What Is Right? Does It Matter?" p. 5.

116. Susanne K. Langer, *Philosophy in a New Key: A Study in the Symbolism of Reason, Rite, and Art,* 3rd edition (Cambridge, Mass.: Harvard University Press, 1967 [1942]), p. 292.
117. Allan Carlson, "The Total Army Family," *Free Market,* June 1998, pp. 1–2.
118. Sharon Begley and Pat Wingert, "Teach Your Parents Well," *Newsweek,* April 28, 1997, p. 72.
119. Stephen Baskerville, "The Fathers' War," *American Conservative,* October 24, 2005, p. 17.
120. Quoted in "As War Deployments Increase, So Does Army Divorce Rate," Associated Press, *Batavia Daily News,* June 30, 2005.
121. Carlson, "The Total Army Family," p. 2.
122. Macer Hall, "Armed Forces Are Bad for Marriage," *Telegraph,* March 19, 2000.
123. "Live with Caspar Weinberger," *American Enterprise,* January–February 1997, pp. 24–27. The question did not make the final cut.
124. Bill Kauffman, *With Good Intentions?: Reflections on the Myth of Progress in America* (Westport, Conn.: Praeger, 1998), pp. 103–16.
125. Grace and Fred M. Hechinger, "Should School Keep All Year Round?" *New York Times Magazine,* January 24, 1960, p. 9.
126. *A Nation at Risk,* National Commission on Excellence in Education (Washington, D.C.: Government Printing Office, 1983), p. 5.
127. Ray Bradbury, *Fahrenheit 451* (New York: Simon and Schuster, 1967 [1953]), p. 66.
128. "Seven Questions," *Partisan Review* (Summer–Fall 1939): 105.
129. *Congressional Record,* 83rd Congress, 1st session, March 9, 1953, p. 1781.
130. Robertson Davies, *The Diary of Samuel Marchbanks* (Toronto: Clarke, Irwin, 1947), p. 75.
131. Benjamin Franklin, "An Economical Project," in *The Life of Benjamin Franklin, Written by Himself, to Which Is Added His Miscellaneous Essays* (Auburn, N.Y.: Miller, Orton and Mulligan, 1857), pp. 256–58.
132. Quoted in Michael Downing, *Spring Forward: The Annual Madness of Daylight Saving Time* (Washington, D.C.: Shoemaker and Hoard, 2005), p. 5.
133. Michael O'Malley, *Keeping Watch: A History of American Time* (New York: Viking, 1990), p. 139.
134. Quoted in ibid., p. 133.
135. Downing, *Spring Forward,* p. 10.

136. Ibid., p. 2. The *New York Times,* smugly middlebrow and dismissive of American dissenters throughout its history, editorialized of DST that "nobody is opposed to it except possibly a few people who are opposed on principle to any alteration of established habits." Well, that settles things, doesn't it? Ibid., p. 2.
137. *The Papers of Woodrow Wilson,* vol. 62, edited by Arthur S. Link (Princeton, N.J.: Princeton University Press, 1990), pp. 304–5.
138. Quoted in O'Malley, *Keeping Watch,* p. 262.
139. Ibid., pp. 284–85.
140. Downing, *Spring Forward,* p. 69.
141. Quoted in *Getting a Better Understanding of the Metric System— Implications If Adopted by the United States,* report to Congress by the comptroller general of the United States (Washington, D.C.: General Accounting Office, October 20, 1978), p. 5.
142. Quoted in Alex Groner and George A.W. Boehm, *Going Metric: An AMA Survey Report* (New York: American Management Association, 1973), p. 16.
143. Frederick A. Halsey, *The Metric Fallacy* (New York: Van Nostrand, 1904), p. 12.
144. Quoted in Frank Donovan, *Prepare Now for a Metric Future* (New York: Weybright and Talley, 1970), p. 30.
145. Quoted in Charles Davis, *The Metric System* (New York: A. S. Barnes, 1871), p. 39.
146. Quoted in Halsey, *The Metric Fallacy,* p. 128.
147. Herbert Spencer, *Against the Metric System* (London: Williams and Norgate, 1904 [1901]), introduction.
148. Quoted in Donovan, *Prepare Now for a Metric Future,* p. 152.
149. Ibid., pp. 149–50.
150. Ibid., p. 152.
151. Quoted in Halsey, *The Metric Fallacy,* epigraph.
152. Donovan, *Prepare Now for a Metric Future,* p. 150.
153. Quoted in Michael Chapman, "Metrics: Mismeasuring Consumer Demand," *Consumers' Research,* February 1994, p. 24ff.
154. *The Metric Debate,* edited by David F. Bartlett (Boulder: Colorado Associated University Press, 1980), p. 4.
155. Ibid., p. 9.
156. Quoted in Chapman, "Metrics: Mismeasuring Consumer Demand." See also "The Meter and Liter Don't Measure Up, Says Seaver Leslie," *People,* June 22, 1981, p. 42.
157. Quoted in Donovan, *Prepare Now for a Metric Future,* p. 85.

158. Groner and Boehm, *Going Metric,* p. 29.
159. For instance, see *Highway Signs: Conversion to Metric Units Could Be Costly,* report to the Honorable John J. Duncan Jr., General Accounting Office, July 1995.
160. Carlson, " 'You're in the Army Now,' " p. 11.

Conclusion: Come Home, America

1. Morley, *Freedom and Federalism,* p. 128.
2. Daniel McCarthy, "Does Lieberman Belong on the Right?" www .ToryAnarchist.com, August 10, 2006.
3. Bill Kauffman, "Free Vermont," *American Conservative,* December 19, 2005, p. 17.
4. Morley, *The Power in the People,* p. 266.
5. Nisbet, *Twilight of Authority,* p. 276.
6. See Bill Kauffman, *Dispatches from the Muckdog Gazette* (New York: Holt, 2003), pp. 117–41.
7. N. P. Willis, "April," in *The Poets and Poetry of America,* edited by Rufus Wilmot Griswold (Philadelphia: Parry and McMillan, 1858), p. 380.

ACKNOWLEDGMENTS

Paul Buhle suggested that I write this book. His career as a gutsy, passionate, and wise radical historian is an inspiration. Steve Fraser was an exacting editor who improved every chapter. I thank him. For advice, assistance, and venues along the way I am grateful to the lovely town supervisor Lucine Kauffman, Allan Carlson, Tom Woods, Jeremy Beer, Kara Beer, Karl Zinsmeister, Erich Eichman, Marty Zupan, Tim Rives, Alan Crawford, Scott McConnell, Kara Hopkins, Dan McCarthy, Leonard Liggio, Elaine Hawley, Gore Vidal, Scott Walter, Wayne S. Cole, Justus D. Doenecke, Chris Check, Chris Kauffman, Jason Peters, Jesse Walker, Joe and Sandy Kauffman, and the staffs of the Richmond Memorial Library and the University of Rochester and Genesee Community College libraries.

Gretel Kauffman, our daughter, generously loaned me her computer when mine (damned machine!), as if on orders from Ned Ludd, broke down. It is for her that I write. May she live in a peaceful, literate America of baseball, poetry, and simple kindnesses.

INDEX

ABOUT THE AUTHOR

BILL KAUFFMAN is the author of six books, most recently *Look Homeward, America* (named one of the best books of 2006 by the American Library Association) and *Dispatches from the Muckdog Gazette* (which won the 2003 national Sense of Place award from Writers & Books). Kauffman has written for *The Wall Street Journal*, the *Los Angeles Times*, *Orion*, and *The American Conservative*, among other publications. He lives in his native upstate New York with his family.

THE AMERICAN EMPIRE PROJECT

In an era of unprecedented military strength, leaders of the United States, the global hyperpower, have increasingly embraced imperial ambitions. How did this significant shift in purpose and policy come about? And what lies down the road?

The American Empire Project is a response to the changes that have occurred in America's strategic thinking as well as in its military and economic posture. Empire, long considered an offense against America's democratic heritage, now threatens to define the relationship between our country and the rest of the world. The American Empire Project publishes books that question this development, examine the origins of U.S. imperial aspirations, analyze their ramifications at home and abroad, and discuss alternatives to this dangerous trend.

The project was conceived by Tom Engelhardt and Steve Fraser, editors who are themselves historians and writers. Published by Metropolitan Books, an imprint of Henry Holt and Company, its titles include *Hegemony or Survival, Failed States, Imperial Ambitions,* and *What We Say Goes* by Noam Chomsky; *Blowback, The Sorrows of Empire,* and *Nemesis* by Chalmers Johnson; *Crusade* by James Carroll; *How to Succeed at Globalization* by El Fisgón; *Blood and Oil* by Michael Klare; *Dilemmas of Domination* by Walden Bello; *War Powers* by Peter Irons; *Devil's Game* by Robert Dreyfuss; *Empire's Workshop* by Greg Grandin; *A Question of Torture* by Alfred McCoy; *The Seventh Decade* by Jonathan Schell; *The Complex* by Nick Turse; *A People's History of American Empire* by Howard Zinn, Mike Konopachi, and Paul Buhle; and *In the Name of Democracy*, edited by Jeremy Brecher, Jill Cutler, and Brendan Smith.

For more information about the American Empire Project and for a list of forthcoming titles, please visit www.american empireproject.com.